The Letters of

SAMUEL JOHNSON

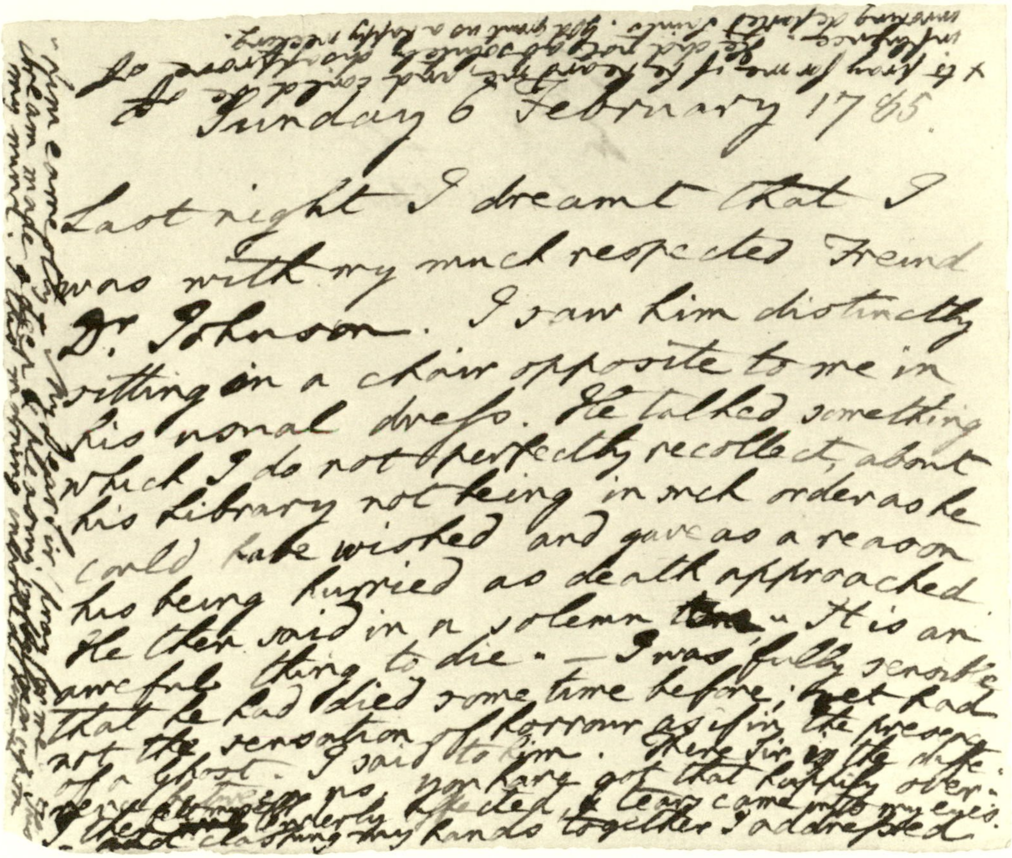

Sunday 6 February 1785.

Last night I dreamt that I was with my much respected Freind Dr. Johnson. I saw him distinctly sitting in a chair opposite to me in his usual dress. He talked something which I do not perfectly recollect, about his Library not being in such order as he could have wished and gave as a reason his being hurried as death approached. He then said in a solemn tone "It is an awful thing to die." — I was fully sensible that he had died some time before; but had not the sensation of horrour as if in the presence of a ghost. I said to him. "There Sir is the difference betwixt us, you have got that happily over." I then was tenderly affected, & tears came into my eyes & clasping my hands together I addressed

JAMES BOSWELL'S DREAM, 6 FEBRUARY 1785

of "my much respected Freind Dr. Johnson"

(Hyde Collection)

The Letters of
SAMUEL JOHNSON

VOLUME V · APPENDICES AND
COMPREHENSIVE INDEX

Edited by

BRUCE REDFORD

PRINCETON, NEW JERSEY

PRINCETON UNIVERSITY PRESS

MCM · LXXXXIV

94-375

PUBLISHED BY PRINCETON UNIVERSITY PRESS, 41 WILLIAM STREET
PRINCETON, NEW JERSEY 08540

LIBRARY OF CONGRESS CATALOGING-IN-PUBLICATION DATA
(REVISED FOR VOLUMES 4 AND 5)

JOHNSON, SAMUEL, 1709–1784.
THE LETTERS OF SAMUEL JOHNSON.
INCLUDES BIBLIOGRAPHICAL REFERENCES AND INDEX.
CONTENTS: V. 1. 1731–1772 — [ETC.] — V. 4. 1 JANUARY 1782 TO
10 DECEMBER 1784 — V. 5. APPENDICES AND COMPREHENSIVE INDEX.
1. JOHNSON, SAMUEL — 1709 – 1784 — CORRESPONDENCE.
2. AUTHORS, ENGLISH — 18TH CENTURY — CORRESPONDENCE.
3. LEXICOGRAPHERS — GREAT BRITAIN — CORRESPONDENCE.
I. REDFORD, BRUCE. II. TITLE.
PR3533.A4 1992   828'.609 [B]   90 – 8806
ISBN 0–691–06881–X (V. 1)   ISBN 0–691–06977–8 (V. 4)
ISBN 0–691–06978–6 (V. 5)

PRINCETON UNIVERSITY PRESS BOOKS
ARE PRINTED ON ACID-FREE PAPER, AND MEET THE
GUIDELINES FOR PERMANENCE AND DURABILITY OF
THE COMMITTEE ON PRODUCTION GUIDELINES
FOR BOOK LONGEVITY OF THE COUNCIL
ON LIBRARY RESOURCES

PRINTED IN THE UNITED STATES OF AMERICA
BY THE STINEHOUR PRESS, LUNENBURG, VERMONT
1 3 5 7 9 10 8 6 4 2

CONTENTS

EDITORIAL PROCEDURES   *page* vii

CHRONOLOGY   xi

CUE TITLES AND ABBREVIATIONS   xiii

APPENDIX I   *Letters of Uncertain Date*   3

APPENDIX II   *Letters Substantiated by Mention*   37

APPENDIX III   *Translations of Letters in Latin*   49

ADDENDA   55

ALPHABETICAL TABLE OF CORRESPONDENTS   59

COMPREHENSIVE INDEX   73

POLICIES of annotation and transcription have been modeled on the style sheet for the Yale Research Edition of the Private Papers of James Boswell. The most detailed version in print appears in the front matter to *The Correspondence of James Boswell with David Garrick, Edmund Burke, and Edmond Malone*, ed. P. S. Baker et al. (1986). The statement that follows adheres closely to this version.

THE TEXTS

Choice and Arrangement of Letters

The letters are presented in chronological order. Letters written for others, as well as public dissertations in the guise of letters, have been excluded. Undated letters that cannot be assigned with confidence to a specific year appear in Appendix I, where they are ordered alphabetically by correspondent. Appendix II gathers together the evidence for letters whose texts have not been recovered. Translations of Johnson's letters in Latin appear in Appendix III.

The copy-text has been the MSS of letters sent, whenever such MSS were available. In the absence of originals, we have used MS copies. When no MSS at all have been recovered, we have used printed texts as copy.

Transcription

In accordance with the policy of the Yale Research Series, "manuscript documents in this edition have been printed to correspond to the originals as closely as is feasible in the medium of type. A certain amount of compromise and apparent inconsistency seems unavoidable, but change has been kept within the limits of stated conventions."

The following editorial conventions are imposed silently:

Addresses. Elements appearing on separate lines in the MS are run together and punctuated according to modern practice. On franked covers, handwriting is that of the franker unless otherwise specified.

Datelines. Places and dates are joined at the head of the letter regardless of their position in the MS. Punctuation has been normalized.

Salutations. Abbreviations are expanded. Commas and colons after salutations are retained; in the absence of punctuation, a colon is supplied.

Complimentary closes. Abbreviations are expanded. Punctuation has been normalized. Elements appearing on separate lines in the MS are run together. Complimentary closes paragraphed separately in the MS are printed as continuations of the last line of text.

Endorsements. Handwriting is that of the recipient unless otherwise specified.

Punctuation. At the ends of completed sentences periods may replace commas or dashes and are always supplied when omitted. A sentence following a period always begins with a capital letter.

Changes. Substantive additions and deletions in Johnson's hand are recorded in the notes.

Lacunae. Words and letters missing through a tear or obscured by a blot are supplied within angle brackets. Inadvertent omissions are supplied within square brackets. Nonauthorial deletions are not reported unless the reading is in doubt.

Abbreviations, contractions, and symbols. The following abbreviations, contractions, and symbols, and their variant forms, are expanded: abt (about), acct (account), agst (against), Bp (Bishop), cd (could), compts (compliments), Dr (Dear), Ld (Lord), Lop (Lordship), Ly (Lady), Lyship (Ladyship), recd (received), sd (should), Sr (Sir), wc (which), wd (would), yr (your), & (and), &c (etc.). All retained abbreviations and contractions are followed by a period. Periods following ordinals have been removed.

Superior letters. Superior letters are lowered.

Brackets. Parentheses replace square brackets in the text, brackets being reserved for editorial use.

Spelling. The original spelling has been retained, except for obvious inadvertencies, which are corrected in the text and recorded in the notes.

Capitalization and paragraphing. Original capitalization and paragraphing have been retained.

ANNOTATION

Headnotes. Postmarks, although partly illegible on some letters, are left unbracketed when not in doubt. Marks on the wrappers other than addresses, postmarks, endorsements, and stamped and written franks have been ignored.

Footnotes. When an abbreviated source is given, the full citation may be found in the list of cue titles and abbreviations on pp. xiii–xv. All other reference titles in the footnotes are sufficiently complete to enable ready identification; for each letter, these citations are presented in full the first time they occur and are shortened in all subsequent occurrences in the notes to that letter. Except where a work has been directly quoted, no source is given when the information is available in the *Dictionary of National Biography,* an encyclopedia, or other general reference work.

Reference to all letters is made by correspondent and date. *Post* and *Ante* references supplement but do not replace the index, which should be consulted whenever the identity of names or places is in doubt.

CHRONOLOGY

1709	Is born at Lichfield, 18 Sept.
1717–25	Attends Lichfield Grammar School.
1728	Enters Pembroke College, Oxford, in October.
1729	Leaves Oxford in December.
1731	Death of his father Michael.
1732	Usher at Market Bosworth School.
1733	Resides in Birmingham; translates Lobo's *Voyage to Abyssinia*.
1735	Marries Elizabeth Porter; opens school at Edial.
1737	Leaves for London in March; begins work for Edward Cave.
1738	*London.*
1744	*An Account of the Life of Richard Savage*; *Harleian Miscellany*.
1746	Signs contract for the *Dictionary*.
1749	*Irene* produced; *The Vanity of Human Wishes*.
1750	Begins *Rambler*.
1752	Death of Elizabeth Johnson; final *Rambler*.
1755	Oxford M.A.; publication of the *Dictionary*.
1758	Begins *Idler*.
1759	Death of his mother Sarah; publication of *Rasselas*.
1760	Final *Idler*.
1762	Is granted annual pension.
1763	Meets James Boswell.
1764	Founding of The Club.
1765	Meets Henry and Hester Thrale; Dublin LL.D.; *The Dramatic Works of William Shakespeare*.
1770	*The False Alarm.*
1771	*Thoughts on the late Transactions respecting Falkland's Islands.*
1773	Hebridean tour.
1774	*The Patriot*; tour of Wales.
1775	*A Journey to the Western Islands of Scotland*; *Taxation No Tyranny*; Oxford D.C.L.; trip to Paris.

1777   Trial of Dr. Dodd; begins work on *Lives of the Poets*.

1779   First installment of *Lives*.

1781   Death of Henry Thrale; second installment of *Lives*.

1783   Founding of Essex Head Club.

1784   Final break with Hester Thrale; dies 13 Dec.

CUE TITLES AND ABBREVIATIONS

Adam Cat.	R. B. ADAM, *The R. B. Adam Library Relating to Dr. Samuel Johnson and His Era*, 4 vols., 1929–30.
Alum. Cant. I	JOHN and J. A. VENN, *Alumni Cantabrigienses*, Part I (to 1751), 4 vols., 1922–27.
Alum. Cant. II	J. A. VENN, *Alumni Cantabrigienses*, Part II (1752–1900), 6 vols., 1940–54.
Alum. Oxon. I	JOSEPH FOSTER, *Alumni Oxonienses . . . 1500–1714*, 4 vols., 1891–92.
Alum. Oxon. II	JOSEPH FOSTER, *Alumni Oxonienses . . . 1715–1886*, 4 vols., 1887–88.
Baker	*The Correspondence of James Boswell with David Garrick, Edmund Burke, and Edmond Malone*, ed. P. S. Baker et al., 1986.
Bibliography	W. P. COURTNEY and DAVID NICHOL SMITH, *A Bibliography of Samuel Johnson*, 1915, 1925.
Bibliography Supplement	R. W. CHAPMAN and A. T. HAZEN, *Johnsonian Bibliography: A Supplement to Courtney*, 1939.
Bloom	E. A. BLOOM, *Samuel Johnson in Grub Street*, 1957.
Burke's Correspondence	*The Correspondence of Edmund Burke*, ed. T. W. Copeland et al., 1958–70.
Chapman	*The Letters of Samuel Johnson, with Mrs. Thrale's Genuine Letters to Him*, ed. R. W. Chapman, 3 vols., 1952.
Clifford, 1952	J. L. CLIFFORD, *Hester Lynch Piozzi*, 2d ed., 1952.
Clifford, 1955	J. L. CLIFFORD, *Young Samuel Johnson*, 1955.
Clifford, 1979	J. L. CLIFFORD, *Dictionary Johnson*, 1979.
Croker	JAMES BOSWELL, *The Life of Samuel Johnson, LL.D.*, ed. J. W. Croker, rev. John Wright, 10 vols., 1868.
SJ's *Dictionary*	SAMUEL JOHNSON, *Dictionary of the English Language*, 4th ed., 1773.
DNB	*Dictionary of National Biography.*

Earlier Years	F. A. POTTLE, *James Boswell: The Earlier Years, 1740–1769*, 1966.
Fifer	*The Correspondence of James Boswell with Certain Members of The Club*, ed. C. N. Fifer, 1976.
Fleeman	SAMUEL JOHNSON, *A Journey to the Western Islands of Scotland*, ed. J. D. Fleeman, 1985.
GM	*The Gentleman's Magazine*, 1731–1907.
Greene, 1975	DONALD GREENE, *Samuel Johnson's Library*, 1975.
Hawkins	SIR JOHN HAWKINS, *The Life of Samuel Johnson, LL.D.*, 2d ed., 1787.
Hazen	A. T. HAZEN, *Samuel Johnson's Prefaces and Dedications*, 1937.
Hebrides	*Boswell's Journal of a Tour to the Hebrides with Samuel Johnson, LL.D., 1773*, ed. from the original MS by F. A. Pottle and C. H. Bennett, 1961.
Hendy	J. G. HENDY, *The History of the Early Postmarks of the British Isles*, 1905.
Hill	*Letters of Samuel Johnson, LL.D.*, ed. G. B. Hill, 1892.
Hyde, 1972	MARY HYDE, *The Impossible Friendship: Boswell and Mrs. Thrale*, 1972.
Hyde, 1977	MARY HYDE, *The Thrales of Streatham Park*, 1977.
JB	James Boswell.
Johns. Glean.	A. L. READE, *Johnsonian Gleanings*, 11 vols., 1909–52.
Johns. Misc.	*Johnsonian Miscellanies*, ed. G. B. Hill, 2 vols., 1897.
JN	*Johnsonian Newsletter.*
Later Years	FRANK BRADY, *James Boswell: The Later Years, 1769–1795*, 1984.
Life	*Boswell's Life of Johnson, Together with Boswell's Journal of a Tour to the Hebrides and Johnson's Diary of a Journey into North Wales*, ed. G. B. Hill, rev. L. F. Powell, 6 vols., 1934–50; vols. V and VI, 2d ed., 1964.
Lit. Anec.	JOHN NICHOLS, *Literary Anecdotes of the Eighteenth Century*, 9 vols., 1812–15.
Lit. Car.	F. A. POTTLE, *The Literary Career of James Boswell, Esq.*, 1929.
Lives of the Poets	*Johnson's Lives of the English Poets*, ed. G. B. Hill, 1905.

Lond. Stage	*The London Stage*, Part III (1729–47), ed. A. H. Scouten, 1961; Part IV (1747–76), ed. G. W. Stone, Jr., 1962; Part V (1776–1800), ed. C. B. Hogan, 1968.
Namier and Brooke	
	SIR LEWIS NAMIER and JOHN BROOKE, *The House of Commons, 1754–1790*, 3 vols., 1964.
OED	*Oxford English Dictionary.*
Piozzi, *Letters*	HESTER LYNCH PIOZZI, *Letters to and from the Late Samuel Johnson, LL.D.*, 2 vols., 1788.
Piozzi	Annotated presentation copy, given to Sir James Fellowes, of H. L. Piozzi's *Letters to and from the Late Samuel Johnson, LL.D.*, 1788 (Birthplace Museum, Lichfield).
Plomer	H. R. PLOMER et al., *Dictionary of Printers and Booksellers, 1668–1725; 1726–1775*, 2 vols., 1922, 1932.
Poems	*The Poems of Samuel Johnson*, ed. David Nichol Smith and E. L. McAdam, rev. J. D. Fleeman, 1974.
Reades	A. L. READE, *The Reades of Blackwood Hill and Dr. Johnson's Ancestry*, 1906.
RES	*Review of English Studies.*
SJ	Samuel Johnson.
Sledd and Kolb	J. H. SLEDD and G. J. KOLB, *Dr. Johnson's Dictionary*, 1955.
Thraliana	*Thraliana: The Diary of Mrs. Hester Lynch Thrale*, ed. K. C. Balderston, 1942.
TLS	*Times Literary Supplement.*
Waingrow	*The Correspondence and Other Papers of James Boswell Relating to the Making of the "Life of Johnson,"* ed. Marshall Waingrow, 1969.
Walpole's Correspondence, Yale ed.	
	The Yale Edition of Horace Walpole's Correspondence, ed. W. S. Lewis et al., 1937–83.
Wheatley and Cunningham	
	H. B. WHEATLEY and PETER CUNNINGHAM, *London Past and Present*, 3 vols., 1891.
Works, Yale ed.	*The Yale Edition of the Works of Samuel Johnson*, J. H. Middendorf, gen. ed., 1958–.

The Letters of

SAMUEL JOHNSON

APPENDIX I
Letters of Uncertain Date

Frances Burney

SATURDAY[1]

MS: Berg Collection, New York Public Library.

Saturday

Mr. Johnson begs of Miss Burney that she will favour him with a copy of Cecilia to lend a friend.

1. This letter, placed in 1783 by Hill and by Chapman, could have been written anytime after the publication of Burney's *Cecilia*, 12 June 1782.

Thomas Cadell

MS: Hyde Collection.

Mr. Johnson desires Mr. Cadel to send him, if he has it, Xenophon de Rebus Græcorum, the Scotch Edition.[1]

1. SJ refers to the octavo edition of Xenophon's *Hellenica* published in 1762 by the Foulis Press (Philip Gaskell, *Bibliography of the Foulis Press*, 2d ed., 1986, p. 248). SJ owned a copy at the time of his death (Greene, 1975, p. 119).

Edward Cave[1]

1. Hill (1.10) follows JB (*Life* 1.155–57) in dating this letter to 1742; Chapman (1.22) assigns it conjecturally to Autumn 1743, but does not explain his decision. The contents do not justify such a precise dating, even if one follows Thomas Kaminski in connecting it to the "Historical Design" of SJ's letter to Cave, Autumn 1743 (Kaminski, *Early Career of SJ*, 1987, p. 251 n. 50).

MS: Hyde Collection.

Sir:

You did not tell Me Your determination about the *Soldier's Letter*,[2] which I am confident was never printed. I think it will not do by itself, or in any other place so well as the Mag. extraordinary.[3] If You will have it at all. I believe You do not think I set it high, and I will be glad if what You give for it You will give quickly.

You need not be in care about something to print, for I have got the State tryals[4] and shall extract Layer,[5] Atterbury,[6] and Macclesfield[7] from them and shall bring[8] them to You in a fortnight, after which I will try to get the Southsea re⟨port⟩,[9] and then I hope to proceed regularly. I am etc.

SAM. JOHNSON

2. JB notes that "I have not discovered what this was" (*Life* 1.156 n. 4). Neither has any subsequent inquirer.

3. The annual supplement to the *GM*, published every December.

4. *A Complete Collection of State-Trials, and Proceedings for High-Treason etc.* (1719, 1730, 1742).

5. Christopher Layer (1683–1723), Jacobite conspirator, whose plot to restore the Pretender was foiled in 1722. Convicted of high treason, Layer was executed in May 1723.

6. Francis Atterbury (1662–1732), Bishop of Rochester, was arrested in 1722 on suspicion of involvement with the Stuart cause and tried before the House of Lords in May 1723. The Lords voted 83–43 against Atterbury, who was stripped of all his ecclesiastical positions and banished for life.

7. Thomas Parker (1667–1732), first Earl of Macclesfield and Lord Chancellor (1718–25). Macclesfield was tried before the House of Lords in May 1725 on charges of bribery and fraud. He was found guilty by a unanimous vote, fined, and briefly imprisoned.   8. MS: "not" del. before "bring"

9. Possibly *The Report from the Trustees of the South Sea Company to the Honourable House of Commons* (London, 1724).

Thomas Davies

PRINTED SOURCE: JB's *Life*, 1791, II.460.[1]

1. "He indeed loved Davies cordially, of which I shall give the following little

Come, come dear Davies, I am always sorry when we quarrel; send me word that we are friends.

---

evidence. One day, when he had treated him with too much asperity, Tom, who was not without pride and spirit, went off in a passion; but he had hardly reached home, when Frank, who had been sent after him, delivered this note" (*Life* IV.231).

Robert Dodsley

MS: Folger Shakespeare Library.
ADDRESS: To Mr. Dodsley.

Sir:

I have as You see written my Letter, and am yet in doubt whether I shall send it, I cannot see what good it can do you, however if you think differently from me I do not love the reputation of obstinacy or perverseness. I have dated the Letter for Monday. You may think on it, whatever you do it will please me if You can please yourself. If You have a Shakespeare pray send it though in sheets.[1] I will return it in[2] two or three days. I am, etc.

SAM. JOHNSON

1. If one assumes that SJ is referring to his own edition, then this letter could have been written anytime between the autumn of 1761 and the late summer of 1765 (the period when, by a conservative reckoning, substantial portions of the edition were "in sheets").   2. MS: "for" del. before "in"

James Elphinston

PRINTED SOURCE: James Elphinston, *Forty Years' Correspondence*, 1791, I.34.

[In one letter (among many now lost) he said] My health seems to be returning; and with health of mind and body a man may supply or bear the remainder of his wants.

David Garrick

MS: Free Library of Philadelphia.
ADDRESS: To David Garrick, Esqr., Adelphi.[1]

Dear Sir: May 25[2]

You have many requests, and many of them must be denied, but I hope this will not be of the number, by which you are desired to order your Boxkeeper, to reserve four places for Dr. Bell of Westminster,[3] any night on which You intend to appear, before Friday. I am, sir, your most humble servant,

SAM. JOHNSON

1. Address added in pencil in an unidentified hand.

2. The indisputable *terminus ad quem* for this letter is 1776, when Garrick retired from the stage (10 June). If the address is accurate, it cannot have been written before he moved into the Adelphi (Mar. 1772) (*Letters of David Garrick*, ed. D. M. Little and G. M. Kahrl, 1963, II.775). The most reliable *terminus a quo* is the date of William Bell's doctoral degree, 1767.

3. William Bell (1731–1816), D.D., Prebendary of Westminster and brother of John Bell (1745–1831), the London bookseller.

Edmund Hector[1]

MS: Hyde Collection.
ADDRESS: To Mr. Hector in Birmingham.
POSTMARK: 28 AV.

Dear Sir:

That You and dear Mrs. Careless should have care or curiosity about my health gives me that pleasure which every man feels from finding himself not forgotten. In age we feel again that

1. As the postmark makes clear, this letter was misplaced by JB (*Life*, 1791, II.421), who dated it *c.* Mar. 1782. It is inconceivable that it could have been written in Aug. 1782, given SJ's serious and protracted illness during that period. I follow Hill (*Life* IV.147 n. 1) and Chapman (II.473) in accepting 1780 as the *terminus ad quem* (Henry Thrale died in Apr. 1781, and, as Hill observes, "What he says of friendship renders it almost certain that the letter was written while he had still Thrale"). 1778 and 1780 are both possible dates.

love of our native place and our early friends, which in the bustle or amusements of middle life were overborn and suspended. You and I should now naturally cling to one another, we have outlived most of those who could pretend to rival us in each other's kindness. In our walk through life we have dropped our companions and are now to pick up such as chance may offer us, or[2] to travel on alone. You indeed have a sister with whom you can divide the day, I have no natural friend left, but Providence has been pleased to preserve me from neglect, I have not wanted such alleviations of life as friendship could supply. My Health has been from my twentieth year such as has seldom afforded me a single day of ease, but it is at least not worse, and I sometimes make myself believe that [it] is better. My disorders are however still sufficiently oppressive.

I think of seeing Staffordshire again this autumn, and intend to find my way through Birmingham, where I hope to see You and dear Mrs. Careless well. I am, Sir, Your affectionate Friend,

SAM. JOHNSON

2. MS: "o" superimposed upon "t"

John Hoole[1]

PRINTED SOURCE: Chapman III.261.

Mr. Johnson returns thanks to Mr. and Mrs. Hoole for their kind attention and enquiries.

1. In all likelihood this note belongs to the last few years of SJ's life, *c.* 1780–84. Its indisputable *terminus a quo*, however, is 1761, the year in which Hoole was introduced to SJ (Hazen, p. 60 n. 2).

Griffith Jones [1]
9 OCTOBER

MS: Hyde Collection.
ADDRESS: To Mr. Jones.

Sir: Oct. 9

You are accustomed to consider advertisements and to observe what stile has most effect upon the publick. I shall think it a favour if you will be pleased to take the trouble of digging twelve lines of common sense out of this strange scribble, and insert it ⟨three times⟩[2] in the daily Advertiser at the expence of, Sir, your humble servant,

SAM. JOHNSON

Please to return me the paper.

1. Griffith Jones (1722–86), printer, translator, and for "many years" editor of the *London Chronicle*, the *Daily Advertiser*, and the *Public Ledger* (*Lit. Anec.* III.465). "The native goodness of his heart endeared him to a numerous and respectable literary acquaintance, among whom he reckoned the philanthropic Mr. John Newbery ... Dr. Oliver Goldsmith, and the pious and learned Dr. Samuel Johnson; to the latter of whom he was for several years a near neighbour in Bolt-court, Fleetstreet" (*Lit. Anec.* III.465).

2. MS: mutilated; "three times" from text in *European Magazine* 34, 1798, p. 163.

Thomas Lawrence
14 JUNE

MS: Houghton Library.
ADDRESS: To Dr. Laurence.

Dear Sir: June 14

I have enclosed some account of your Son, with which, upon the whole, I think you will be pleased, otherwise I should not wish to be the reporter.

The Lady's Letter you must not show, as it contains secret

history.[1] I am, Sir, Your most obliged and most humble Servant,

SAM. JOHNSON

1. It is likely that SJ refers to a report from Sir Robert Chambers on William Chauncy Lawrence (*Ante* To Robert Chambers, 30 Sept. 1773), and that the "secret history" came from Lady Chambers (cf. *Ante* To Robert Chambers, 31 Oct. 1779). If that interpretation is correct, then the letter must date from the period between W. C. Lawrence's departure for India in 1773 and his death in 1783.

Alexander Lennox [1]

MS: Houghton Library.
ADDRESS: To Mr. Lennox in Gerrard Street, Soho.
ENDORSEMENT: Mr. S. Johnson.

Sir:

I beg the favour of you to lend[2] me another Guinea, if you can by Frank. My compliments to dear ———. I am, sir, your most humble servant,

SAM. JOHNSON

1. The address and the reference to Francis Barber date this note to the period between Mar. 1753 and late 1756 (Duncan Isles, "The Lennox Collection," *Harvard Library Bulletin* 19, 1971, p. 418 n. 190).
2. MS: "lend" altered from "send"

Charlotte Lennox [1]

MS: Houghton Library.
ADDRESS: To Mrs. Lenox.
ENDORSEMENT: Saml. Johnson.

1. Given the general nature of this letter's contents, it is impossible to suggest a period more precise than virtually the full term of their acquaintance, *c.* 1749–84. The confident handwriting establishes, however, that the letter could not have been written at the very end of SJ's life.

Dearest Madam:

I am sorry you misunderstood me, I did not write for my Books but for their names which you did not send me.

I wish you would for once resolve to use any method of transacting with your friends but that of letters. You will, in whatever part of the World you may be placed, find mankind extremely impatient of such letters as you are inclined to favour them with. You can send your letters, such as the last but one, only[2] to two sorts of people, those whom you cannot pain, and those whom you can, and surely it is not eligible either to give mirth to your enemies or to raise anger in your friends. I have no[3] pleasure in saying this, and am glad that I have delayed beyond the time in which I might have been inclined to say more. I have no inclination to continue quarrels, and therefore hope you will again allow me, now I have vented my resentment, ⟨to be⟩,[4] Dear Madam, your most obedient, and most humble servant,

SAM. JOHNSON

2. MS: "only" superimposed upon "any"
3. MS: "not" with "t" partially erased
4. MS: tear in bottom left-hand corner

Charlotte Lennox
THURSDAY NIGHT[1]

MS: Houghton Library.
ADDRESS: To Mrs. Lennox.
ENDORSEMENT: Mr. Saml. Johnson.

Dear Madam: Thursday night

When friends fall out the first thing to be considered is how to fall in again, and he is the best that makes the first advances, I have designed to come to you ever since half an hour after you ran from me but I knew not whither. I did not when I began

1. The handwriting suggests that this letter dates to *c.* 1779–84.

intend to say more [than] the first sentence, nor when I left off, to have a final quarrel. Pray, my dear, think no more of it, but come to me or let me know when I can come to you, for the thought of driving you away will be very painful to, Dearest Parlet,[2] your most obedient etc.

SAM. JOHNSON

I have not read your Letter nor will read it, till I know whether it is peevish or no, for if it be you shall have it again.

2. It is probable that SJ has in mind Falstaff's question to Dame Quickly: "How now, dame Partlet the hen, have you enquired yet who picked my pocket?" (*I Henry IV* iii.iii.50–51). For a discussion of the biographical and literary resonances, see Duncan Isles, "The Lennox Collection," *Harvard Library Bulletin* 19, 1971, p. 420 n. 194.

Charlotte Lennox
25 JANUARY[1]

MS: Houghton Library.
ADDRESS: Westminster.[2]

Madam: Jan. 25

That mistake may not gather strength by time, I make this haste to assure you, that between hurry and sickness joined with other causes of confusion, I did not on Yesterday morning know either your Face or your Voice; and that the answer which I happened to give you was intended for another, very unlike you, so that you must not be angry with, Madam, Your humble servant,

SAM. JOHNSON

1. The address indicates that this letter cannot predate 1779. During his last six winters SJ was often ill, most severely in 1782 and 1784. According to Duncan Isles, "1782 appears to have the better claim" ("The Lennox Collection," *Harvard Library Bulletin* 19, 1971, p. 179 n. 162). The available evidence is far from conclusive, however, and 1779–84 remains the least debatable indication of date.
2. The preceding part of the address has been torn away.

John Levett[1]

MS: Hyde Collection.

Sir: Golden Anchor, Holborn, Sat. Morning[2]

I have been hindred from writing to You by an imagination that it was necessary to write more than I had time for, but recollecting that Business may be despatched much more expeditiously by conversation, I beg to be informed when I can wait on You with most convenience to Yourself. I believe I shall find means of accommodating the affair so as to give You reasonable satisfaction.[3] You forgot to send me word what interest is due which I mention that You may examine, for though Mr. Aston[4] has a receipt for Interest which I got him to pay to Your Father, I[5] cannot conveniently wait on him about it. I am, Sir, Your most humble Servant,

SAM. JOHNSON

1. John Levett (1721–99), son of Theophilus, called to the Bar in 1743, M.P. for Lichfield (1761–62) (Namier and Brooke III.39).

2. In all likelihood this letter, as well as the two that follow, was written between May 1746 (the death of Theophilus Levett) and Nov. 1748 (the death of Henry Hervey Aston; see below, n. 4).

3. SJ continued to owe interest on the mortgage Theophilus Levett had granted him and his mother in 1740 (*Ante* To Theophilus Levett, 1 Dec. 1743 and n. 3).

4. The Hon. and Rev. Henry Hervey (1701–48), fourth son of the first Earl of Bristol. Hervey, who had known SJ since 1730, befriended him during his first years in London (Clifford, 1955, pp. 126–27, 175). When in 1744 Hervey's wife Catherine inherited the estates of her brother, Sir Thomas Aston, Bt., he changed his name to "Aston" (*Johns. Glean.* V.246).   5. MS: "but" del. before "I"

John Levett

MS: Hyde Collection.

Sir:

I am very ill, and unable to wait on You or meet with you. I have been disappointed by two to whom I applied, and either of whom might have done it without inconvenience. The Gentleman whom I have desired to come with this has effected it, on terms which may make a little longer delay, but if you have any one with whom You can leave the things necessary it may now be done. I am, sir, Your humble servant,

SAM. JOHNSON

I had sent to You but I had forgot your lodging which you have not mentioned in your notes.

John Levett

MS: Hyde Collection.
ADDRESS: To ⟨Mr. Levett.⟩

Saturday

I am very much obliged to You for your concession, which though, I think, not absolutely necessary to me, will be extremely convenient, as it will rescue me from the necessity of soliciting a favour, which, you know all mankind is apt ⟨to ra⟩te not according to its real value ⟨but to⟩ the exigence of him that asks it. I have all the assurance that human life allows, of being able by the time you mention of settling the affair without any trouble, and shall consider this exemption from the pain of borrowing as a very considerable favour to, Sir, Your humble servant,

SAM. JOHNSON

As You mention nothing of my coming to You, I suppose it is not convenient. May I have the pleasure of seeing you? I am almost always at home.

Will You spend an evening with me?

Andrew Millar

MS: Michael Silverman.

Mr. Johnson's compliments to Mr. Millar. He begs the favour of seeing the Elements of Criticism.[1]

1. The *terminus a quo* for this letter is the publication (by Millar) of Lord Kames's *Elements of Criticism* (1762), the *terminus ad quem* the death of Millar (1768). According to SJ, Kames took "the right method in his 'Elements of Criticism.' I do not mean that he has taught us any thing; but he has told us old things in a new way" (*Life* II.89–90).

Hannah More
THURSDAY[1]

MS: Folger Shakespeare Library.

                                                            Thursday

Mr. Johnson will wait on Miss Moore to morrow, about seven in the Evening.

1. The *terminus a quo* for this note is SJ's introduction to More, June 1774 (*Life* IV.341 n. 6), the *terminus ad quem* some few months before SJ's death, 13 Dec. 1784.

Hannah More
FRIDAY[1]

PRINTED SOURCE: John Grant Catalogue, Mar. 1931, p. 1.
ADDRESS: To Miss Moore.

Madam: Friday

I will wait on Mrs. Garrick and you on friday, it was by mere

1. The *terminus a quo* is the death of David Garrick, 20 Jan. 1779 (*Ante* To Hannah More, 12 Apr. 1781, n. 1), the *terminus ad quem* some few months before SJ's death, 13 Dec. 1784.

forgetfulness, not inadvertence, that I made an improper appointment before. I am, Madam, Your most humble servant,

SAM. JOHNSON

John Nichols
FRIDAY AFTERNOON[1]

MS: British Library.

Friday afternoon

Mr. Johnson is going to tea, and begs the favour of Mr. Nichol's company.

1. In his ordering of SJ's "little billets" to Nichols, F. W. Hilles places this note between 12 Apr. 1784 and 20 Oct. 1784 ("Johnson's Correspondence with Nichols," *Philological Quarterly* 48, 1969, p. 228). It could in fact belong anywhere in the series (1778–84).

Lewis Paul [1]

MS: Birmingham Public Library.

Dear Sir: Saturday

I have been really much disordered—when your last message came I was on the bed, and had not resolution to rise, having had no sleep all night, I indeed had for two days no audible voice, but am now much better, though I cannot hope to go out very quickly. I am, sir, your humble servant,

SAM. JOHNSON

1. Both Hill (1.66) and Chapman (1.94) assign this letter to 1756; neither one discusses his reasons for doing so. The mere fact that SJ and Paul were corresponding regularly during that year does not justify their conjectural dating. The date ("21 Dec.") added to the bottom of the letter in an unidentified hand offers no real clue (the twenty-first of December did not fall on a Saturday in 1756); neither does the direction on the verso ("To Mr. Johnson in Gauf's Square, fleet Street"). Paul's "last message" may concern the flurry of business dealt with in dated letters of this time (*Ante* To Lewis Paul, 13 Jan. 1756 and Late Feb. or Early Mar. 1756), but then again it may not. At the very least we can say that the letter probably predates SJ's removal from the Gough Square house in 1758.

Thomas Percy[1]

MS: Hyde Collection.
ADDRESS: To the Reverend Dr. Percy.

Sir:

I have sent you home a parcel of books, and do not know that I now retain any except Gongora,[2] and Araucana.[3] If you can spare Amadis,[4] please to return it to, Sir, your most humble,

SAM. JOHNSON

1. The *terminus a quo* for this letter is Dec. 1769 (when Percy proceeded D.D. from Cambridge), the *terminus ad quem* 1782 (when he became Bishop of Dromore). The handwriting would seem to indicate that it comes from the early to middle 1770s, when Percy was working on his collection of Spanish ballads in translation, "Ancient Songs, chiefly on Moorish Subjects" (Gisela Beutler, *Thomas Percy's spanische Studien*, 1957, p. 146). This miscellany was not published in Percy's lifetime (see *Ancient Songs*, ed. David Nichol Smith, 1932).

2. Luis de Gongora (1561–1627), prolific Spanish poet, who wrote in various forms, including the sonnet and the ballad.

3. SJ refers to *La Araucana* (1569), an epic poem by Alonso de Ercilla (1533–94).

4. *Amadis de Gaule*, a fifteenth-century Spanish romance, possibly translated from the Portugese.

John Perkins[1]

MS: Hyde Collection.
ADDRESS: To Mr. Perkins.

Sir:

I have sent a receipt for the interest. I have a draught of 200£ upon the house. When shall I bring it? I am, Sir, your most humble servant,

SAM. JOHNSON

1. Soon after the acquisition of the Thrale brewery by John Perkins and his partners, June 1781 (*Thraliana* 1.498–99), SJ began to use Perkins as his private banker (*Ante* To John Perkins, 6 Aug. 1781). At the time of his death, he had £300 on deposit with the firm (*Life* IV.402 n. 2). This note therefore belongs to the period between the summer of 1781 and the autumn of 1784.

John Perkins
24 JANUARY[1]

MS: Hyde Collection.
ADDRESS: To Mr. Perkins.

Dear Sir: Jan. 24

I am sorry for You all, and shall hope soon to see You all well;
when You come, allow your selves time for talk and tea, else I
shall be discontented. I am, dear Sir, your most humble servant,

SAM. JOHNSON

My compliments to Mrs. Perkins.

1. The form, content, tone, and handwriting of this and the following note
(dated 3 Feb.) suggest that they belong to 1782–84 (cf. *Ante* To John Perkins, 8
Oct. 1781; 23 Jan. 1784).

John Perkins
3 FEBRUARY

MS: Hyde Collection.

Febr. 3

Mr. Johnson expected Master Perkins's yesterday, and sup-
poses there was some mistake in the message. He begs the
favour of seeing them to day, or as soon as is convenient to
them.

Frances Reynolds[1]

MS: Hyde Collection.

1. This letter may date to *c.* 1769, if James Northcote's account is to be trusted.
See below, n. 2.

Dear Madam:

This is my letter which at least I like better than yours. But take your choice, and if you like mine alter any thing that you think not ladylike.[2]

2. SJ encloses a letter he had written for Frances Reynolds to send to her brother. In it he expresses her concern over Sir Joshua's lack of "notice," and asks for "a degree of attention . . . as may set me above the contempt of your servants" (MS: Hyde Collection). James Northcote appears to describe this letter when he reports: "Johnson, who participated with her in her troubles . . . voluntarily offered to write a letter himself, which when copied should pass as her own. This accordingly he performed; but when this letter was produced by him for her approval, she felt herself obliged to reject it, as the whole contents of it were so very unlike her own diction, and so decidedly like his, that the intended deception would no more have passed with Sir Joshua, than if Johnson had attired himself in her cap and gown, and endeavoured to impose his identical person upon Sir Joshua as his own sister" (*Life of Sir Joshua Reynolds*, 1818, 1.203). For similar instances of mediation, *Ante* To Frances Reynolds, 15 Feb. 1779; 28 May 1784.

Frances Reynolds[1]

MS: Hyde Collection.

ADDRESS: To Mrs. Reynolds.

Bolt court, 2 in the afternoon

Mr. Johnson will wait [on] dear Miss Reynolds in about two hours.

1. The Bolt Court address places this note sometime in the period 1776–84.

Joshua Reynolds[1]

MS: Hyde Collection.

ADDRESS: To Sir Joshua Reynolds.

Sir:

This is brought You by a young artist who is going to persue

1. The *terminus a quo* for this letter is 1769, when Reynolds received his knighthood. The handwriting suggests a date in the 1770s.

his studies in Italy, and thinks it disgraceful to leave England, without having had the honour of a conversation with you. Of his skill I cannot judge, all else that I know of him is to his advantage. I am, Sir, your most humble servant,

SAM. JOHNSON

Joseph Simpson[1]

MS: Beinecke Library. A copy sent to JB by Mary Adey,[2] 26 Feb. 1785.[3]

Dear Sir:

Your[4] Fathers Inexorability not only grieves but amazes me,[5] he is your Father, he was always accounted a Wise Man nor do I remember any thing to the disadvantage of his good nature, but in his refusal to assist you, there is neither good nature, Fatherhood nor Wisdom. It is the practice of good Nature to over look Faults which have already by the consequences[6] punish'd the[7] Delinquent. It is natural for a Father to think more favorably than others of[8] Children, and it is always wise to give Assistance while a little help will prevent the Necessity

1. *Ante* To John Levett, 17 Mar. 1752, n. 3. The *terminus a quo* for this letter is the death of SJ's mother, Jan. 1759, the *terminus ad quem* Lucy Porter's move into her new house, early 1766. It is most likely to have been written before Lucy Porter inherited her brother's fortune, Apr. 1763 (*Ante* To Lucy Porter, 6 Feb. 1759 and n. 3; 12 Apr. 1763).

2. Mary Adey was Joseph Simpson's first cousin (*Reades*, p. 212 n. 4).

3. Three other copies of this letter have been recovered: one by the Rev. Daniel Astle, sent to JB in Dec. 1786 (Beinecke Library); another by Mary Adey, sent to H. L. Piozzi on 29 Oct. 1787 (Rylands Library); and one sent by a "Mrs. Clerke" to a "Miss Simpson," ?21 Sept. 1802 (Beinecke Library). Substantive variants have been recorded. For more extensive commentary, see Waingrow, pp. 67–70.

4. "Mr. Simpson communicates your Letters regularly" (Astle); "Communicate your letters regularly" (Piozzi)

5. Stephen Simpson (?1700–74), lawyer and landowner in Lichfield (*Johns. Glean.* IV.150, 160; Clifford, 1955, p. 92). In 1719 he married Jane Adey (1702–67), daughter of Joseph Adey the elder, attorney of Lichfield, and sister of Joseph Adey the younger, father of Mary (*Reades*, p. 212 n. 4; *Johns. Glean.* XI.5).

6. "consequence" (Astle, Piozzi)   7. "their" (Astle)   8. "of his" (Astle)

of greater; If you married imprudently, you miscarried[9] at your own hazard at an Age when you had a right of choice.[10] It wou'd be hard if the[11] Man might not chuse his own Wife who has a right to plead before the Judges of his Country.[12]

If your imprudence has ended in difficulties and inconveniences,[13] You are yourself to support them,[14] and with the help of a little better health you wou'd Support them and conquer them. Surely that want which Accident and Sickness produces[15] is to be supported[16] in every Region of Humanity, tho' there were neither Friends nor Fathers in the World, You have certainly from your Father, the highest claim of Charity tho' none[17] of right, and therefore I wou'd counsel you to omit no decent nor Manly degree of Importunity. Your debts in the whole are not large, and of the whole but a small part is troublesome. Small debts are like small shot, they are ratling on[18] every Side, and can scarcely be Escaped without a Wound. Great debts are like Cannon of loud Noise but little danger. You must therefore be enabled to discharge petty debts[19] that you may have leisure with Security to Struggle with the rest. Neither the great nor little debts disgrace you. I am sure you have my Esteem for the Courage with which you contracted them, and the Spirit with which you endure them. I wish my Esteem cou'd be of more use. I have been invited, or have invited Myself to Several parts of the Kingdom, and will not incommode my Dear Lucy by coming to Lichfield while her present Lodging is of any use to her. I hope in a few Days to be at leisure and to make Visits. Wither I shall fly is

9. "married" (Astle, Piozzi)

10. Joseph Simpson had first been married, "at least as early as 1754," to Elizabeth Gravenor, the daughter of a silk merchant in Coventry (*Johns. Glean.* IV.149, 157); "the imprudent marriage which SJ speaks of in his letter was presumably his second" (Waingrow, p. 68 n. 17).   11. "a" (Clerke)

12. At this point Astle's text includes the following quotation, whose source has not been traced: "Cui se clientum Capita fortunae / fides tutanda credunt."

13. "inconvenience" (Astle)

14. "and to conquer them" (Astle)

15. "produce" (Piozzi)   16. "succoured" (Astle)   17. "to none" (Clerke)

18. "in" (Clerke)   19. "demands" (Astle, Piozzi)

Matter[20] of no Importance, A Man unconnected is at home every where, unless he maybe said to be at home no where.

I am sorry Dear Sir[21] that where you have Parents, a Man of your Merits[22] shou'd not have an[23] home.[24] I wish I cou'd give it you. I am, my Dear Sir,[25] Affectionately Yours,

SAML. JOHNSON[26]

20. "a matter" (Astle)

21. "dear Simpson" (Astle)   22. "merit" (Astle)   23. "a" (Piozzi)

24. See above, n. 5. "I am sorry to Say my Aunt Simpson was more implacable than my Uncle, which was very Strange, as She had generosity and Charity to *others*, and was Esteem'd a very Sensible Polite Woman" (Mary Adey to JB, 26 Feb. 1785: Waingrow, pp. 70–71).

25. "I am, Dear Simpson" (Astle); "I am, Dear Sir" (Piozzi)

26. MS: "Johson," corrected by JB; "Sam. Johnson" (Astle, Clerke)

Percival Stockdale

PRINTED SOURCE: Percival Stockdale, *Memoirs*, 1809, pp. 128–29.

[I was once expressing to him (I think it was in the year 1778) my anxiety for a permanent establishment in the church. I told him that as I had some personal acquaintance with Burke; if I was assisted with his friendly, and warm recommendation to that gentleman, I had no doubt that he would exert his interest to procure me a benefice. Johnson replied, that if I would engage to *him*, to be conscientiously attentive to my clerical duties, he would write to Burke in my favour. I sincerely made him the promise that he required of me. Dr. Johnson gave me his letter of recommendation to read; it was a short, but kind one. ... I, at this time, took several occasions to express my dislike of the measures of government; as I detested the american war. To this circumstance, a humorous, and ironical remark in the doctor's letter alluded. ... After he had spoken well of my orthodoxy, he added;] to his political heresies, I wish that *you* were more an enemy.

Margaret Penelope Strahan

20 SEPTEMBER

MS: Beinecke Library.
ADDRESS: To Mrs. Strahan.

Dear Madam: Sept. 20

When you kindly invited me to dine with [You] to morrow, I had forgotten that I had my self invited a friend to dine with me. I will therefore wait on You any other day. I am, Madam, your most humble servant,

SAM. JOHNSON

William Strahan[1]

MS: Hyde Collection.
ADDRESS: To Mr. Strahan.

Dear Sir:

What you tell me, I am ashamed never to have thought on—I wish I had known it sooner—Send me back the last sheet and the last copy for correction. If you will promise me henceforward to print a sheet a day, I will promise you to endeavour that you shall have every day a sheet to print, beginning next tuesday.[2] I am, Sir, Your most, etc.

SAM. JOHNSON

1. The contents of this letter suggest a period early in the printing of the *Dictionary*—sometime between the autumn of 1749 and the summer of 1750.

2. J. L. Clifford explains the background to this letter: "We know that Johnson was, at some point, supposed to receive a guinea for carefully prepared copy which would make a printed sheet. This was paid on delivery, and every guinea parcel was then tied up at the printers and 'put upon a shelf in the collector's room till wanted.' Printed sheets were sent back to Gough Square for revision" (Clifford, 1979, p. 55). The problem at issue here may have involved "clipping close" (*Ante* To William Strahan, Spring or Summer 1753, n. 6).

William Strahan[1]

MS: Hyde Collection.
ADDRESS: To Mr. Strahan.

Dear Sir:

I must desire you to add to your other civilities this one, to go to Mr. Millar and represent to him our manner of going on, and inform him that I know not how to manage, I pay three and twenty shillings a week to my assistants, in truth without having much assistance from them, but they tell me they shall be able to fall better in method, as indeed I intend they shall.[2] The point is to get two Guineas for, Your humble Servant,

SAM. JOHNSON

1. According to J. L. Clifford, this letter could have been written "as early as late 1749" (Clifford, 1979, p. 55). It is unlikely to have been written later than mid 1750, by which time SJ's assistants would have fallen "better in method."

2. "If he was paying only 23s. a week to his amanuenses, that would mean that he probably had only two working at the time (one receiving 12s. and the other 11s.), or possibly three, with lower wages (9, 7, 7)" (Clifford, 1979, p. 55).

John Taylor
THURSDAY NIGHT[1]

MS: Beinecke Library.
ADDRESS: To the Revd. Dr. Taylor in Market Bosworth, near Leicester.
POSTMARK: 11 OC.
ENDORSEMENT: Thursday Night.

Dear Sir: Thursday Night

I received on Monday your kind Letter, which I am now, I hope able to answer. I know not what to think of your affair with Mr. Broderic,[2] if he has not yet answered your Letter

1. The *terminus a quo* for this letter is Taylor's nomination to the rectory of Market Bosworth in 1740 (*Life* 11.542). The handwriting points to a date in the early to middle 1740s.

2. "Mr. Broderic," who has not been identified, must have been living in the London area; otherwise he could not have been reached by the penny post.

which I thought very rational and polite and therefore sent immediately to the penny post, you must I think write to him again, so as to keep the affair alive, though it will be like playing at Chess by messages,[3] Life may be ended before the Game. I hope I shall grow better and I perceive You hope so too, but you forgot to direct the Bill so that I knew not whither to carry it. I am, Dear Sir, Your humble Servant,

SAM. JOHNSON

3. According to J. M. Osborn, "Johnson's reference to 'Chess by messages' [now known as 'correspondence chess'] is one of the earliest in the history of the noble game" ("Johnson to Taylor No. 90," *TLS*, 24 Dec. 1964, p. 1171).

John Taylor

MS: Hyde Collection.[1]

With regard to your last scheme it is probably too late to mention it, for I suppose Wills[2] may before now have resigned his preferments. You laid I remember some stress upon the Kings Journey, which as I am well informed, is now no lon⟨   ⟩

1. This fragment appears to have been cut from a letter to John Taylor that relates to Taylor's campaign for preferment to the deanery of Lincoln through the patronage of the Duke of Devonshire (*Ante* To John Taylor, 24 Sept. 1781 and n. 1). If this hypothesis is correct, then the letter must date to late 1781 or early 1782. On the verso appears part of the draft of a letter (also in SJ's hand), designed presumably for Taylor to copy over and send to the Duke: "⟨   ⟩ly imply a want of Confidence in your Grace's Promise. I feel less concern for my present obligations to reside here, because ⟨I am⟩ myself absolutely unable to promote the efficacy of your Grace's kind Intentions ⟨*half a line*⟩ must be wholly your Grace's act, as ⟨   ⟩." Cf. To John Taylor, 20 Oct. 1774.
2. Possibly John Wills (*c.* 1741–1806), D.D. (1783), Fellow of Hertford College, Oxford, and Rector of Tydd St. Mary, Lincolnshire (*Alum. Oxon.* II.iv.1578).

Hester Maria Thrale

THURSDAY MORN[1]

1. It is likely that this note belongs to the period after the death of Henry

MS: Hyde Collection.

ADDRESS: To Miss Thrale.

Thursday Morn

Mr. Johnson begs the favour of Miss Thrale, that she will write him word whether Lady (Langton) Rothes, dines with them, for, if she does not, Mr. Johnson will set down Mrs. Williams in Welbeck Street.

Thrale, Apr. 1781, and before the family's departure for Bath, Apr. 1783. A definite *terminus ad quem* is provided by the death of Anna Williams, Sept. 1783. The most plausible date is 1782 or early 1783.

Hester Thrale

MS: Hyde Collection.

ADDRESS: To Mrs. Thrale.

Johnson's Court, Oct. 2[1]

Mr. Johnson flatters himself that there is no need of informing Mr. Thrale that the application required was made to Mr. Burke, or Mrs. Thrale that he wishes her every thing that friendship can wish her. He has sent her a pamphlet to amuse her in her confinement, which he would not have shown to more than Mr. Thrale, and Mrs. Salisbury.

1. The *terminus a quo* for this letter is Jan. 1765 (SJ's first meeting with the Thrales), the *terminus ad quem* June 1773 (the death of Mrs. Salusbury). If one assumes that "Oct. 2" is correct, then the likeliest date is 1765, when Hester Thrale was recovering from the birth of Frances (27 Sept.). The "pamphlet" may be associated with SJ's services for W. G. Hamilton (*Ante* To Charles Jenkinson, 26 Oct. 1765, n. 3).

Hester Thrale

MS: Hyde Collection.[1]

ADDRESS: To Mrs. Thrale.

1. This fragment of a letter consists of four lines of text and a separate scrap with the direction.

⟨   ⟩ bleeding, and Physick, and ⟨*four or five letters*⟩,[2] and innumerable miseries. There are many Ups and Downs in the world, and my dearest Mistress, ⟨has⟩[3] been down, and up, and down again. When you are up again, keep up.

2. MS: one word heavily del.
3. MS: one word heavily del.

Hester Thrale

SATURDAY[1]

MS: Hyde Collection.
ADDRESS: To Mrs. Thrale.

Dearest Madam: Saturday

I long to come to that place which my dear Friends allow me to call HOME. Pray come, or send for me on Wednesday. I am, Madam, your most humble servant,

SAM. JOHNSON

1. This letter cannot be dated more precisely than 1766–80.

Hester Thrale

21 MAY[1]

MS: Hyde Collection.

Madam: May 21

I have now got more books for Mr. Thrale than can be carried in the coach, and, I think, he may better send a cart than we can get one, because he may send with it baskets or sacks for the smaller volumes. We have of all sizes more than four

1. This letter could have been written in 1770, 1771, 1772, 1773, 1774, or 1778. I am inclined to date it to 1770—two days before the birth of Susanna Arabella Thrale.

hundred. If I could know when the cart would come I would take care to have somebody in the way. But perhaps there is no haste; yet I now care not how soon they are gone. Please to send me word that you are pretty well, at least tell me how you are. I am, Madam, your most obedient,

SAM. JOHNSON

Hester Thrale[1]

MS: Alderman Library, University of Virginia.
ADDRESS: To Mrs. Thrale.

Dear Madam:

I know not, nor ever shall know, the ingenious writer. Steevens has been with me this morning, and told me of it. He says Cinna is Shebeare.[2] I am, Madam, Your most humble,

SAM. JOHNSON

1. Though it is impossible to date this note with any degree of precision, the likeliest period is that of 1770–75, when SJ produced his four political tracts and involved himself intensively in Henry Thrale's political career. See below, n. 2.

2. John Shebbeare (1709–88) trained as a surgeon in Paris, then in 1754 began a career as a polemical writer. He was convicted of libel in 1758 for writing against the Hanoverian monarchy; three years later he was released from prison and granted a pension. "From the time of that event we find Dr. Shebbeare a uniform defender of the measures of Government, and the mark against whom every opposer of administration considered himself at liberty to throw out the grossest abuse" (*European Magazine* 14, 1788, p. 87). Shebbeare was the author of numerous political tracts, including *An Essay on the Origin, Progress, and Establishment of National Society* (1776) (*European Magazine* 14, 1788, p. 168). He may have been the pseudonymous "Cinna" who contributed extensively to the *Public Advertiser* in 1770, attacking Junius and the "patriotic" Whigs (*Public Advertiser*, 9 Oct. 1770, p. 1; *The Letters of Junius*, ed. John Cannon, 1978, p. 364 n. 2).

Hester Thrale

MS: Princeton University Library.
ADDRESS: To Mrs. Thrale.

⟨ ⟩ could be expected. To advise or help a daughter to run a way, is an intrusion into the domestick rights of another man, and a violation of his authority such as is not easily ⟨ ⟩ Dear Madam, your most etc.[1]

SAM. JOHNSON

1. This letter may relate to the elopement of Fanny Plumbe, though it appears to contradict SJ's sentiments on paternal authority (*Ante* To Hester Thrale, 17 May 1773).

Hester Thrale[1]

MS: Johnson House, London.
ADDRESS: Mrs. Thrale.

Mr. Johnson will wait for dear Mrs. Thrale to morrow, and shall be to the last degree unwilling to do any thing which she shall forbid. He will go with her to Streatham, for he longs to be again with so much kindness, and prudence.

1. This letter might conceivably fall anytime during the period 1766–80. I am inclined, however, to place it *c.* 1773, the era of SJ's French letter (*Ante* To Hester Thrale, Early June 1773).

Hester Thrale

MS: Hyde Collection.

Dear Madam: Lichfield, July 7, 1771[1]

Once more I sit down to write, and hope you will once more be willing to read it.

1. This letter is misdated: from 29 June to 31 July 1771, SJ was in Ashbourne. Various conjectural redatings are possible from the period 1770–79, depending on whether one assumes SJ to have mistaken the year or the month (or both). The other years in which the letter might have been written are 1770, 1775, 1777, and 1779.

Last Sunday an old acquaintance found me out, not, I think, a Schoolfellow, but one with whom I played perhaps before I went to School. I had not seen him for forty years, but was glad to find him alive. He has had as he phrased it *a matter of four wives,* for which neither you nor I like him much the better, but after all his marriages he is poor, and has now at sixty six two very young children.

Such, Madam, are the strange things of which we that travel come to the knowledge. We see mores hominum multorum.[2] You that waste your lives over a book at home, must take life upon trust. I am, Dear Madam, your most obedient servant,

SAM. JOHNSON

2. *dic mihi, Musa, virum, captae post tempora Troiae / qui mores hominum multorum vidit et urbes:* "Sing, Muse, for me the man who on Troy's fall / Saw the wide world, its ways and cities all" (Horace, *Ars Poetica,* ll. 141–42, trans. H. R. Fairclough, Loeb ed.).

Hester Thrale[1]

MS: Hyde Collection.

Qu'il vous plaise, Madame, de m'envoyer le son que vous trouvez bon que je prenne;[2] il pourra venir a l'aide de ma medicine. Pour vous, mon illustre maîtresse, il faut toutefois conserver vôtre gaietè, et esperer tout le meilleur.

1. It is likely that all three of SJ's notes in French belong to the period 1773–75. Cf. *Ante* To Hester Thrale, Early June 1773.
2. Decoctions of bran were "supposed to have a laxative and detergent quality," and to be efficacious on occasion "against coughs" (William Lewis, *Materia Medica,* 3d ed., 1784, pp. 310–11).

Hester Thrale

MS: Hyde Collection.

Je ne saurois me dispenser d'âvouer, Madame, qu'apres avoir

soûtenù durant trois heurs un chaleur et une amértûme assez penible, les consequences[1] de la medicine que vous me faisiez l'honeur de me mêtre, je lavois ma bouche au moment du coûcher, pour ne perdre mon sommeil. Je me jette a vos pies, si j'ai fait trop, il ne reste qu'a vous, Madame, de venger vos droits.

1. MS: "effets" del. before "consequences"

Hester Thrale

MS: Hyde Collection.

Vous me chargiez hier, Madame, de tant de pain, que je n'en pouvois prendre qu'une partie, il en reste assez pour ce jour.

Hester Thrale

TUESDAY[1]

MS: Hyde Collection.

Tuesday

Mr. Johnson is much obliged by Mrs. Thrales enquiry. He came home on Saturday. He is still very much disordered, but would have come to Streatham if Mrs. Thrale had called. Quo me vertam, nescio.[2]

1. This note may have been written after SJ's return from Lichfield, Aug. 1775.
2. *Quo me vertam, nescio:* "I do not know where to turn."

Hester Thrale

MS: Hyde Collection.

Thursday, Febr. 21[1]

Mr. Johnson will be ready to attend Mrs. Thrale and Miss Burgoyne to morrow.[2]

1. If SJ's date is correct, then this note belongs either to 1771 or to 1782. The handwriting suggests the later date, but in late Feb. 1782 SJ was recovering from a severe cold (*Ante* To Hester Thrale, 21 Feb. 1782; *Ante* To Edmond Malone, 27 Feb. 1782).

2. Miss Burgoyne, the godmother of Ralph Thrale and the daughter of Sir Roger Burgoyne (*c.* 1710–80), sixth Bt., of Sutton Park, Bedfordshire (Hyde, 1977, p. 85).

Unidentified Correspondent[1]

MS: Hyde Collection.

ENDORSEMENT in an unidentified hand: from Sam. Johnson.

⟨Dear⟩ Sir: Thursday night[2]

⟨I⟩ have been waiting on you every ⟨day⟩ and have not done it. I hear you take subscriptions for your two subsequent volumes, I beg to put my name amongst your other friends, if you favour me with a few receipts, I will push them.

My Lord Corke did me the honour to leave his name, I went to Mr. Andrew Millar to enquire where he resides,[3] but could not learn. I am impatient to know. I am, Sir, your most humble servant,

SAM. JOHNSON

1. Chapman's conjectural identification of the recipient as Samuel Richardson (i.51) is disproved by T.C.D. Eaves ("Dr. Johnson's Letters to Richardson," *PMLA* 75, 1960, pp. 378–79). Eaves has no alternative candidate to propose.

2. The letter could not have been written before 3 Dec. 1753, when Lord Orrery succeeded to the title of Cork. Orrery died in 1762.

3. Millar had published Orrery's *Remarks on the Life and Writings of Dr. Jonathan Swift* (1751).

Unidentified Correspondent
29 NOVEMBER

MS: Hyde Collection.

Dear Sir: Nov. 29

I have seen your proof as I told you, and saw I think only one word that I wished to alter.

Be pleased to make my compliments to the Ladies of[1] your house. I am, Sir, Your most humble servant,

SAM. JOHNSON

1. MS: "of" altered from "at"

Unidentified Correspondent

MS: Pierpont Morgan Library.

My eye tells me that he will work no longer.

Unidentified Correspondent[1]

MS: Houghton Library.

It is great impudence to put Johnsons Poets on the back of books which Johnson neither recommended nor revised.[2]

He recommended only Blackmore on the Creation[3] and Watts.[4] How then are they Johnson's? This is indecent.

1. This note, which probably dates to 1779 or 1780, may have been sent to John Nichols (cf. *Ante* To John Nichols, *c.* Apr. 1780).
2. *Ante* To John Nichols, *c.* Apr. 1780, n. 1.
3. *The Creation* (1712), a philosophical poem by Sir Richard Blackmore.
4. *Ante* To W. Sharp, 7 July 1777 and n. 2. SJ also recommended Pomfret, Yalden, and Thomson (*Life* III.370; *Ante* To JB, 3 May 1777).

Unidentified Correspondent
19 AUGUST[1]

PRINTED SOURCE: Chapman III.274.

Aug. 19

Mr. Johnson is this day engaged to the Bishop of Dromore. To refuse invitations from great friends is very vexatious. Do not think it perverseness in, dear Madam,

1. The *terminus a quo* is the consecration of Thomas Percy as Bishop of Dromore, May 1782. In Aug. 1784 SJ was visiting Ashbourne. This note therefore dates to either 1782 or 1783.

Unidentified Correspondent
FRIDAY NIGHT[1]

MS: Hyde Collection.

Fryday night

I have not yet seen the Doctor, but will have his help to morrow, for I have no news to write at which my friends can rejoice.

1. The handwriting dates this note to the period 1782–84.

Joseph or Thomas Warton

MS: Pierpont Morgan Library.
ADDRESS: Revd. ⟨   ⟩ Warton.[1]

Dear Sir:

I wish you had given me notice a little sooner before I had parcelled out the day, but I will come to you if I can, and I believe I can. I am, Dear Sir, etc.

SAM. JOHNSON

1. MS: mutilated

Thomas Warton
MONDAY NIGHT[1]

MS: Trinity College, Oxford.
ADDRESS: To the Revd. Mr. Warton.

Sir: Monday Night

I beg the favour of you when you send for your books not to let the table be forgotten. Make my compliments to your Brother and do not forget your affectionate,

SAM. JOHNSON

1. It is possible that this note was written at the same time as To Robert Chambers, 4 Aug. 1755, which is also dated "Monday night." If this conjecture is correct, then the books and table to which SJ refers may well have been loaned to him for use in Kettell Hall (*Ante* To Thomas Warton, 13 May 1755, n. 5) (information supplied by Dr. David Fairer).

Elizabeth Way
JULY[1]

PRINTED SOURCE: Chapman III.339.
ADDRESS: South Sea House.

July

Mr. Johnson returns his sincere thanks to dear Mrs. Way for her kind enquiries.

1. It is likely that this note dates to the same period (1782–84) as SJ's other letters to Elizabeth Way.

Charles Wesley[1]

1. John Telford includes this note in the chapter devoted to Charles Wesley's "old age and death," and places it immediately before SJ's note to Sarah Wesley, 28 Oct. 1783 (Telford, *The Life of the Rev. Charles Wesley, M.A.*, 1900, pp. 279–80). The handwriting and the reference to SJ's "disordered state of . . . health" point as well to the period 1781–84.

MS: Hyde Collection.

Sir: Wednesday

I beg that You, and Mrs.,[2] and Miss Wesley will dine with your Brother and Mrs. Hall, at my house in Bolt court, Fleetstreet, to morrow.

That I have not sent sooner, if You knew the disordered state of my health, You would easily forgive me. I am, Sir, Your most humble Servant,

SAM. JOHNSON

2. Sarah Gwynne (1726–1822), third daughter of Marmaduke Gwynne, of Garth, Breconshire, married Charles Wesley in 1749.

APPENDIX II
Letters Substantiated by
Mention

TO SARAH JOHNSON, *Whitsuntide* 1719

"I staid after the vacation was over some days; and remember, when I wrote home, that I desired the horses to come on Thursday of the first school week; and then, and not till then, they should be welcome to go. I was much pleased with a rattle to my whip, and wrote of it to my mother."
(*Works*, Yale ed. 1.20)

TO EDMUND HECTOR, 1732

"This employment was very irksome to him . . . and he complained grievously of it in his letters to his friend Mr. Hector, who was now settled as a surgeon in Birmingham. The letters are lost; but Mr. Hector recollects his writing 'that the poet has described the dull sameness of his existence in these words, '*Vitam continet una dies*' (one day contains the whole of my life); that it was unvaried as the note of the cuckow; and that he did not know whether it was more disagreeable for him to teach, or the boys to learn, the grammar rules'."
(*Life* 1.84)

TO JOHN TAYLOR, 2 *Jan.* 1742

"Speaking of Mrs. Johnson's illness."
(Sotheby's Catalogue, 31 Mar. 1875, Lot No. 260, p. 36)

TO AN UNIDENTIFIED CORRESPONDENT, 17 *July* 1742

(date fragment in Hyde Collection)

TO LUCY PORTER, *Dec.* 1743

(To Theophilus Levett, 3 Jan. 1744)

TO AN UNIDENTIFIED CORRESPONDENT, *Birmingham*,
Dec. 1743

(To Theophilus Levett, 3 Jan. 1744)

TO JOHN *or* PAUL KNAPTON, ?*June* 1746
(To Robert Dodsley, June 1746)

TO JOHN TAYLOR, 17 *Mar.* 1752
"The dreadful shock of separation [on Elizabeth Johnson's death] took place in the night; and he immediately dispatched a letter to his friend, the Reverend Dr. Taylor, which, as Taylor told me, expressed his grief in the strongest manner he had ever read; so that it is much to be regretted that it has not been preserved."
(*Life* 1.238)

TO HILL BOOTHBY, *c.* 17 *May* 1754
"How was I surprized this morning, when, on opening a letter from you."
(Hill Boothby to SJ, 20 May 1754, *An Account of the Life of Dr. Samuel Johnson*, ed. Richard Wright, 1805, p. 58)

TO FRANCIS WISE, *Feb.* 1755
(To Thomas Warton, 4 Feb. 1755)

TO FRANCIS WISE, *Mar.* 1755
(To Thomas Warton, 20 Mar. 1755)

TO ROBERT CHAMBERS, 6 *Aug.* 1755
(To Robert Chambers, 7 Aug. 1755)

TO CATHERINE TALBOT, *Jan.* 1756
"Before your Letter came I had been honored with one from Mr. Johnson himself, so highly polite and complimental that it infinitely distressed me."
(Catherine Talbot to Elizabeth Carter, 24 Feb. 1756, *A Series of Letters between Mrs. Elizabeth Carter and Miss Catherine Talbot*, 1809, II.221)

TO WILLIAM COLLINS, *c.* 1756
(To Joseph Warton, 15 Apr. 1756)

TO SARAH JOHNSON, 21 *June* 1757
(To John Levett, 21 June 1757)

TO GEORGE HUDDESFORD, *June* 1757
(To Thomas Warton, 21 June 1757)

TO CHARLES BURNEY, *Mar.* 1758
(To Charles Burney, 8 Mar. 1758)

TO WILLIAM SHENSTONE, *c.* 1759
"Did I tell you I had a letter from Johnson, inclosing Vernon's Parish-clerk."
(William Shenstone to Mr. Graves, 26 Oct. 1759, William Shenstone, *Works*, 1764–69, III.340–41)

TO THOMAS HERVEY, ?1763
"Johnson interfered as their friend [in a dispute between Hervey and his wife] and wrote him a letter of expostulation, which I have not been able to find."
(*Life* II.32, 480)

TO FRANCIS ANDREWS, *c.* 17 *Oct.* 1765
(To Thomas Leland, 17 Oct. 1765)

TO HENRY *and* HESTER THRALE, *Autumn* 1765
"Mr. Johnson . . . in the autumn of the next year . . . followed us to Brighthelmstone, whence we were gone before his arrival; so he was disappointed and enraged, and wrote us a letter expressive of anger, which we were very desirous to pacify, and to obtain his company again if possible."
(*Johns. Misc.* I.233)

TO MR. WESLEY, *c.* 3 *Mar.* 1768
(To Hester Thrale, 3 Mar. 1768)

TO AN UNIDENTIFIED CORRESPONDENT, 7 *July* 1770
(To Hester Thrale, 7 July 1770)

TO THOMAS CADELL, 1771
"Johnson's (Dr. Sam.) Note to his Publisher to bind two copies of 'False Alarm' and 'Falkland Islands,' written in 1771."
(Fletcher's Catalogue, 30 May 1845, Lot No. 115, p. 8)

TO THOMAS GRIFFITH, *July* 1771
(To Frances Reynolds, 29 July 1771; To Henry Thrale, 31 July 1771)

TO HESTER THRALE, 4 *May* 1773
(To Hester Thrale, 4 May 1773)

TO ANNA WILLIAMS, 28 *Aug.* 1773
"Mr. Johnson wrote tonight both to Mrs. Thrale and Mrs. Williams."
(*Hebrides*, p. 95)

TO EDMUND ALLEN, 21 *Sept.* 1773
"The last letter we received from Dr. Johnson was dated the 21st of
last month, he was then in the Isle of Sky."
(Edmund Allen to Thomas Percy, 30 Oct. 1773, MS: Hyde Collection)

TO ?RICHARD TWISS, *before* 30 *Mar.* 1774
"He [Twiss] then put into my Hand a Letter from that awful *Colossos*
of Literature, as he [SJ] is often called. I told him that I *had* seen his
Writing (which is scarse legible) . . . in a Letter to my Father. However,
he shewed me one Word; (it was *Testimony*) that I could not possibly
make out."
(*The Early Journals and Letters of Fanny Burney*, ed. Lars Troide, 1990,
II.18)

TO ?CHARLES SIMPSON, *c.* 25 *Feb.* 1775
(To Lucy Porter, 25 Feb. 1775)

TO HENRY THRALE, 6 *May* 1775
"Asking for news of Mrs. Thrale's health, apparently on the birth of
a child."
(Sotheby's Catalogue, 30 Jan. 1918, Lot No. 226, p. 34)

TO GEORGE FAULKNER, *May* 1775
(To Hester Thrale, 12 May 1775)

TO THOMAS LELAND, *May* 1775
(To Hester Thrale, 12 May 1775)

TO EDMUND ALLEN, 16 *June* 1775
(To Edmund Allen, 17 June 1775)

TO JOSHUA REYNOLDS, 16 *June* 1775
(To Edmund Allen, 17 June 1775)

TO THOMAS DAVIES, *c.* 19 *June* 1775
(To Edmund Allen, 19 June 1775)

TO RICHARD GREENE, 29 *June* 1775
"Making an appointment."
(Puttick and Simpson Catalogue, 10 Mar. 1862, Lot No. 363, p. 35)

TO HESTER MARIA THRALE, *Early July* 1775
(To Hester Thrale, 11 July 1775)

TO ELIZABETH ASTON *and* JANE GASTRELL, 9 *Sept.* 1775
(To Lucy Porter, 9 Sept. 1775)

TO JOHN TAYLOR, *between* 16 *Nov.* 1775 and 25 *Dec.* 1775
(Conjecture based on Taylor's numeration; see Chapman III.302–4)

TO CHARLES CARTER, *Feb.* 1776
(To Hester Thrale, 11 Feb. 1776)

TO JOHN TAYLOR, *c.* 22 *Mar.* 1776
(To John Taylor, 23 Mar. 1776)

TO COUNT MANUCCI, *May* 1776
(To Hester Thrale, 16 May 1776)

TO JOHN TAYLOR, *between* 3 *Sept.* 1776 *and* 23 *Jan.* 1777
(Conjecture based on Taylor's numeration; see Chapman III.302–4)

TO WILLIAM STRAHAN, *c.* 4 *Oct.* 1776
(To William Strahan, 14 Oct. 1776)

TO ANNA WILLIAMS, *Oct.* 1776
(To Robert Levet, 21 Oct. 1776)

TO LUCY PORTER, *Dec.* 1776
(To William Strahan, 24 Dec. 1776)

TO AN UNIDENTIFIED CORRESPONDENT, *Feb.* 1777
(To Bennet Langton, 13 Feb. 1777)

TO JOHN TAYLOR, *between* 19 *May* 1777 *and* 9 *Mar.* 1779 (I)
(Conjecture based on Taylor's numeration; see Chapman III.302–4)

TO JOHN TAYLOR, *between* 19 *May* 1777 *and* 9 *Mar.* 1779 (II)
(Conjecture based on Taylor's numeration; see Chapman III.302–4)

TO HESTER THRALE, 11 *June* 1777
"Giving a list of his engagements."
(Sotheby's Catalogue, 30 Jan. 1918, Lot No. 230, p. 34)

TO WILLIAM BEATTIE, *c.* 24 *June* 1777
"I have given him [Seward] letters to you and Beattie."
(SJ to JB, 28 June 1777)

TO WILLIAM VYSE, *c. July* 1777
(*Life* III.125)

TO HESTER THRALE, 11 *Sept.* 1777
(To Hester Thrale, 15 Sept. 1777)

TO THOMAS DAVIES, 13 *Sept.* 1777
(*Works*, Yale ed. I.275)

TO ROBERT LEVET, 13 *Sept.* 1777
(*Works*, Yale ed. I.275)

TO LUCY PORTER, 13 *Sept.* 1777
(*Works*, Yale ed. I.275)

TO ROBERT WATSON, 13 *Sept.* 1777
(*Works*, Yale ed. I.275)

TO ANNA WILLIAMS, 13 *Sept.* 1777
(*Works*, Yale ed. I.275)

TO JOSEPH WARTON, *c. Jan.* 1778
"The same year [1778] Dr. Johnson not only wrote to Dr. Joseph War-

ton in favour of Dr. Burney's youngest son, who was to be placed in the college of Winchester, but accompanied him when he went thither."
(*Life* III.367; J. Warton to SJ, 27 Jan. 1778, MS: Winchester College)

TO AN UNIDENTIFIED CORRESPONDENT, 30 *June* 1778
(Sotheby's Catalogue, 25 Apr. 1843, Lot No. 175, p. 17)

TO THOMAS CADELL, 17 *Oct.* 1778
"Apologises for the delay in returning the proof sheets, mentioning those of the Life of Dryden."
(Sotheby's Catalogue, 10 May 1875, Lot No. 96, p. 11)

TO JOHN TAYLOR, *between* 4 *May* 1779 *and* 3 *Aug.* 1779
(Conjecture based on Taylor's numeration; see Chapman III.302–4)

TO HESTER THRALE, *before* 11 *Oct.* 1779
(To Hester Thrale, 11 Oct. 1779)

TO LUCY PORTER, *c. Oct.* 1779
(To Lucy Porter, 19 Oct. 1779)

TO FRANCES BURNEY, *c. Apr.* 1780
(To Hester Thrale, 20 Apr. 1780)

TO HESTER MARIA THRALE, *c. Apr.* 1780
(To Hester Thrale, 20 Apr. 1780) Possibly the same as To Hester Maria Thrale, 19 May 1780.

TO LORD THURLOW, 19 *Oct.* 1780
(*Life*, III.441)

TO GEORGE FLETCHER, ?1780
"The rev. George Fletcher, rector of Cubley in Derbyshire, informed me, that the Doctor had formerly applied to him for extracts relative to his father and his family, who are registered as the natives of that village."
(Stebbing Shaw, *The History and Antiquities of Staffordshire*, 1798–1801, I.323)

TO MARY ADEY, *Mar.* 1781
(To Lucy Porter, 8 Mar. 1781)

?TO AN UNIDENTIFIED CORRESPONDENT, 17 *Apr.* 1781
(Chapman No. 727.1, II.423) Possibly the same as To Hester Thrale,
17 Apr. 1781.

TO BATEMAN ROBSON, *Apr.* 1781
(To Hester Thrale, 16 Apr. 1781)

TO ELIZABETH ASTON, 19 *Mar.* 1782
(*Works*, Yale ed. I.314)

TO WILLIAM GERARD HAMILTON, 22 *Mar.* 1782
(*Works*, Yale ed. I.316)

TO JOHN TAYLOR, 22 *Mar.* 1782
(*Works*, Yale ed. I.316)

TO EDWARD EDWARDS, *June* 1782
(To Hester Thrale, 11 June 1782)

TO CATHERINE HERVEY, 26 *Aug.* 1782
(*Works*, Yale ed. I.327)

TO JOHN TAYLOR, 26 *Aug.* 1782
(*Works*, Yale ed. I.327)

TO WILLIAM VYSE, 9 *Sept.* 1782
(*Works*, Yale ed. I.330)

TO JOHN TAYLOR, *between* 3 *Oct.* 1782 *and* 7 *Dec.* 1782
(Conjecture based on Taylor's numeration; see Chapman III.302–4)

TO GEORGE STRAHAN, 18 *Oct.* 1782
(*Works*, Yale ed. I.342)

TO AN UNIDENTIFIED CORRESPONDENT, *Lichfield, Oct.* 1782
(To John Taylor, 3 Oct. 1782)

TO LORD ASHBURTON, 7 *Nov.* 1782
(*Works*, Yale ed. 1.348)

TO HESTER THRALE, 9 *Dec.* 1782
(*Works*, Yale ed. 1.355)

TO LORD ASHBURTON, *c.* 15 *Dec.* 1782
(To Hester Thrale, 18 Dec. 1782)

TO JOSHUA REYNOLDS, 26 *Dec.* 1782
"Declining an invitation on account of illness."
(Sotheby's Catalogue, 10 May 1875, Lot No. 126, p. 14)

TO HESTER THRALE, 30 *Dec.* 1782
"About attending a meeting of executors."
(Sotheby's Catalogue, 30 Jan. 1918, Lot No. 236, p. 35)

TO WILLIAM LANGLEY, *Early Feb.* 1783
(*GM* 1878, pp. 699–700)

TO AN UNIDENTIFIED CORRESPONDENT, 15 *Feb.* 1783
(date and signature fragment in Hyde Collection)

TO WARREN HASTINGS, *c.* 16 *Apr.* 1783
(To Thomas Cadell, 16 Apr. 1783)

TO HESTER THRALE, *Apr.* 1783
"I have just taken a Vomit, and just received your Letter."
(Hester Thrale to SJ, 18–19 Apr. 1783, MS: Rylands Library)

TO PASQUALE PAOLI, 1 *May* 1783
(To Hester Thrale, 1 May 1783)

TO ANNA WILLIAMS, *July* 1783
(To William Strahan, 15 July 1783)

TO WILLIAM HEBERDEN, *Sept.* 1783
(To Hester Thrale, 23 Sept. 1783)

TO FRANCIS BARBER, 8 *Sept.* 1783
(*Works*, Yale ed. 1.365)

TO RICHARD BROCKLESBY, 8 *Sept.* 1783
(*Works*, Yale ed. 1.365)

TO FRANCES REYNOLDS, 2 *Oct.* 1783
(Anderson Galleries, 30 Nov. 1920, Lot No. 244, p. 56)

TO JOHN TAYLOR, *between* 20 *Dec.* 1783 *and* 3 *Jan.* 1784
(Conjecture based on Taylor's numeration; see Chapman III.302–4)

TO SOPHIA THRALE, ?*Dec.* 1783
(To Hester Thrale, 13 Dec. 1783) This conjectural letter may never
have been written.

TO SUSANNA THRALE, ?*Dec.* 1783
(To Hester Thrale, 13 Dec. 1783) This conjectural letter may be that
of 25 Mar. 1784.

TO JOHN RYLAND, 5 *Jan.* 1784
"Begging him to bring young Mr. Ryland and Mr. Payne, and eat the
Hare with him."
(Sotheby's Catalogue, 12 June 1876, Lot No. 109, p. 15)

TO RICHARD MUSGRAVE, *Jan.* 1784
(To Hester Thrale, 12 Jan. 1784)

TO ELIZABETH ASTON *and* JANE GASTRELL, ?*Early* 1784
(To Elizabeth Aston and Jane Gastrell, 11 Mar. 1784) This conjectural
letter may be that of 22 Sept. 1783.

TO WILLIAM ADAMS, *Early* 1784
(To William Adams, 30 Mar. 1784)

TO FRANCESCO SASTRES, *Apr.* 1784
(To Charlotte Lewis, 4 Apr. 1784)

TO JOHN RYLAND, *c.* 21 *Aug.* 1784
(To John Ryland, 23 Aug. 1784)

TO JOHN HAWKINS, *between* 18 *Sept.* 1784 *and* 8 *Nov.* 1784
"In his [SJ's] return to London, he stopped at Lichfield, and from
thence wrote to me several letters."
(Hawkins, p. 576)

TO AN UNIDENTIFIED CORRESPONDENT, 2 *Dec.* 1784
"Your most humble Servant, SAM. JOHNSON, Dec. 2, 1784."
(MS: National Library of Wales)

TO WILLIAM SEWARD, 1784
(To Francesco Sastres, 20 Oct. 1784)

TO GEORGE COLMAN, *n.d.*
"To George Colman, Esq., at Mr. Davies's Bookseller in Russel Street,
Covent Garden, London."
(address fragment in Hyde Collection)

TO DAVID GARRICK, *n.d.*
"An Interesting Letter to Garrick, *n.d.*"
(Sotheby's Catalogue, 3 Dec. 1856, Lot No. 1151, p. 74)

TO ?GEORGE JOHNSTONE, *n.d.*
"In a Debate on the Copyright Bill on May 16, 1774, Governor
Johnstone said:—'It had been urged . . . that Dr. Johnson had received an after gratification from the booksellers who employed him
to compile his Dictionary; . . . he [Governor Johnstone] had in his
hand a letter from Dr. Johnson, which he read, in which the doctor
denied the assertion, but declared that his employers fulfilled their
bargain, and that he was satisfied'."
(*Life* 1.304 n. 1)

TO A STEWARD OF TRINITY COLLEGE, *Dublin, n.d.*
(G. J. Kolb, "Notes on Four Letters by Dr. Johnson," *PQ* 38, 1959,
pp. 379–80)

TO HENRY THRALE, *n.d.*
"To Henry Thrale, Esq."
(address fragment in Hyde Collection)

TO HESTER THRALE, *n.d.*
(address fragment in Gwin J. Kolb Collection)

Translations of Letters
in Latin

GEORGE HUDDESFORD, 26 Feb. 1755

Both you and I would think me thoroughly ungrateful did I not convey in writing (inadequate as it must be) how much joy I took in the honors which the Academic Senate recently conferred on me—I believe at your instance. I would appear ungrateful indeed unless I were to acknowledge and praise the graciousness with which the distinguished gentleman personally delivered the testimony of your regard. If anything can add satisfaction to something already so satisfying, the honor pleases me all the more in that I have been selected to re-enter academic ranks in the very season when crafty (albeit unintelligent) men attempt by all available means to lessen your authority and to injure the reputation of the University—men whom I (insofar as someone on the sidelines can) have always opposed and will always oppose. I hold that any man who shall have betrayed you or the Academy would be the betrayer of virtue and literature and of himself and future generations.

THOMAS FOTHERGILL, 7 Apr. 1775

Many words are not needed to tell you how I receive the commendation with which under your leadership the University has committed my name to posterity. No one fails to take pleasure in thinking well of himself; no one fails to think well of himself who has been able to make you, judges of letters, think well of him. But such a good deed has one disadvantage: from now on I cannot go wrong or fall short without hurting your reputation, and I must always fear that what is an exceptional honor to me may at some time cause shame to you.

THOMAS LAWRENCE, 5 Jan. 1782

From a body in the worst possible condition I run for succor to you, most skilled of men. Since I judge that lesser ailments ought to be passed over, I will speak to the best of my ability of what afflicts me most grievously. When I have gone to bed after a brief sleep (usually very brief) I have felt as if my chest were swollen with matter. The result is that, although pain neither tears nor pierces, sleep is immediately banished, and when I lift my head from the mattress, I am obliged on occasion to sit wrapped in blankets. Hence frequent sighs, and at times gasps, and difficult labor of breathing. For this reason I fear going to bed; nor have I been able to enjoy the daylight hours.

Please give me your opinion as to how these problems can be counteracted. It seems to me in fact that blood should be let, but I am hardly willing to have it done except by your orders. I have tried the results of a stomach purge by means even of mercury—but without success. If blood is to be let, I wish you to be here, lest through fear or boldness a blunder occur.

Don't come to me; after you read this, I will come to you.

THOMAS LAWRENCE, 21 Jan. 1782

Sleep last night was indeed often intermittent—yet so peaceful, that it provided leisure for uninterrupted and harmonious dreams; nor while I slept did coughing cause any distress. But I now feel oppressed, and continue to feel (although better) not free of sickness. My chest remains as if on fire. I know not if I dare be bled again; however, when I feel neither weak nor empty, I do not see what especially is to be feared. I do not doubt that you will proceed gently to this remedy, if you concur. What you have done has protected against the illness, which nevertheless has not been cured. Farewell.

THOMAS LAWRENCE, 13 Mar. 1782

Exhausted by the long duration of my ill-health, I call again to my assistance, most learned man, your skill and your friendship. Coughing, somewhat less violent, does not trouble me frequently or severely—but at the least touch of cold it breaks out again. It is certainly not so bad that I should dwell on it at length. Now the labored and obstructed action of breathing has caused greater discomforts by far. Although this difficulty is not painful, it is difficult to recount in Latin how much weariness it causes. Lying in bed, I must bear some part of that dire torture by which our ancestors overcame the stubbornness of a silent defendant whose chest was piled high with weights. My windpipe is often quiet; what that may mean it will be your task to ascertain.

I bear all these discomforts the more painfully, the more easily I am confident they can be relieved. If I am able to perceive anything by feeling or estimate anything by judging, the effective and safe remedy is the surgical lance. I know that you hope the gout will at last come to my aid. However, the long-awaited gout will perhaps not come, and if it comes, perhaps will bring no relief. In the past, both my chest and my foot hurt at the same time that the gout was at its peak.

Therefore I beg and implore you, most learned of men, not to forbid the letting of blood. Up to now this has been done too cautiously. But now, lest through fear or rashness a mistake be made, I hope that blood can be let before noon, in your presence, and halted according to your directions. I will see you again in the afternoon, so that you may determine whether another letting (easily accomplished when the bandages are removed) would be safe.

I write this in early evening; it must be delivered to you tomorrow morning.

THOMAS LAWRENCE, 15 Mar. 1782

After you finished everything you had to do in the kindest possible way and left me yesterday, I felt no discomfort in any part of my body. I was relaxed, and my energy was scarcely depleted. I consumed very little food and drink, lest the empty veins be filled up. Early in the night I was so troubled by frequent coughing that I took out the laudanum from the drug cabinet; however, soon thereafter the cough was calmed without the help of opium, and left me as I lay abed. Then sleep ensued—sleep of such soundness that from one to eight I do not remember even having dreamed. May God grant that from now on all things be auspicious and joyful for both of us. Farewell.

The History of Music that I did not have with me yesterday I send to you now. You need not be in haste to return it. We have read scarcely anything more delightful or more copious. Goodbye, and enjoy it.

There is no need for you to see me, unless it is convenient.

THOMAS LAWRENCE, 20 Mar. 1782

Now a relaxed spirit goes away and comes back to me with a freer movement; now less harsh coughing lacerates my chest and stomach. So much good does bleeding at the right time accomplish, so much good the sweet poppy with its powerful juice. Now what remains? Provided only that I see how much warm baths might relieve tight skin, tomorrow I intend to go forth whither sweet Thrale recalls me. This too remains, that I express gratitude to the prince of doctors, and pray fervently that the skills that benefit all may not fail their master. Farewell.

THOMAS LAWRENCE, 1 May 1782

Another cold, another cough, and increased difficulty in breathing; these argue for another letting of blood. However, I do not wish to have this done without your advice. I can scarcely come to you, nor is there any reason for you to come to me. You may say, in one word, yes or no, and leave the rest to Holder and me. If you agree, let the messenger be told to bring Holder to me.

When you are gone, where shall I turn?

THOMAS LAWRENCE, Mid-May 1782

New pains require new assistance. After the recent blooding you ordered, I began to hope for better health. My chest calmed down, my breathing grew less impeded, and everything was a little more peaceful.

But now everything regresses. Old diseases harrass me, perhaps more gently than before—but such as I am scarcely equal to bearing. Sleep is brief, interrupted, and precarious. But I am overcome with sleepiness. It appears to me that, once again, a remedy is to be sought from a surgeon. But you, most learned man, will be the judge.

Letters Recently Recovered

David Garrick [1]

LATE MAY 1765

MS: Hyde Collection.

I wish you had named your plays that I might not have [been] suspected of culling the best.[2] You may have any other.

Francis will be much obliged, if you would sometimes favour him with an order.[3]

1. The tone and contents of this note rule out any other possible recipient, as does the provenance: the MS descended through the family of the Rev. Thomas Rackett, the executor of Eva Maria Garrick.

2. The correspondence with David Garrick concerning SJ's forthcoming edition of Shakespeare begins with SJ's letter of 18 May 1765 (I.247–48). It is probable that this undated note constitutes SJ's response to Garrick's (unrecovered) reply. The exchange appears to end with To David Garrick, Spring or Summer 1765 (I.251).

3. SJ refers to Francis Barber.

Lucy Porter

SATURDAY 25 FEBRUARY 1775 [1]

MS: Hyde Collection.

ADDRESS: To Mrs. Lucy Porter, Lichfield.

FRANK: Hfreethrale.

POSTMARKS: 25 FE, FREE, [Undeciphered].

ENDORSEMENT in an unidentified hand: 1775.

1. It is highly likely that this letter is the one to which SJ refers at the end of To Henry Thrale, c. 26 Feb. 1775 (II.182–83). The Thrale letter should therefore be redated to 25 Feb. 1775.

Dear Madam: Febr. 25, 1775

I am glad that you like my little book.[2] I have given one to Mr. Porter.[3] I received a very kind letter from dear Miss Adey, pray make her my compliments.

I have enclosed Mrs. Bond's note, which Mr. Simpson, I suppose, will send for, I have commissioned him in the letter inclosed to settle the affair.[4]

We made our journey through a very great part of North Wales, and into the Isle of Anglesea, and back through Shropshire, Warwickshire, Worcestershire, and Oxfordshire, without one vexatious Accident.[5] I hope to see Staffordshire this summer. I have no long Journey in hand. I am pretty well, not quite well, and hope you, my dear, as well at least as your most humble servant,

SAM. JOHNSON

2. SJ refers to the *Journey.*
3. SJ refers to Joseph Porter.
4. Apparently SJ refers to a transaction involving the tenant of his Lichfield house, the widow of Thomas Bond, who rented the property after Sarah Johnson's death; Mrs. Bond was still the tenant at the time of SJ's death (*Johns. Glean.* IV.20, 23). It is probable that Charles Simpson (1732–96), Lichfield attorney, who also served as Coroner and Town Clerk (1764–92), acted as SJ's agent in this "affair."

5. *Ante* To Bennet Langton, 5 July 1774 and n. 4; *Ante* To JB, 1 Oct. 1774; *Ante* To John Taylor, 20 Oct. 1774.

Sir Richard Worsley[1]

TUESDAY 28 AUGUST 1781

MS: Arthur Rippey.

Sir: Aug. 28, 1781

I return thanks for the use of the Survey of the Isle of Wight which appears to me a work of great knowledge and accuracy.[2]

1. Sir Richard Worsley (1751–1805), 7th Bt., of Appuldercombe, Isle of Wight, M.P. for Newport, Isle of Wight (1774–79, 1780–84), and Newtown, Isle of Wight (1790–93, 1796–1801).
2. Worsley's *History of the Isle of Wight* appeared in June 1781. Upon its publica-

I should be glad of the map,[3] if You have one to spare. I am, Sir, Your humble Servant,

SAM. JOHNSON

tion, Worsley sent copies to various people—among them Thomas Warton and SJ—asking for comments and corrections (information supplied by Professor Donald Eddy).

3. A detailed map of the Isle of Wight, prepared especially for Worsley's *History* by John Haywood, immediately precedes chapter 1.

Supplementary Annotation

To Thomas Warton, 10 June 1755, n. 6: SJ refers to a projected companion volume to Warton's *Observations*, which was to include an essay on the development of pastoral (information supplied by Dr. David Fairer).

To Thomas Warton, 21 June 1757, n. 5: The dates for Mary Jones are 1707–78 (information supplied by Dr. David Fairer).

To George Staunton, 1 June 1762: Professor Marshall Waingrow has convinced me that the sense of the penultimate paragraph compels the insertion of "not" in the final sentence. Therefore, the text should read: "the Peruvian Bark is [not] the only specifick. . . ."

To Charles Burney, 16 Oct. 1765: Holograph MS at University of Basel, Switzerland.

To Thomas Warton, 31 May 1769: Dr. David Fairer argues that this letter was written on 31 May 1775. See the relevant appendix to his forthcoming edition of Thomas Warton's correspondence.

To Thomas Lawrence, 19 Nov. 1774: Sold by Swann Galleries, New York City, 7 Nov. 1991 (Lot 110). The current owner has not been traced.

To Hester Thrale, 23 Aug. 1777: It is likely that SJ alludes in the first sentence of the third paragraph to Pope's *Epistle to Burlington*, l. 106: "His pond an Ocean, his parterre a Down" (information supplied by Professor Carey McIntosh). Therefore, the text should be emended to "a down," with the manuscript reading ("adorn") recorded in a note.

To Hester Thrale, 14 Nov. 1778, and To Hester Thrale, 6 Apr. 1780, are now at the Beinecke Library.

As of July 1993, three previously unknown letters have been recovered: To Eva Maria Garrick and Hannah More (no date), To Eva Maria Garrick and Hannah More (2 May 1782), and To Mary Nollekens (no date).

ALPHABETICAL TABLE OF
CORRESPONDENTS

FOLLOWING is an alphabetical listing of Samuel Johnson's correspondents and the dates of his letters to each of them. The list does not include letters that appear in Appendix I or Appendix II, or those to unidentified correspondents. An asterisk after the date of a letter indicates that it was addressed to more than one person.

Note on Selected Correspondents

The great majority of the letters from Hester Thrale to SJ that have been recovered are now at the John Rylands University Library; the other significant repository is the Hyde Collection. The only recovered letter from John Taylor is a one-sentence note (17 Oct. 1772, MS: Hyde Collection) to which SJ responds in his letter of 19 Oct. 1772. The only letter from Lucy Porter (15 Apr. 1780, MS: Hyde Collection) has appeared as a keepsake printed for The Johnsonians (1979). Hill Boothby's letters to SJ are available in *An Account of the Life of Dr. Samuel Johnson*, ed. Richard Wright (1805). Charles Burney's letters appear in *The Correspondence of Dr Charles Burney*, ed. Alvaro Ribeiro, SJ, vol. 1 (Oxford, 1991). Letters to SJ from Joshua Reynolds will appear in the correspondence volume being prepared by Brian Allen and John Edgcumbe. David Fairer's edition of the Thomas Warton correspondence is forthcoming from the University of Georgia Press.

ADAMS, William
  1776, 29 May
  1778, 7 April
  1784, 30 March
  1784, 31 May
  1784, 11 July

ALLEN, Charles
  1780

ALLEN, Edmund
  1775, 17 June
  1775, 19 June
  1777, 17 June
  1777, 22 June
  1781, 26 November
  1783, 17 June
  1784, 7 June

APPERLEY, Thomas
  1768, 17 March

ARGYLL, Duke of
  1773, 27 October

ASTLE, Thomas
  1781, 17 July

ASTON, Elizabeth
  1767, 17 November
  1769, 26 August
  1777, 8 March
  1777, 15 March
  1777, 13 September
  1777, 20 November
  1779, 2 January
  1779, 4 March
  1779, 4 May
  1779, 25 October
  1779, 5 November
  1782, 30 March*
  1784, 11 March*
  1784, c. 8 November*

BAGSHAW, Thomas
  1773, 8 May
  1784, 12 July

BANKS, Joseph
  1772, 27 February

BARBER, Francis
  1768, 28 May
  1770, 25 September
  1770, 7 December
  1783, 16 September

BARCLAY, David
  1784, 16 September

BARETTI, Giuseppe
  1761, 10 June
  1762, 20 July
  1762, 21 December

BARNARD, Frederick
  Augusta

BARNARD, F. A. (*cont.*)
1768, 28 May
1781, 6 June

BARNARD, Thomas
1777, 17 January

BARRY, James
1783, 12 April

BEATTIE, James
1771, 30 August
1773, 5 August
1780, 21 August

BEAUCLERK, Topham
1762, *c.* October

BENTHAM, Edward
1775, 8 April

BIRCH, Thomas
1743, 29 September
1750, 12 May
1752, 4 November
1753, 20 January
1754, January
1755, 29 March
1755, 8 November
1756, 9 January
1756, 20 March
1756, 22 June

BOND, Phineas
1773, 4 March

BOOTHBY, Hill
1753, *c.* December
1755, 30 December
1755, 31 December
1756, 1 January
1756, 3 January
1756, 3 January
1756, 8 January

BOSWELL, James
1763, 8 December
1766, 14 January
1766, 21 August
1768, 23 March
1769, 9 September
1769, 9 November

1771, 20 June
1772, 15 March
1772, 31 August
1773, 24 February
1773, 5 July
1773, 3 August
1773, 3 August
1773, 11 August
1773, 14 August
1773, 27 November
1774, 29 January
1774, 7 February
1774, 5 March
1774, *c.* 19 March
1774, 10 May
1774, 27 May
1774, 21 June
1774, 4 July
1774, 1 October
1774, 27 October
1774, 26 November
1775, 14 January
1775, 21 January
1775, 28 January
1775, 7 February
1775, 25 February
1775, 27 May
1775, 27 August
1775, 30 August
1775, 14 September
1775, 16 November
1775, 23 December
1776, 10 January
1776, 15 January
1776, 3 February
1776, 9 February
1776, 15 February
1776, 24 February
1776, 5 March
1776, 12 March
1776, 3 April
1776, *c.* 22 April
1776, 2 July
1776, 6 July
1776, 16 November

1776, 21 December
1777, 18 February
1777, 11 March
1777, 3 May
1777, 24 June
1777, 28 June
1777, 22 July
1777, 4 August
1777, 30 August
1777, 1 September
1777, 11 September
1777, 23 September
1777, 25 November
1777, 27 December
1778, 24 January
1778, 23 April
1778, 3 July
1778, 21 November
1779, 13 March
1779, 26 April
1779, 13 July
1779, 9 September
1779, 27 October
1779, 13 November
1780, 8 April
1780, 21 August
1780, 17 October
1781, 14 March
1782, 5 January
1782, 28 March
1782, 3 June
1782, 24 August
1782, 7 September
1782, 21 September
1782, 7 December`
1783, *c.* 4 February
1783, 3 July
1783, 30 September
1783, 24 December
1784, 11 February
1784, 27 February
1784, 2 March
1784, 18 March
1784, 30 March
1784, 11 July

1784, 26 July
1784, *c.* 5 August
1784, *c.* 7 August
1784, 3 November

BOSWELL, Margaret
1776, 16 May
1777, 22 July
1782, 7 December

BOUFFLERS, Mme. de
1771, 16 May

BOWLES, William
1783, 24 July
1783, 30 July
1783, 4 August
1783, 21 August
1783, 25 August
1783, 22 September
1783, 30 September
1783, 7 October
1783, 23 October
1784, 3 January
1784, 14 January
1784, 3 February
1784, 23 February
1784, 5 April
1784, 3 May
1784, 10 July
1784, 7 August
1784, 13 September

BRIGHT, Henry
1762, 12 October
1770, 9 January
1770, 27 January
1770, 24 May

BROCKLESBY, Richard
1783, 29 August
1784, 21 July
1784, 31 July
1784, 5 August
1784, 12 August
1784, 14 August
1784, 16 August
1784, 19 August
1784, 21 August

1784, 26 August
1784, 30 August
1784, 2 September
1784, 9 September
1784, 11 September
1784, 16 September
1784, 29 September
1784, 6 October
1784, 20 October
1784, 25 October
1784, 6 November

BURKE, Edmund
1770, 21 June
1779, 27 April

BURKE, Jane
1775, Mid-to-Late
November

BURNEY, Charles
1755, 8 April
1757, 24 December
1758, 8 March
1765, 16 October
1778, 2 November
1779, 17 June
1780, 19 April
1780, 31 July
1782, 18 March
1783, Early July*
1783, 20 September
1784, 2 August
1784, 23 August
1784, 28 August
1784, 4 September
1784, 1 November
1784, 17 November

BURNEY, Elizabeth
1783, Early July*

BURNEY, Frances
1781, 9 July
1782, 7 June
1783, Early July*
1783, 19 November
1784, 1 November

BURNEY, James
1782, 24 June

BUTE, Lord
1762, 20 July
1762, 3 November

CADELL, Thomas
1778, 28 January
1779, 31 March
1779, 13 April
1781, 5 March
1783, February
1783, 16 April
1784, Late November

CALDER, John
1776, 19 February

CALDWELL, Sir James
1767, 12 February

CARTER, Elizabeth
1756, 14 January

CAVE, Edward
1734, 25 November
1737, 12 July
1738, *c.* April
1738, *c.* April
1738, April
1738, Late April or
Early May
1738, *c.* August
1738, November
1738
1743, Autumn

CAVE, Richard or
William
1756, January

CHAMBERS, Richard
1782, 8 July

CHAMBERS, Robert
1754, 21 November
1755, 4 August
1755, 7 August
1756, 31 July
1758, 8 April
1758, 14 April

CHAMBERS, Robert
  (*cont.*)
  1758, 1 June
  1760, 23 June
  1760, 31 December
  1762, 22 October
  1763, 15 March
  1766, 19 November
  1766, 11 December
  1767, 22 January
  1767, *c.* 6 October
  1770, 24 March
  1771, 6 April
  1772, 11 April
  1772, 3 December
  1773, 14 September
  1773, 30 September
  1773, 15 October
  1773, 27 November
  1774, 30 March
  1779, 31 October
  1783, 19 April
  1783, 4 October

CHAPONE, Hester
  1782, 9 February
  1783, 20 November
  1783, 28 November

CHESTERFIELD, Lord
  1755, 7 February

CHOLMONDELEY, Mary
  1777, 6 May

CLARK, Richard
  1773, 8 February
  1774, 31 January
  1778, 22 April
  1778, 17 July
  1782, 7 December
  1783, 13 December
  1784, 27 January

COLMAN, George
  1767, 19 August
  1769, 17 January

COMPTON, James
  1782, 6 October

1782, 24 October
1782, 7 November

CONGREVE, Richard
  1735, 25 June
  1755, 16 October

COTTERELL, Frances
  1755, 19 July

CRADOCK, Joseph
  1783, 20 January
  1783, 20 January

CROFT, Herbert
  1783, 10 February

CRUIKSHANK, William
  1783, 30 July
  1783, 6 August
  1783, 24 September
  1783, 2 October
  1783, 3 December
  1784, 13 February
  1784, 17 February
  1784, 4 September

CUMMING, Thomas
  1774, 25 May

DARTMOUTH, Lord
  1783, 25 April

DAVIES, Thomas
  1783, 18 June
  1784, 14 August

DESMOULINS, Elizabeth
  1775, 5 August

DILLY, Charles
  1779, 13 July
  1781, 17 July
  1784, 6 January

DODD, William
  1777, 22 June
  1777, 26 June

DODSLEY, Robert
  1746, June
  1746, 26 December

DOUGLAS, John
  1776, 6 March

1776, 9 March

DRUMMOND, William
  1758, 1 October
  1766, 13 August
  1767, 21 April
  1767, 24 October

EDWARDS, Edward
  1778, 2 November

ELIBANK, Lord
  1773, 14 September

ELPHINSTON, James
  1749, 20 April
  1750, 25 September
  1752, Early
  1778, 27 July

FARMER, Richard
  1770, 21 March
  1771, 18 February
  1777, 22 July
  1780, 23 May

FISHER, Philip
  1775, 7 June

FITZMAURICE, Thomas
  1778, 7 December

FLINT, Louise
  1769, 31 March

FORBES, William
  1784, 7 August

FORD, Samuel
  1735, Mid

FOTHERGILL, Thomas
  1775, 7 April

FOWKE, Francis
  1776, 11 July

FOWKE, Joseph
  1783, 19 April

GARRICK, David
  1765, 18 May
  1765, Late May
  1765, Spring or
    Summer
  1765, *c.* 14 September

1766, 10 October
1771, 12 December

GARRICK, Eva Maria
1779, 21 January
1779, 2 February
1784, 15 March*
1784, 2 October

GASTRELL, Jane
1777, 23 December
1782, 30 March*
1783, 22 September
1784, 11 March*
1784, c. 8 November*

GOLDSMITH, Oliver
1773, 23 April

GRANGER, James
1772, 15 December

GREENE, Richard
1784, 2 December

GRENVILLE, George
1765, 2 July

HAMILTON, Anthony
1783, 4 June
1784, 11 February
1784, 17 February
1784, 2 June

HAMILTON, Archibald
1776, 13 February

HAMILTON, William
Gerard
1783, 19 November
1784, 20 October

HARDY, Samuel
1780, 23 September

HARRINGTON, Lady
1777, 25 June

HASTINGS, Warren
1774, 30 March
1774, 20 December
1780, 7 July
1781, 29 January

HAWKESWORTH, John

1756, Early March
1773, 20 January

HAWKINS, John
1773, 15 January
1783, 22 November
1783, 3 December
1784, Summer
1784, 7 November

HAY, George
1759, 9 November

HEBERDEN, William
1784, 6 February
1784, 13 October

HECTOR, Edmund
1755, 15 April
1755, 13 May
1756, 7 October
1756, 11 November
1757, 16 April
1765, 7 December
1767, 3 November
1772, 5 December
1772, 12 December
1775, 4 February
1775, 23 March
1775, 16 November
1776, 7 March
1782, 21 March
1784, 17 November

HEELEY, Humphry
1784, 12 August

HERTFORD, Lord
1776, 11 April

HICKMAN, Gregory
1731, 30 October

HOLLYER, John
1774, 6 December
1784, 27 November

HOOLE, John
1773, 23 April
1774, 19 December
1775, 28 August
1776, 30 October

1776, 9 November
1780, 7 July
1783, Autumn
1783, c. November
1784, 7 August
1784, 4 September
1784, 13 September

HORNE, George
1774, 30 April

HORNECK, Hannah
1770, 13 June

HUDDESFORD, George
1755, 26 February

HUGGINS, William
1754, 9 November
1754, 14 November

HUMPHRY, Ozias
1784, 5 April
1784, 13 April
1784, 31 May

HUNTER, William
1774, 29 December
1778, 2 June

HUSSEY, John
1778, 29 December

JACKSON, Richard
1783, 11 November

JEBB, Sir Richard
1782, 11 June

JENKINSON, Charles
1765, 26 October
1777, 20 June

JESSOP, William
1766, 28 June

JODRELL, Richard Paul
1783, 15 April

JOHNSON, Elizabeth
1740, 31 January

JOHNSON, Sarah
1759, 13 January
1759, 16 January
1759, 18 January

JOHNSON, Sarah (*cont.*)
1759, 20 January

JOHNSON, Thomas
1777, 16 December

JOHNSON, William
Samuel
1773, 4 March

KEARSLEY, George
1782, 20 May

LANGLEY, William
1782, 24 June
1783, May

LANGTON, Bennet
1755, 6 May
1758, 27 June
1758, 21 September
1759, 9 January
1760, 18 October
1766, 8 March
1766, 10 May
1767, 10 October
1770, 24 October
1771, 20 March
1771, 29 August
1772, 14 March
1772, 13 April
1774, 5 July
1775, 17 April
1775, 21 May
1776, 22 June
1777, 13 February
1777, 29 June
1777, 7 July
1778, 29 August
1778, 31 October
1781, 16 June
1782, 20 March
1783, 20 September
1783, 24 September
1783, 11 October
1784, 27 March
1784, 8 April
1784, 13 April
1784, 12 July

1784, 26 August
1784, 29 November

LANGTON, Elizabeth
1771, 17 April

LANGTON, Jane
1784, 10 May

LAWRENCE, Charles
1780, 30 August

LAWRENCE, Elizabeth
1782, 22 May
1782, 9 June
1782, 2 July
1782, 22 July
1782, 26 August
1783, 4 February

LAWRENCE, Thomas
1767, 17 June
1767, 20 June
1774, 19 November
1774, 6 December
1775, 30 January
1775, 7 February
1777, 26 July
1778, 13 October
1778, 5 December
1779, 29 July
1780, 20 January
1782, 5 January
1782, 17 January
1782, 21 January
1782, 4 February
1782, 13 March
1782, 14 March
1782, 15 March
1782, 20 March
1782, 1 May
1782, Mid-May
1783, 16 April

LELAND, Thomas
1765, 17 October

LENNOX, Charlotte
1750, Late
1752, 4 February

1752, 12 March
1753, 6 March
1753, *c.* May
1756, 30 July
1757, 10 March
1775, 2 May
1778, 9 November

LEVET, Robert
1774, 16 August
1775, 18 September
1775, 22 October
1776, 23 September
1776, 21 October

LEVETT, John
1752, 17 March
1752, 26 July
1757, 21 June

LEVETT, Theophilus
1743, 1 December
1744, 3 January

LEWIS, Charlotte
1784, 4 April

LONGMAN, Thomas
1746, June

LOWE, Mauritius
1778, 28 April
1782, 1 January
1782, 22 October
1783, 20 June

LOWTH, Robert
1780, 13 July

LYE, Edward
1765, 17 August
1765, 26 September

MACLEOD OF MACLEOD
1773, 28 September

MACLEOD, John, of
Raasay
1775, 6 May

MACPHERSON, James
1775, 20 January

MALONE, Edmond

1782, 27 February
1782, 2 March

THE MERCERS'
COMPANY
1783, 19 April

METCALFE, Philip
1782, 3 October
1784, 17 November

MILLAR, Andrew
1753, 11 July

MONTAGU, Elizabeth
1759, 9 June
1759, 17 December
1774, 11 January
1775, 15 December
1775, 17 December
1775, 21 December
1778, 5 March
1778, 6 March
1783, 22 September

MORE, Hannah
1781, 12 April
1784, 15 March*

Morning Chronicle,
Editor of
1782, 27 May

MUDGE, John
1783, 9 September
1783, 23 September
1783, 9 October

NEWBERY, John
1751, 15 April
1751, 29 July
1751, 24 August

NICHOLS, John
1778, c. March
1778, 2 May
1778, 27 July
1778, c. Mid-August
1778, 23 November
1778, 26 November
1778, c. December
1779, 1 March

1780, Early
1780, c. February
1780, c. February
1780, c. March
1780, c. April
1780, c. April
1780, c. April
1780 (I), c. May
1780 (II), c. May
1780, May
1780, 24 May
1780, 16 June
1780, Early August
1780, 16 August
1780, 26 October
1780, c. December
1780, Late
1781, Early
1781, c. March
1781, 16 April
1781, c. April
1781, May
1781, 10 June
1781, 26 December
1782, 12 August
1782, 10 October
1782, c. October
1782, 28 October
1783, 10 January
1784, 4 February
1784, 7 February
1784, 12 April
1784, 20 October
1784, 6 December

NICOL, George
1784, 8 June
1784, 19 August
1784, 4 September

NOLLEKENS, Joseph
1776, 24 December
1777, 27 August

NORTH, Lord
1775, c. March

O'CONOR, Charles

1757, 9 April
1777, 19 May

ORRERY, Lord
1751, Late November
1752, 9 July

OWEN, Margaret
1781, 8 March

PALMER, Joseph
1775, February

PARADISE, John
1784, 20 October

PATERSON, Samuel
1772, 6 April

PATRICK, Charles
1782, 14 February

PATTEN, Thomas
1781, 24 September

PAUL, Lewis
1741, 31 January
1741, 31 March
1755, 29 December
1756, 6 January
1756, 13 January
1756, Late February or
Early March
1756, 12 March
1756, 29 September
1756, Autumn
1756, 8 October
1756, Autumn
1756, Autumn

PENNECK, Richard
1768, 3 March

PERCY, Thomas
1760, 4 October
1760, 29 November
1761, 12 September
1763, 3 September
1764, 23 June
1769, 5 November
1770, 27 November
1773, 9 August
1776, 1 December

PERCY, Thomas (*cont.*)
1776, 2 December
1776, 16 December

PERKINS, Amelia
1784, 11 January*
1784, 23 January*
1784, 12 June*

PERKINS, John
1774, 25 October
1777, 4 April
1781, 2 June
1781, 2 July
1781, 6 August
1781, 8 October
1782, 29 January
1782, 7 May
1782, 28 July
1782, 8 November
1782, 3 December
1783, 8 January
1783, Late October
1783, 5 December
1784, 5 January
1784, 11 January*
1784, 21 January
1784, 23 January*
1784, 13 April
1784, 12 June*
1784, 4 October
1784, 25 October

PORTER, Lucy
1749, 12 July
1755, 30 December
1759, 16 January
1759, 20 January
1759, 23 January
1759, 25 January
1759, 27 January
1759, 6 February
1759, 15 February
1759, 1 March
1759, 23 March
1759, 10 May
1759, 9 August

1761, 13 January
1762, 24 July
1763, 12 April
1763, 5 July
1763, 12 July
1764, 10 January
1766, 14 January
1766, 13 November
1768, 18 April
1768, 7 June
1768, 18 June
1768, 12 July
1770, 1 May
1770, 29 May
1775, 25 February
1775, 9 September
1775, 16 November
1775, *c.* 23 December
1777, 20 November
1778, 19 February
1779, 2 January
1779, 4 March
1779, *c.* 22 April
1779, 4 May
1779, 24 August
1779, 19 October
1779, 2 December
1780, 8 April
1781, 8 March
1781, 12 April
1781, 9 June
1781, 15 October
1782, 2 March
1782, 19 March
1783, *c.* 12 April
1783, 25 June
1783, 5 July
1783, 10 November
1783, 29 November
1784, 23 February
1784, 10 March
1784, 26 April
1784, 8 July
1784, 31 July
1784, 14 August

1784, 11 September
1784, 2 December

PORTMORE, Lord
1784, 13 April

PROWSE, Mary
1780, 14 August
1780, 9 December
1781, 7 May
1782, 4 June
1784, 17 February

REPINGTON, Gilbert
1735, 18 May

REYNOLDS, Frances
1762, 21 December
1764, 27 October
1771, 25 July
1771, 29 July
1774, 28 June
1776, 11 April
1776, 15 April
1776, 15 June
1776, 21 June
1776, 3 August
1779, 15 February
1779, *c.* 29 June
1779, 19 October
1779, 21 October
1780, 16 June
1781, 25 June
1781, 21 July
1782, 8 April
1782, 14 July
1783, March
1783, 18 August
1783, 24 August
1783, 1 October
1783, 23 October
1783, 27 October
1783, 27 November
1783, 8 December
1783, 23 December
1784, 9 February
1784, 12 April
1784, 30 April

1784, 28 May

REYNOLDS, Joshua
1764, c. 10 August
1771, 17 July
1772, 27 February
1776, 16 May
1776, 22 June
1776, 3 August
1778, 14 August
1781, 4 April
1781, 23 June
1782, 14 November
1783, 19 February
1783, 4 March
1783, 12 April
1783, 2 May
1783, 2 June
1783, 6 September
1783, 4 December
1784, 1 June
1784, 8 July
1784, 21 July
1784, 19 August
1784, 2 September
1784, 9 September
1784, 18 September
1784, 2 October

RICHARDSON, Samuel
1751, 9 March
1751, 10 December
1751-52
1753, 17 April
1753, 26 September
1754, 28 March
1755, 3 February
1756, 16 March
1756, 19 March

RICHARDSON, William
1783, 23 February

RIVINGTON, John
1771, 2 February

ROGERS, Mary see
PROWSE, Mary

ROLT, Mrs.
1771, 7 May

RYLAND, John
1756, January
1776, 21 September
1776, 14 November
1777, 12 April
1783, 8 July
1783, 24 July
1784, 12 July
1784, 23 August
1784, 2 September
1784, 18 September
1784, 29 September
1784, 6 October
1784, 30 October
1784, 4 November

ST. ALBYN, Lancelot
1782, 15 May

SALUSBURY, Hester
1767, 14 February

SASTRES, Francesco
1782, 25 April
1784, 21 August
1784, 2 September
1784, 16 September
1784, 20 October
1784, 1 November
1784, 17 November

SCOTT, John
1774, 27 May
1774, 2 June

SCOTT, William
1783, 4 March
1783, 17 March
1784, 10 October

SHARP, W.
1777, 7 July

SMART, Anna Maria
1758, Late

SMITH, Joseph
1770, 1 March
1771, 29 January

1771, 12 December

SOUTHWELL, Lady
1780, 9 September

STAUNTON, George
1762, 1 June

STEEVENS, George
1774, 7 February
1774, 21 February
1774, 5 March
1777, 25 February

STRAHAN, George
1763, 19 February
1763, 26 March
1763, 16 April
1763, 14 July
1763, 20 September
1765, 25 May
1782, 19 August
1782, 10 October
1783, 16 January
1783, January
1784, 16 October

STRAHAN, Margaret
1781, 23 April
1782, 4 February

STRAHAN, William
1751, 1 November
1753, 22 March
1753, Spring or
    Summer
1754, Late July or Early
    August
1759, 20 January
1764, 24 October
1772, 8 October
1774, 7 March
1774, 30 November
1774, 22 December
1775, 14 January
1775, 1 March
1775, 3 March
1775, 6 March
1775, 20 July
1776, 14 October

STRAHAN, William (*cont.*)
1776, 24 December
1778, 27 July
1778, 7 November
1780, 13 September
1781, 5 March
1782, 24 October
1782, 14 November
1782, 11 December
1783, 15 July
1784, 16 August
1784, 30 September
and 16 October
1784, 29 November
1784, 7 December
1784, 10 December

TAYLOR, John
1732, 27 July
1742, 10 August
1743, 2 January
1752, 18 March
1755, 11 April
1756, 31 July
1756, 18 November
1763, 13 August
1763, 18 August
1763, 25 August
1763, 3 September
1763, 29 September
1764, 22 May
1765, 15 July
1765, 1 October
1769, 5 October
1770, 2 July
1772, 17 April
1772, 15 August
1772, 31 August
1772, 6 October
1772, 13 October
1772, 19 October
1773, 27 February
1773, 20 March
1773, 22 June
1773, 5 August
1774, 15 January

1774, 26 March
1774, 20 October
1774, 22 December
1775, 14 January
1775, 9 February
1775, 23 March
1775, 8 April
1775, 13 April
1775, 27 May
1775, 16 November
1775, 23 December
1776, 15 January
1776, 17 February
1776, 7 March
1776, 23 March
1776, 4 April
1776, 13 April
1776, 29 April
1776, 25 June
1776, 3 September
1777, 23 January
1777, 3 May
1777, 19 May
1779, 9 March
1779, 4 May
1779, 3 August
1779, 9 September
1779, 19 October
1779, 9 December
1780, 20 April
1780, 6 June
1781, 12 May
1781, 24 September
1782, 2 March
1782, 14 March
1782, 13 June
1782, 8 July
1782, 22 July
1782, 3 August
1782, 12 August
1782, 17 August
1782, 21 September
1782, 3 October
1782, 7 December
1782, 9 December

1782, 31 December
1783, 16 January
1783, 21 January
1783, 17 June
1783, 24 July
1783, 3 September
1783, 20 September
1783, 24 September
1783, 20 October
1783, 10 November
1783, 19 November
1783, 22 November
1783, 29 November
1783, 20 December
1784, 3 January
1784, 24 January
1784, 22 March
1784, 12 April
1784, 8 June
1784, 19 June
1784, 23 June
1784, 7 July
1784, 16 October
1784, 20 October
1784, 23 October

THRALE, Henry
1769, 29 June
1771, March
1771, 31 July
1773, 15 October
1773, 23 October
1773, 26 October
1775, 2 January
1775, *c.* 26 February
1776, 3 June
1777, 9 April
1777, 31 July
1779, *c.* 20 June
1779, 23 June
1780, 30 May

THRALE, Hester Maria
1771, 29 July
1772, 2 November
1772, 28 November
1777, 4 September

1778, 24 October	1768, 11 November	1772, 3 December
1779, 11 November	1768, 2 December	1772, 5 December
1779, 25 December	1768, 14 December	1773, 26 January
1779, 29 December	1769, 18 May	1773, 19 February
1780, 8 April	1769, c. 21 June	1773, 9 March
1780, 19 May	1769, 29 June	1773, 11 March
1780, 18 July	1769, 6 July	1773, 12 March
1780, 28 August	1769, 14 August	1773, 15 March
1781, 19 April	1770, 13 January	1773, 16 March
1781, 7 November	1770, 6 April	1773, 17 March
1781, 28 November	1770, Early July	1773, 19 March
1782, 21 December	1770, 7 July	1773, 20 March
1783, 17 February or	1770, 11 July	1773, 23 March
March	1770, 14 July	1773, 25 March
1783, 26 April	1770, 20 July	1773, 2 April
1783, 22 May	1770, 23 July	1773, 3 April
1783, 2 June	1770, 28 July	1773, 27 April
1783, 24 July	1771, 15 June	1773, 4 May
1783, 23 August	1771, 20 June	1773, 8 May
1783, 3 September	1771, 22 June	1773, 17 May
1783, 30 September	1771, 25 June	1773, 22 May
1783, 20 October	1771, 3 July	1773, 23 May
1783, 20 December	1771, 7 July	1773, 24 May
1784, 31 January	1771, 8 July	1773, 29 May
1784, 3 June	1771, 10 July	1773, Early June
1784, 1 July	1771, 15 July	1773, 12 August
1784, 3 July	1771, 17 July	1773, 17 August
1784, 6 July	1771, 20 July	1773, 25 August
1784, 12 August	1771, 22 July	1773, 28 August
1784, 2 September	1771, 24 July	1773, 6 September
	1771, 3 August	1773, 14 September
THRALE, Hester	1771, 5 August	1773, 21 September
1765, 13 August	1772, 15 October	1773, 24 September
1767, 11 May	1772, 19 October	1773, 30 September
1767, 20 July	1772, 24 October	1773, 15 October
1767, 3 October	1772, 29 October	1773, 23 October
1767, 10 October	1772, 31 October	1773, 28 October
1768, 29 February	1772, 4 November	1773, 3 November
1768, 3 March	1772, 7 November	1773, 12 November
1768, 14 March	1772, 9 November	1773, 18 November
1768, 18 March	1772, 14 November	1774, 11 March
1768, 24 March	1772, 19 November	1774, 17 December
1768, 19 April	1772, 21 November	1775, Early January
1768, 28 April	1772, 23 November	1775, 3 February
1768, 23 May	1772, 27 November	1775, 4 February
1768, 17 June		

THRALE, Hester (*cont.*)

1775, 3 March	1776, 11 February	1777, 22 October
1775, 6 March	1776, 16 March	1777, 25 October
1775, 8 March	1776, 23 March	1777, 27 October
1775, 1 April	1776, 25 March	1777, 29 October
1775, 3 April	1776, 30 March	1777, 3 November
1775, 9 May	1776, 1 April	1777, 6 November
1775, 12 May	1776, 4 April	1777, 10 November
1775, 20 May	1776, 9 April	1778, 30 April
1775, 22 May	1776, 6 May	1778, 15 October
1775, 24 May	1776, 11 May	1778, 24 October
1775, 25 May	1776, 14 May	1778, 31 October
1775, 26 May	1776, 16 May	1778, 9 November
1775, 1 June	1776, 18 May	1778, 14 November
1775, 5 June	1776, 22 May	1778, 21 November
1775, 6 June	1776, 23 May	1779, 10 March
1775 (I), 7 June	1776, 4 June	1779, 18 March
1775 (II), 7 June	1776, 5 June	1779, 9 April
1775, 10 June	1776, 6 June	1779, 20 May
1775, 11 June	1776, 8 June	1779, 29 May
1775, 13 June	1777, 11 January	1779, 10 June
1775, 17 June	1777, 15 January	1779, 12 June
1775, 19 June	1777, 16 January	1779, 14 June
1775, 21 June	1777, 19 March	1779, 17 June
1775, 23 June	1777, 27 March	1779, 19 June
1775, 26 June	1777, 19 May	1779, 24 June
1775, 1 July	1777, 2 June	1779, 26 June
1775, Early July	1777, 4 August	1779, 4 October
1775, *c.* 3 July	1777, 7 August	1779, 5 October
1775, 6 July	1777, 9 August	1779, 8 October
1775, 9 July	1777, 13 August	1779, 11 October
1775, 11 July	1777, 23 August	1779, 16 October
1775, 12 July	1777, 27 August	1779, 21 October
1775, 13 July	1777, 6 September	1779, 25 October
1775, 15 July	1777, 8 September	1779, 28 October
1775, 17 July	1777, 13 September	1779, 2 November
1775, 20 July	1777, 15 September	1779, 4 November
1775, 21 July	1777, 18 September	1779, 7 November
1775, 24 July	1777, 20 September	1779, 8 November
1775, 26 July	1777, 22 September	1779, 16 November
1775, 29 July	1777, 25 September	1779, 20 November
1775, 1 August	1777, 27 September	1780, 6 April
1775, 2 August	1777, 29 September	1780, 11 April
1775, 5 August	1777, 6 October	1780, 15 April
1775, 29 August	1777, 13 October	1780, 18 April
	1777, 16 October	1780, 20 April

1780, 25 April

1780, 1 May

1780, 7 May

1780, 8 May

1780, 9 May

1780, 23 May

1780, 25 May

1780, 6 June

1780, 9 June

1780, 10 June

1780, 12 June

1780, 14 June

1780, 15 June

1780, 21 June

1780, 4 July

1780, 10 July

1780, 27 July

1780, 1 August

1780, 8 August

1780, 14 August

1780, 18 August

1780, 24 August

1780, 25 August

1780, 16 October

1781, 5 April

1781, 7 April

1781, 9 April

1781, 11 April

1781, 12 April

1781, 14 April

1781, 16 April

1781, 17 April

1781, 22 May

1781, 28 May

1781, 17 October

1781, 20 October

1781, 23 October

1781, 27 October

1781, 31 October

1781, 3 November

1781, 10 November

1781, 12 November

1781, 14 November

1781, 24 November

1781, 3 December

1781, 8 December

1782, 5 January

1782, 6 January

1782, 28 January

1782, 16 February

1782, 17 February

1782, 21 February

1782, 14 March

1782, 16 March

1782, 24 or 25 April

1782, 30 April

1782, 2 May

1782, 4 May

1782, 7 May

1782, 8 May

1782, 9 May

1782, 21 May

1782, 26 May

1782, 4 June

1782, 5 June

1782, 7 June

1782, 8 June

1782, 11 June

1782, 12 June

1782, 13 June

1782, 17 June

1782, 9 November

1782, 30 November

1782, 11 December

1782, 16 December

1782, 17 December

1782, 18 December

1782, 20 December

1782, 26 December

1782, 28 December

1783, 17 January

1783, 23 March

1783, 30 March

1783, 31 March

1783, 1 May

1783, 8 May

1783, 5 June

1783, 13 June

1783, 19 June

1783, 20 June

1783, 21 June

1783, 23 June

1783, 24 June

1783, 28 June

1783, 30 June

1783, 1 July

1783, 3 July

1783, 5 July

1783, 8 July

1783, 23 July

1783, 13 August

1783, 20 August

1783, 26 August

1783, 22 September

1783, 23 September

1783, 6 October

1783, 9 October

1783, 21 October

1783, 27 October

1783, 1 November

1783, 13 November

1783, 20 November

1783, 24 November

1783, 27 November

1783, 29 November

1783, 1 December

1783, 13 December

1783, 27 December

1783, 31 December

1784, 12 January

1784, 21 January

1784, 9 February

1784, 2 March

1784, 10 March

1784, 16 March

1784, 15 April

1784, 19 April

1784, 21 April

1784, 26 April

1784, 13 May

1784, 31 May

1784, 17 June

1784, 26 June

1784, 2 July

1784, 8 July

THRALE, Sophia
  1783, 24 July

THRALE, Susanna
  1783, Late Spring or
    Early Summer
  1783, 26 July
  1783, 9 September
  1783, 18 November
  1784, 25 March

THURLOW, Lord
  1784, 9 September

TOMKISON, Mr.
  1783, 1 October

TONSON, Jacob
  1758, 10 February
  1765, 9 October
  1765, 19 October

"MR. URBAN"
  1743, August

VYSE, William
  1777, 19 July
  1777, 22 July
  1780, 30 December
  1781, 10 April
  1784, 29 November

WARTON, Joseph
  1753, 8 March
  1754, 8 March
  1754, 24 December
  1756, 15 April
  1765, 9 October
  1770, 27 September
  1780, 23 May

WARTON, Thomas
  1754, 16 July
  1754, 28 November
  1754, 21 December
  1755, 1 February
  1755, 4 February
  1755, 13 February
  1755, 25 February
  1755, 20 March
  1755, 25 March
  1755, 13 May
  1755, 10 June
  1755, 24 June
  1755, 7 August
  1757, 21 June
  1758, 14 April
  1758, 1 June
  1769, 31 May
  1770, 23 June
  1780, 9 May

WAY, Elizabeth
  1782, 4 May
  1782, 6 May
  1782, 12 June
  1783, 23 April
  1784, 23 November

WELCH, Saunders
  1778, 3 February

WESLEY, John
  1776, 6 February
  1779, 3 May

WESLEY, Sarah
  1783, 28 October

WESTCOTE, Lord
  1780, 27 July
  1780, 28 July

WESTON, Phipps
  1768, 22 April
  1768, 28 April
  1768, 3 May

WETHERELL, Nathan
  1776, 12 March
  1779, 14 June

WHEELER, Benjamin
  1775, 30 March
  1775, 15 April
  1778, 2 November

WHITE, Mrs.
  1784, 2 November

WHITE, William
  1773, 4 March

WILKES, John
  1783, 24 May

WILSON, Thomas
  1782, 31 December
  1782

WINDHAM, William
  1783, 31 May
  1784, c. 20 August
  1784, 2 October
  1784, 17 November

WORSLEY, Richard
  1781, 28 August

Comprehensive

INDEX

COMPREHENSIVE INDEX

SJ's writings, opinions, and principal topics of commentary have been indexed separately. The reader should therefore go directly to the relevant entry, for example, "*Rasselas*," "friendship," "solitude."

The primary authority for locating letters to a given correspondent is the Alphabetical Table of Correspondents (v.59–72). However, as a supplementary guide to the reader, the entries for SJ's correspondents end with a comprehensive listing (by volume and page number) of all letters to the individual in question.

The following abbreviations are used: Bt. (Baronet), Kt. (Knight), ment. (mentioned). Peers are listed under their titles, with cross-references from the family name.

Letters and supplementary annotation that appear in the *Addenda* (v.55–58) have not been indexed.

A

Abbess, Mrs., housekeeper, III.258 and n6

Aberbrothick *see* Arbroath

Abercrombie, James, businessman, II.12 and n2

Aberdeen, Scotland, II.57, 58–59, III.9n11

Abingdon School, I.332n2

Abington, Frances, actress, II.205 and nn6,7

Abrahami Couleii Angli, Poemata Latina (ed. Sprat), I.340 and n1

Abrégé de la Vie des Peintres (de Piles), III.89n1

Abridgment of Law and Equity (Viner), I.161n2

Absalom and Achitophel (Dryden): quoted, III.79n15

abstinence: as calmer of thoughts, III.28; Dr. Lawrence recommends, III.261; effects of compared with those of parsimony, III.366; *see also* Johnson, Samuel —diet; health

Account of an Attempt to Ascertain the Longitude at Sea (Williams/Johnson), I.44n5

Account of a Series of Pictures in the Great Room of the Society of Arts, Manufactures, and Commerce (Barry), IV.135n8

Account of Corsica (Boswell), I.273 and n11, 298n2, 328–29 and n4

Account . . . of Mr. Blacklock (Spence), II.53n15

Account of the . . . Commemoration of Handel (C. Burney), IV.357 and n1, 384–85 and nn1,14, 431 and n4; and SJ's dedication, IV.357 and n1, 384 and nn1,14, 392 and n2

Account of the Loss of the Grosvenor, Indiaman (A. Dalrymple), IV.227 and n4

Account of the Trial of the Letter Y, Alias Y (Edwards), I.70 and nn3,9

Account of the Voyages undertaken . . . in the Southern Hemisphere (Hawkesworth), III.50 and n6

Adair, James, II.210 and n13

Adam, Robert, architect, II.52n1, 108n2, III.70n4, IV.135n8

Adams, Sarah (later Sarah Adams Hyett), IV.55 and n1, 346; SJ thanks for visits, IV.327; and SJ's stay in Oxford, IV.332 and n2

Adams, Sarah Hunt (Mrs. William), IV.346 and n9

Adams, Rev. William, D.D., Oxford don: ment., I.80 and n6; and Father Wilkes, III.75; and SJ's request for K. Macaulay's son, III.111–12; SJ dines with, III.361–62, IV.51, 52, 54; and E. Edwards's edition of Xenophon's *Memorabilia*, IV.304 and n2, 345–46; ment. as host at Oxford, IV.334; copies of SJ's books sent to, IV.441
— LETTERS: II.338, III.111–12, IV.304–5, 345–46

Addenbrooke, John, Dean of Lichfield, I.380 and n1, II.157 and n4

Addison, Joseph, essayist and literary critic, I.37n5; quoted, I.366n2, II.160n2, 339n4, III.249n9, IV.191n6; and *Lives of the Poets*, III.226nn1,2, 228, 229n7, 237, 254; and *The Tatler*, IV.241 and n2

Adelphi, The, I.26n1, IV.135n8

Adey, Felicia Hammond (Mrs. Joseph), I.301 and nn3,4; ment., II.254, 282, III.48, 149; death of, III.154 and n4, 163

Adey, Jane *see* Simpson, Jane Adey

Adey, Joseph (the elder), attorney: ment., v.19n5

Adey, Joseph (the younger), Lichfield Town Clerk, I.301n3; ment., v.19n5

Adey, Mary (later Mrs. John Sneyd), daughter of Joseph and Felicia, I.317 and n3; and SJ's visit to Lichfield, II.224, 228, 230, 263n1; ment., III.149, 328, IV.15, 22, 294, v.19 and nn2,5

"Ad Urbanum" (Johnson), I.14 and n2

Adventurer, The, I.67 and nn2,4, 77n1, 88n6, III.17

Advertisement touching an Holy War (Bacon), II.295 and n6

Aelian (Claudius Aelianus), rhetorician, I.11 and n4

Aeneid (Virgil), I.51n4, 52 and n5; quoted, I.100n6, 172n7, 273 and n10, 286n2, 376 and n2, II.35 and n4, 37

and n12, 125 and n3, 230 and n16, 309 and n8, III.19 and n3, 61 and n7, 77 and n10, 301n2, IV.130n5; Dryden's translation ment., III.119n6, IV.232 and n2

age and aging, III.68, 88, IV.127; "one of the old man's miseries is, that he cannot easily find a companion to partake with him of the past," III.107; on growing old, IV.90; *see also* youth

Agricola (Tacitus), IV.145 and n3

Akenside, Mark, poet and physician: medical advice, III.4n2, 52 and n2, IV.365; *Lives of the Poets*, ment., III.233n5, 301

Akerman, Richard, Keeper of Newgate Prison, III.268 and n6

Alaric ou Rome Vaincue (Scudéry), I.95n7

Albemarle, 3d Earl of (George Keppel), I.211n2

Aldine Press, I.312n27

Aldrich, Henry, Dean of Christ Church, Oxford, I.7n2; musical collection, III.136n2, 137n3

Alexander, Thomas, II.17 and nn1,5, 20, 22 and n3

Alexander et al. v. *Paterson et al.*, II.205 and n10

Alexander's Feast (Dryden): quoted, II.232 and n6, III.90n2

Alfred (Alfred the Great), King of England, III.354 and n3

"Allegro, L'" (Milton), IV.178n2

Allen, Rev. Charles, III.321–22

Allen, Edmund, printer: ment., I.155n1, 156n3, 175n4, 251, 253, IV.100, 152, 199, 282, 319; and Dodd case, III.27–28, 29n1, 31n2; recommended to continue as printer for Royal Academy, III.104–5 and n3; SJ owes rent to, III.361; death of, IV.355–56n2; death ment., IV.358, 369, 390, 406, 424
— LETTERS: II.225, 227, III.27–28, 376, IV.148, 331–32

Allen, Mrs. Edmund: ment., II.227; death ment., IV.160

Allen, Elizabeth (daughter of Elizabeth Allen Burney) *see* Meeke, Elizabeth Allen

Allen, Hollyer, of Magdalen Hall, I.163 and *n*5

Allestree, Richard, author, III.158*n*2

Almoran and Hamet (Hawkesworth), III.17 and *n*4

Alnwick Castle, II.45 and *n*2, 46*n*3, 50, 51–52 and *n*1

Althorp, Viscount (later 2d Earl Spencer), III.195*n*3, IV.96 and *n*4

Althorp, Viscountess *see* Bingham, Lavinia

Alzuma (Murphy), II.24*n*4

Amadis de Gaule (Spanish romance), V.16 and *n*4

America, I.203

American Traveller (James), I.27*n*4

American War (American Revolution), II.259 and *n*5, III.95 and *nn*9,10, 156*n*3, 197*n*4, 207*n*4, IV.27*n*4, 29*n*4, V.21

Ames, Joseph, antiquarian, I.357*n*4

Amores (Ovid), IV.185*n*2

Amphitryon (Dryden), II.356*n*1

Anacreon, poet, I.393 and *n*4

Anacreon (Baxter), IV.113 and *n*3, 209 and *n*2, 299

Analysis of the Gaelic Language (Shaw), III.12 and *nn*3,5

Anatomy of Melancholy (Burton), II.118 and *n*3

"Ancient Translations from Classic Authors" (Farmer), I.335*n*3, 355

Andrews, Francis, Provost of Trinity College, Dublin, I.257 and *n*3

Anecdotes of Some Distinguished Persons (Seward), III.229*n*7

Anecdotes of William Bowyer (Nichols), IV.84*n*7

Anfossi, Pasquale, composer, IV.99*n*2

Angel, The (inn, Stilton), II.47 and *n*2

Angell, George (the younger), III.113 and *nn*2,3

Angliae Notitiae, or the Present State of England (Chamberlayne), I.72*n*9

Annals of Scotland (Hailes), II.139*n*3, III.157 and *n*4; SJ sent manuscript for comments, II.145 and *n*4, 150, 154; SJ sends manuscript back, II.213, 295, 298*n*1; SJ makes few alterations on, II.266, 269 and *n*1; and "character" of Robert the Bruce, II.274 and *n*5; SJ receives first volume of, II.284 and *n*4, 295

Anne (Lucy Porter's maid): suffers from worms, III.49, 52

Another Traveller (Paterson), I.389*n*1

Antimachus, II.290*n*3

Antonius Musa, physician, I.55*n*17

Apollonius Rhodius, poet, I.108 and *n*2

Apothecaries Hall (London), III.126 and *n*3

Appeal to all that Doubt or Disbelieve the Truths of the Gospel (Law), I.123*n*1

Appendix Virgiliana, IV.391 and *n*7

Apperley, Thomas, of Leominster, Herefordshire, ment., I.190–91 and *n*3

— LETTER: I.296–97

Appius and Virginia (Dennis), I.52–53 and *n*8

Araucana, La (de Ercilla), V.16 and *n*3

Arbroath (Aberbrothick) Abbey, II.57 and *n*12

Archaeological Dictionary; or Classical Antiquities of the Jews, Greeks, and Romans, Alphabetically Arranged (Wilson), III.357–58 and *n*5

Archer, Thomas, architect, I.411*n*3

Aretinus, Leonardus, II.59*n*28

Argyll, Duchess of (Elizabeth Gunning) (wife of 5th Duke), II.109 and *n*3, 110; and JB, III.76 and *n*3, 79

Argyll, 4th Duke of (John Campbell), II.105*n*17

Argyll, 5th Duke of (John Campbell):

Argyll, 5th Duke of (*cont.*)
SJ dines with, II.108 and *n*1, 109–10;
Maclean's lawsuit, III.35*n*16, 40 and
*n*5; and SJ's Hebridean tour, III.76
and *n*3
— LETTER: II.109

Ariosto, Ludovico, poet, I.83*n*1, 92 and
*n*2; Hoole translation of *Orlando Furioso*, III.323 and *nn*3,4,6

Aristotle, II.59*n*28, III.122*n*7

Arithmetique Made Easie (Wingate),
IV.138 and *n*5

Armadale (Skye), II.81*n*52, 87*n*1

Arnold, Richard, author, III.293*n*1

Ars Amatoria (Ovid), III.69*n*12, 280*n*6

Ars Poetica (Horace): quoted, V.29*n*2

Art of Painting of Charles Alphonse du Fresnoy . . . with Annotations by Sir Joshua Reynolds, Knt., IV.115*n*1

Art Poétique, L' (Boileau-Despréaux),
I.95*n*7, IV.349*n*4

Asbridge, John, of Lichfield, I.154

Ascham, Roger, author, II.48 and *n*15

Ashbourne: ment. of plans for visit in
1770, I.254*n*4, 327, 344*n*1, 347 and
*n*4; The Mansion, I.347 and *n*3; SJ visits in 1771, I.366–67; SJ's 1772 visit,
I.397*n*2; SJ's stay in 1775, II.192*n*2,
247*n*11, 255; Thrales visit in 1774,
II.235*n*1, III.60*n*3; SJ and JB visit in
1776, II.309*n*4, 309–10 and *nn*1,2,
316 and *n*2; SJ's 1777 visit to, III.20*n*6,
56, 57, 64*n*1, 73 and *n*6; JB's visit to,
III.39–40 and *nn*2,3; a barren place,
III.63; no evil but very little good in,
III.85; SJ's stay in 1781, IV.68*n*4; SJ
visits in 1784, IV.340–41 and *n*1, 373–
74, 383; vacancy of SJ's life in, IV.381;
SJ wishes to leave, IV.406; as a solitary
place, IV.414

Ashbourne Grammar School, I.4 and
*n*3, 394*n*2

Ashburton, 1st Baron (John Dunning),
politician, lawyer, III.42, IV.95–96 and

*n*1, 98, 99; and J. Taylor, II.286 and
*n*2

Astle, Daniel, soldier, II.179 and *n*2

Astle, Thomas, antiquarian: ment.,
II.179 and *n*2
— LETTER: III.354–55

Aston, Catherine (Mrs. Henry Hervey
Aston), V.12*n*4

Aston, Elizabeth, daughter of Sir
Thomas: ment., I.344, 364, 372–73,
414 and *n*2, 415, II.222 and *n*5, 229,
258–59 and *n*3, 311, III.45*n*2, 53, 92,
166, 200, 285, 378, IV.166, 384*n*1; on
Harry Thrale's death, II.311; health
of discussed and ment., III.10–11, 13,
48 and *n*2, 51, 60, 64–65, 86, 87, 91,
96–97 and *n*5, 100, 148–49, 152–53,
167, 364, 365, 367–68, IV.202, 341;
SJ visits, III.48 and *n*2, 55–56, 361,
364, 365, 367–68; struck with palsy,
III.48*n*2, 58, 172; improved health
ment., IV.410 and *n*1, 412, 421
— LETTERS: I.292–93, 328, III.10–11,
13, 64–65, 96–97, 152–53, 164, 197,
207–8, IV.29–30, 296, 437

Aston, Henry Hervey, son of 1st Earl
of Bristol, V.12 and *nn*2,4; lends SJ
money, I.38*n*3, 60, 154, V.12 and
*nn*2,4; ment., I.292*n*1, 375*n*1; and JB,
III.98*n*1

Aston, Sophia *see* Prujean, Sophia
Aston

Aston, Sir Thomas, 3d Bt., I.292*n*1,
375*n*1, III.86*n*4

Astronomica (Manilius): quoted, IV.308
and *n*2

Athenae Oxonienses (Wood), I.115 and *n*2,
133*n*2; and R. Rawlinson, IV.79*n*3

Atterbury, Francis, Bishop of Rochester
(1713–23): ment., I.55 and *n*17; trial
before House of Lords, V.4 and *n*6

Auchinleck, Alexander Boswell, Lord,
JB's father, I.238 and *n*5, 262 and *n*6;
and JB's legal career, II.9 and *n*10; SJ
plans to visit, II.99, 100, 102; SJ and

JB visit, II.116–17 and nn36,37; and advance copy of *Journey*, II.166; JB to visit, II.265 and n1; and entail dispute, II.284–85 and n1, 287, 289, 294 and n3, 329; JB's desire to be independent of, II.328 and n7; JB's relations with, II.360 and n1, 364–65, III.8 and n2, 19 and n5, 142, 215 and n9; and case of J. Knight, III.42 and n18, 104; health of ment., III.181 and n2; death of, IV.71–72 and n1; death ment., IV.73n1, 77, 126

Auchinleck, Ayrshire: SJ ment. plans to visit, II.102 and n3, 108, 111; SJ and JB visit, II.102 and n3, 116–17 and n37; JB visits, III.19 and n5; distance from Carlisle, III.215 and nn7,8; Mrs. Boswell invites SJ to, IV.91–92 and n2

Auchinleck, Elizabeth Boswell, Lady (2d wife of Lord Auchinleck), II.209 and n3, 364, III.142n3; inheritance of, IV.72n2

Auchnashiel (Auknashealds): Inverness-shire, II.74

Aureng-Zebe (Dryden), I.374 and n3

Ausonius, Decimus Magnus, II.260n9

Austrian Succession, War of the, I.29n14

Autobiographical and Literary Anecdotes of William Bowyer (Nichols), IV.78

Ayrshire: and JB, IV.263n4

B

Bach, Johann Christian, composer: ment., III.248n3

Bach-y-Graig (Salusbury estate), II.58n19, 147n4, III.66 and n4

Bacon, Francis, Viscount St. Albans, essayist and philosopher, II.295 and n6

Bagnall, John, IV.126n18

Bagot, Sir Walter Wagstaffe, 5th Bt., I.299 and n3

Bagshaw, Thomas, chaplain of Bromley

College: and E. Johnson's burial and tombstone, IV.348 and n1, 350

– LETTERS: II.29–30, IV.348–49

Bahadur, Raja Nandakuma, IV.129 and nn2,3

Baillet, Adrien, scholar, I.312 and n26

Baker, David Erskine, author, I.290n5

Baker, Eliza Clendon (widow of David), I.290 and n5

Baker, Sir George, Bt., M.D., IV.377 and n2

Baker, Thomas, antiquarian and biographer, III.43 and n3

Baker-Holroyd, John *see* Sheffield, 1st Baron

Balbi, Giovanni, II.257n3

Ballard, Mr., I.103

Ballencrieff, II.69n2

balloons and ballooning, IV.204 and n1, 218, 222, 235, 259, 268, 272, 279 and nn2,5, 281, 377, 404, 407 and n2, 438 and n1; as amusement, IV.408–9; fiery demise of Sheldon-Keegan balloon, IV.415 and n7; have no use until can be guided, IV.415–16

Bamff *see* Banff

Banff (Banffshire), II.63

Bank of England, III.272 and n1

Banks, Sir Joseph, Bt., explorer: ment., I.387, II.57 and n15, 118, III.317; elected to The Club, III.132 and n5, 142; SJ dines with, IV.138

– LETTER: I.386

Barber, Elizabeth Ann, daughter of Francis: birth of, III.375n6, 376

Barber, Elizabeth Ball (Betsy) (Mrs. Francis), II.357 and n3; ment., II.358, IV.332, 433; daughter born, III.375 and n6, 376

Barber, Francis (Frank), SJ's servant, I.115 and n3, 145 and n1, 222, 327n2, 364, 368, 379, 398, 413 and n2, III.4, 49, 62, 86; SJ petitions for release of, I.187–88 and nn1,5,6; and Mrs. Coxeter, I.357n3; ment., II.37, 159n1, 211,

Barber, Francis (*cont.*)
220, 238, 273, 323, 358, III.66, 117 and $n3$, 140, 184, 361, 376, IV.177 and $n3$, V.4$n1$, 9 and $n1$; marriage of, II.357 and $n3$; and proof sheets of *Lives of the Poets*, III.156–57 and $n2$; daughter born, III.375 and $n6$; health ment., IV.15; and package from Lisbon, IV.110$n1$; and ballooning, IV.438
– LETTERS: I.315, 350, 353, IV.199

Barbeyrac, Jean, savant, I.101$n2$

Barclay, Alexander, poet and scholar, I.89–90 and $nn3,4$

Barclay, David, banker: ment., III.345 and $n1$, 348$n1$; and J. Scott's biography, IV.404 and $n1$
– LETTER: IV.404

Barclay, Mrs. Robert, IV.415 and $n1$

Barclay, Robert, brewer, III.348$n1$; and sale of brewery, III.353; ment., IV.37 and $n3$, 86, 163$n6$, 315 and $n2$, 415 and $n1$

Baretti, Giuseppe, I.87 and $n8$, 92 and $n4$, 111, 155$n1$, 163, 164–65, 346$n2$, 348 and $n6$, IV.19$n1$; ment., I.74$n5$, II.26, 190 and $n9$, 194$n8$, 228, 229, 273, 337, 339 and $n5$, IV.241; gold watch incident, I.83–86 and $nn1$–7; on SJ's reaction to H. Boothby's death, I.123$n2$; quarrels with T. Davies, II.9 and $n7$; tutors H. M. Thrale, II.118 and $n5$, 151, 218 and $n6$; and proposed trip to Italy, II.223$n12$, 299$n2$; and regatta, II.234$n1$; and F. Chambers, II.244 and $n4$, 252; Hester Thrale's relationship with, II.248 and $n3$, 253 and $n5$; trip to France, II.271$n1$, 276; leaves for Bath with the Thrales, II.313 and $nn1,6$, 314$n1$; health ment., II.325; quarrels with and leaves Thrales, II.365–66 and $n15$; translates *Discourses* of Sir J. Reynolds, II.366$n17$; musical scheme of, III.144 and $n9$, 156; dines with SJ, III.212

– LETTERS: I.196–201, 205–7, 212–15

Barker, Edmund: death ment., IV.259$n6$

Barker, Mr., possible servant of the Dukes of Devonshire, III.359

Barnard, Edward, Provost of Eton, III.235 and $n1$; and *Evelina*, III.236 and $n3$

Barnard, Frederick Augusta, librarian: and formation of Royal Library, I.303–4 and $n3$, 307–14; ment., I.306, III.156, IV.395$n1$
– LETTERS: I.307–14, III.348–49

Barnard, John, page of the backstairs, I.307$n1$

Barnard, Thomas, Bishop of Killaloe (1780–94), Bishop of Limerick (1794–1806), II.261$n2$
– LETTER: III.6

Barrett, William, surgeon and antiquarian, II.336 and $n9$, 339

Barrington, Daines, lawyer, antiquarian, and naturalist, IV.240 and $n2$

Barrington, 1st Viscount (John Shute), IV.240$n2$

Barrington, Samuel, admiral, IV.31$n4$

Barry, Sir Edward, Bt., M.D., IV.266 and $n6$

Barry, James, painter: and Essex Head Club, IV.120, 257 and $n4$; and M. Lowe's painting, IV.121 and $nn2,3$, 135 and $n8$, 154; and Sir J. Reynolds, IV.135 and $n8$, 257$n4$; ment., IV.189
– LETTER: IV.120–21

Barwell, Richard, II.351$n2$

Bas Bleu, Le (More), III.335$n1$, IV.297 and $n1$, 317

Baskerville, John, printer and typographic designer, I.105 and $nn6,7$, 323

Baskett, Mark, printer, I.246$n10$

Bassette Table, The (Montagu), I.371 and $n2$

Bath: Hester and H. M. Thrale and Baretti at in 1776, II.313$nn1,6$, 314$n1$,

317 and n1; SJ accompanies Thrales to in 1776, II.317n7; JB visits SJ and the Thrales in 1776, II.323 and n2; Conte Manucci invited to, II.325 and n3; Thrales return from in 1776, II.334n3; Thrales and F. Burney visit in 1780, III.228 and n1; warm waters of ment., III.245 and n7; SJ on, III.262; violence against Catholics in, III.273 and nn6,8, 274; Thrales leave because of violence in, III.273 and n8, 279n1; good roads between London and, III.331 and n4

Bathurst, 2d Earl (Henry Bathurst): and Dodd case, III.27n1

Bathurst, Richard (the elder), West Indian planter, I.115n3

Bathurst, Richard (the younger), physician and writer, I.68–69 and n3, 115n3; death of, I.211, 215, IV.259n6

Baxter, Richard, author, II.150n7, IV.271 and n4

Baxter, William, author: Anacreon, IV.113 and n3, 209n2

Bayley, Ann Hinckley (Mrs. Francis), IV.22n5

Bayley, Francis, of Lichfield, IV.22n5

Bayley, Hester, daughter of Francis, IV.22 and n5

Beach, Thomas, wine merchant and poet, I.16n2

Beaton (Bethune), David, Archbishop of St. Andrews, II.56 and n9

Beattie, James (the elder), poet and philosopher: ment., I.388 and n3, 393n1, II.8 and n2, 43, 46, III.35, 347 and n1; and pension issue, II.41–42 and n8, 44, 111; calls on SJ while staying with B. Porteus, II.210 and n14; F. Reynolds wishes to send O. Goldsmith's epitaph to, II.344n3, 345; on SJ, III.347n1
– LETTERS: I.382–83, II.44, III.301–2

Beattie, James (the younger), son of James and Mary, III.302n3, 347n1

Beattie, Mary Dun (Mrs. James, the elder), I.388 and n3, II.44; ment., III.302

Beauclerk, Charles George, son of Topham, III.231 and n6

Beauclerk, Lady Diana (wife of Topham), II.170 and n7, III.210n3, 231 and n6

Beauclerk, Elizabeth, daughter of Topham, III.231 and n6

Beauclerk, Mary, daughter of Topham, III.231and n6

Beauclerk, Lady Sidney (Mary Norris), mother of Topham, III.231 and n5, IV.126

Beauclerk, Lord Sidney, M.P., I.192n2

Beauclerk, Topham, I.192 and nn1,2, 205 and n2, 207, 213, 360n1, III.210–11 and n3, 214; and The Club, II.27n1, 126n1, 128n5; health of, II.170 and n6, III.9 and n6, 216 and n10; ment., II.213; and H. Hervey incident, III.98–99 and nn1,2; and portrait of SJ, III.127n5; death of, III.216n10, 231 and nn3,5,8, IV.126; library of, III.231 and n8
– LETTER: I.211

Beauties of Johnson: Consisting of Maxims and Observations . . . Accurately extracted from the Works of Dr. Samuel Johnson, III.361n1, IV.28 and n5, 40nn3,4, 41

Beauvoir, Osmund, headmaster of King's School, IV.31n6

Becket, Thomas: and Macpherson manuscripts, II.177n6

Becket, Thomas à see Thomas à Becket

Beckford, William, M.P., London alderman, I.278n2

Belford, Northumberland, II.52 and n2

Bell, John, bookseller, III.226n1; ment., V.6n3

Bell, John, schoolmaster, III.102 and n1

Bell, Robert, printer, II.13nn5,6

Bell, William, Prebendary of Westminster, V.6 and nn2,3; ment., III.244; and

Bell, William (*cont.*)
   almshouses, IV.270 and *n*5
Bellamy, George Anne, actress, I.172
   and *n*10
Bellum Catilinarium (Sallust), I.221*n*6
Bembo, Pietro, IV.390 and *n*6
Bentham, Edward, D.D., II.196–97
Bentley, Richard, D.D., I.396 and *n*7
Berkeley, George, Bishop of Cloyne,
   III.235 and *n*2
Bernard, Edward, astronomer, I.86*n*2
Berwick: ment., II.50
Bethune, David *see* Beaton, David
"Better Answer (To Chloe Jealous)"
   (Prior), IV.220*n*6
Bevan, Amelia *see* Perkins, Amelia
   Bevan
Bevan, Silvanus, banker, III.348*n*1
Bevan, Timothy Paul, banker, III.334*n*1
Bewley, William, surgeon, III.353 and
   *n*1; death ment., IV.199 and *n*1
Bible, The, IV.77; SJ advocates transla-
   tion into Gaelic, I.269–70 and *nn*2,9;
   early printing of, I.313 and *nn*31–34;
   quoted, IV.153*n*19; Polyglot Bible,
   IV.395–96 and *nn*2–4
Biblia Sacra Polyglotta (B. Walton),
   IV.395*n*2
Bibliotheca Græca, I.312 and *n*28
Bibliothecæ Regiæ Catalogus, I.307*n*2
*Bibliothèque raisonnée des Ouvrages des Sa-
   vans* (Barbeyrac), I.101*n*2
Biggin, George, balloonist, IV.408*n*3
Bingham, Anne, daughter of 1st Baron
   Lucan, III.204 and *n*3, 213
Bingham, Sir Charles, Bt. *see* Lucan, 1st
   Baron
Bingham, Lavinia, daughter of 1st
   Baron Lucan (later Viscountess Al-
   thorp), III.195 and *n*3, 204 and *n*3,
   213, IV.266
Bingham, Louisa, daughter of 1st
   Baron Lucan, III.204 and *n*3, 213
Bingham, Margaret Smith *see* Lucan,
   Baroness

Bingham, Margaret, daughter of 1st
   Baron Lucan, III.204 and *n*3, 213
Bingham, Richard *see* Lucan, 2d Earl of
Biographia Britannica, III.226*n*2; SJ requests copy of, III.76 and *n*11, 93
*Biographical and Literary Anecdotes of Wil-
   liam Bowyer* (Nichols), IV.66*n*2, 424
Biographical History (Granger), I.416*n*1,
   417*n*4
biography: SJ's comments on in *Rambler*, I.266 and *nn*4,6; SJ's fundamental premise concerning, I.345–46 and
   *n*5
Birch, Thomas, literary scholar, 157
   and *n*5
   — LETTERS: I.36–37, 44, 65, 76–77,
   101–2, 115, 124, 133, 135
Birmingham, IV.26*n*3; SJ passes
   through in 1767, I.260*n*4; Edinburgh
   compared to, II.52; SJ and JB visit in
   1776, II.310; SJ visits in 1777, III.20
   and *n*6, 46*n*8, 48, 90; SJ visits in 1781,
   III.362
Biron *see* Byron
Bishop's Palace (Lichfield), I.223–24
   and *n*5
Bishop Stortford Grammar School,
   I.350*n*3
Blackamoor's Head Inn, III.74 and *n*2
Blackfriars Bridge, III.45*n*2
Blacklock, Thomas, Scots poet, II.53
   and *n*15
Blackmore, Sir Richard, poet and phy-
   sician: and *Lives of the Poets*, III.225
   and *n*3, 233*n*5, 260 and *n*3, 286 and
   *n*13, 301; essays of ment., III.260 and
   *n*3; ment., v.32 and *n*3
Blackstone, Sir William, Kt., jurist,
   I.162*n*3, 276*n*1, III.112*n*1; and grain
   embargo, I.275–76 and *n*5; and
   copyright law, II.130*n*3
Blackwall, Anthony, IV.104*n*1
Blair, Hugh, clergyman and critic,
   II.128 and *n*6; and Ossian controversy, II.177 and *n*4, 339*n*6; publica-

tion of sermons of, II.367 and n1; sermons of ment., III.8, 19, 99

Blenheim, III.3n4

bloodletting see Johnson, Samuel—health; medicine

Blount, Thomas (1618–79), lexicographer, I.66n2

Blount, Sir Thomas Pope (1649–97), 1st Bt., writer, I.65–66 and n2

Bluestockings, I.185n1, II.175nn5,6, III.14n5; prominent hostesses, I.185n1, III.27n5, 116n4, 236n7, 242n2, 251n8; SJ attends party of, IV.52n2; and Hester Thrale's marriage to G. Piozzi, IV.351n1

Bodleian Library, II.219n3, III.135, 136; SJ presents books to, II.150 and nn7,8

Bodward, Thomas, tenant at Gough Square, I.255n5

Boece, Hector see Boethius, Hector

Boethius (Boece), Hector, Scots historian, II.126 and n3, IV.299

Boileau-Despréaux, Nicolas, poet, I.305–6 and n3; quoted, I.95n7, IV.349 and n4

Bolingbroke, 1st Viscount (Henry St. John), I.60 and n4

Bolingbroke, 2d Viscount (Frederick St. John), IV.163n3

Bolingbroke, Viscountess (Lady Diana Spencer): divorce and remarriage of, II.170 and n7

Bolt Court (London), III.8n3, 93, 96n1; SJ moves to, II.316 and n1; and G. Jones, V.8n1

Bond, Phineas, attorney, II.11–12

Book of Common Prayer, II.21n3; quoted, III.122n8, IV.128 and n28

book publishing see printing and publishing

books: on collecting, I.307–14; and illustrations, I.311nn19,21; on dictionaries, IV.379; see also printing and publishing

Boothby, Hill, SJ's friend: discrepant

theological views, I.119–21; death of, I.123n2

– LETTERS: I.76, 116–18, 119–24, 139

Bordesley Hall, I.416n2

Bosville, Godfrey, JB's "Yorkshire Chief," II.77n29, III.46 and n5

Boswell, Alexander see Auchinleck, Alexander Boswell, Lord

Boswell, Alexander (Sandy), son of JB: birth of, II.146 and n9, 273 and n1; ment., II.280, 284, 296, 329, 360, III.8, 12, 35n13, 36, 99, 103, 215, 304

Boswell, David, son of JB: birth of, II.364 and n4; death of, III.12 and n9, 20

Boswell, Elizabeth see Auchinleck, Elizabeth Boswell, Lady

Boswell, Elizabeth, daughter of JB: ment., III.304

Boswell, Euphemia, daughter of JB: birth of, II.144 and n5, 146; ment., II.156, 214, 284, 296, 360, III.12, 35n13, 99, 103, 215, 232, 304

Boswell, Euphemia, mother of JB: death of, I.262n6

Boswell, James: and Grand Tour, I.261–62; relationship with his father, I.262, 272, II.360 and n1, 364–65, III.19, 318, IV.71–72; defends thesis, I.271–72 and nn1,2; marriage of, I.329 and n7, 332; ment., II.25, 69, 84, 92, III.42–43, 45, 62, 70 and nn1,4, 71, 74, 76n3, 79 and nn17,21, 207, 220, 255 and n3; elected to The Club, II.27 and n1; affection for SJ, II.43 and n2; apartment of, II.52–53 and n9; controversy with Sir A. Macdonald, II.77 and n30, 114; expects SJ to visit his father, II.99, 100; and lawsuit of Sir A. Maclean, II.105n17, 214; projected Baltic trip, II.156; receives, reads, and comments on Journey, II.166 and nn1,3; and Memis case, II.176 and n1, 178; and Ossian controversy, II.176–78 and n2, 180–81

Boswell, James (*cont.*)

and *nn*2,3,5,6; and SJ-Raasay controversy over clan supremacy, II.203, 206, 214, 228–29; and the English bar, II.205 and *n*9; ment. of law case tried and money received, II.205 and *n*10, 209; opinion of in Lichfield, II.224; SJ's love for, II.267, 330, III.63, 103, 318; and entail dispute, II.284–85 and *n*1, 286–89, 291, 294 and *n*3, 298 and *n*3, 299, 329; suffers from melancholy, II.298–99 and *n*1, 348, 349; comes to London, and then accompanies SJ to Oxford and Lichfield, II.299*n*4; with SJ in Lichfield and Ashbourne, II.309–10 and *nn*1,2, 311; visits SJ and the Thrales in Bath, II.323 and *n*2; seeks a "place," II.328 and *n*7; and "Rowley" poems, II.332*n*9; and Mrs. Rudd, II.334 and *n*6; SJ pays in books, balance due from Hebridean tour, II.348 and *n*3, 349; and *Lives of the Poets*, III.20 and *n*10; visits SJ in Ashbourne in 1777, III.65 and *n*2, 66–67, 68, 73, 76–77; SJ-Percy dispute, III.113–14; wishes to come to London in 1778, III.125 and *n*4; visits SJ in London in 1779, III.125*n*4, 186 and *n*4; SJ hopes to send some *Lives* to read, III.143 and *n*7; SJ's letter of introduction to J. Wesley, III.162; SJ's concern over not hearing from, III.177 and *n*1, 178, 181; on Henry Thrale's health and appearance, III.185; visits Chester, III.191 and *n*11; visits Lichfield in 1779, III.191 and *n*11, 199–200 and *n*2; financial problems, III.230 and *n*2, IV.77; SJ on melancholy of, III.232; SJ unable to meet for interview with, III.317–18; melancholy at thoughts of predestination, III.328 and *n*1; in London, III.335*nn*2,3; and proposed trip in 1782 to London, IV.27 and *n*3, 73*n*1; SJ's advice on frugal living,

IV.27–28, 45, 112, 347; and Society of Solicitors, IV.28 and *n*7; SJ's advice on remaining with Mrs. Boswell, IV.73*n*2; SJ gives R. Chambers news of, IV.126; SJ informs of his stroke, IV.164; and Essex Head Club, IV.257*n*2, 345; concern over SJ's health, IV.284 and *n*1, 286 and *n*6, 291 and *n*1; political ambition of, IV.299*nn*3,6, 310; SJ's advice on election campaign, IV.306; and trip to Oxford, IV.332 and *n*1; hopes to visit Lichfield with SJ in 1784, IV.335–36; involved in plans for SJ's augmented pension and trip to Italy, IV.342 and *n*3; SJ's advice on projected move to London in 1784, IV.347 and *n*1, 361–63; on Seward's *Louisa*, IV.412*n*3; on last letters from SJ, IV.434*n*2; on SJ's affection for T. Davies, V.4*n*1

— HEBRIDEAN TRIP: ment. while in St. Andrews, II.55, 56; at Arbroath Abbey, II.57; in Aberdeen, angry that professors would not talk, II.60; ment., II.69, 84, 92; shares bread, II.74; ment. at Inn in Glenelg, II.76–77; fears ghosts in chapel on Inchkenneth, II.105 and *n*18; desires to be on dry ground, II.107; keeps register of weather conditions, II.110; offers tip to keeper at deer park, II.111; SJ on as traveling companion, II.115; and visit with Countess of Eglinton, II.116

— LETTERS: I.237–40, 261–62, 271–73, 298, 328–29, 331–32, 362–63, 388–89, 393–94, II.7–10, 41–43, 51, 119–20, 123, 124–25, 127–28, 132–34, 140, 142, 144, 145–47, 149–50, 153–54, 155–56, 166–67, 170–72, 176–78, 180–82, 213–14, 265–67, 269, 270, 273–74, 280–81, 283–85, 286–89, 291–92, 294–96, 304, 315–16, 323–24, 348–50, 360–61, 364–66, III.11–12, 19–20, 31, 33–36, 39–42, 47–48, 56–58, 63–64, 74, 98–100,

101–4, 113–14, 118–20, 141–43, 156–57, 161, 178, 181–82, 199–201, 214–16, 230–32, 303–4, 317–18, 328–29, IV.3–4, 27–28, 44–45, 70, 71–73, 90–91, 112–13, 164–65, 209–10, 262–64, 284–86, 290–92, 298–99, 305–6, 346–48, 354–55, 358–59, 360, 433–34

Boswell, James (the younger), son of JB: birth of, III.142 and *n*1; illness ment., IV.165*n*7

Boswell, John, uncle of JB, III.35*n*13

Boswell, Margaret Montgomerie (Mrs. James), I.329 and *n*7; SJ meets, I.389 and *n*8; Hester Thrale hopes she will accompany JB to London, II.10*n*11; relationship with SJ, II.42, 120, 123, 125, 128, 182, 213, 214, 265, 266–67, 273, 281, 284, 289, 292, 296, 329, 360, III.8, 11, 19, 42–43, 79, 99, 318; concern over JB's and SJ's health during Hebridean trip, II.77; mien and manners of, II.111; SJ on relationship between JB and, II.133, 329–30; ment., II.144, 150, 154, 156, 167, 171, 178, 270, 304, 350, III.12, 57, 181, 215, 216, 232, 304, IV.28, 45, 306, 434; SJ on birth of son, II.146 and *n*9; and gift for JB's stepmother, II.209; and entail dispute, II.273*n*2, 284–85 and *n*1, 298 and *n*3; and orange marmalade, III.11 and *n*1, 19, 33 and *n*2, 42–43, 46, 157; health ment., III.35*n*13, 47 and *n*2, 103 and *nn*1–3, 118, 142 and *n*2, IV.3*n*1, 4, 27 and *n*2, 70, 73, 92, 112, 292; pregnant, III.142 and *nn*1,2; sent set of *Lives of the Poets*, III.157 and *n*3, 177 and *n*2, 304 and *n*8, 325; SJ's advice to JB concerning, IV.73 and *n*2, 77; invites SJ to Auchinleck, IV.91–92; SJ thanks for attention from, IV.298–99

– LETTERS: II.329–30, III.42–43, IV.91–92

Boswell, Thomas David, brother of JB,

III.280 and *n*9, 318, IV.164*n*1, 165

Boswell, Veronica, daughter of JB, II.111 and *n*4; birth of, II.42 and *n*11; ment., II.128, 144, 156, 167, 171, 178, 280, 284, 296, 360, III.8, 12, 20, 35*n*13, 36, 47, 99, 103, 157, 215, 232, 304; SJ on relationship with, II.213, 214, 329

Boufflers-Rouverel, Comtesse de (Marie Charlotte Hippolyte), I.360–61

Boulton, Matthew, manufacturer and engineer, II.310 and *n*3

Bouquet, Joseph, bookseller, I.47*n*3

Bourke, Joseph Dean, Archbishop of Tuam, IV.186 and *n*8

Bourne, Thomas, usher, I.4*n*3

Bouverie, Harriet, IV.239*n*9

Bouverie, William Henry, politician, IV.289*n*5

Bowen, Mr., bookseller, III.188–89 and *n*5, 195, 198

Bowker, Mr., cotton manufacturer, I.144 and *n*5

Bowles, Dinah Frankland (Mrs. William), IV.177 and *n*5, 195; ment., IV.202, 210, 219, 230, 274, 281, 324, 345, 361, 403

Bowles, Rev. William (the elder), Canon of Salisbury, III.245*n*4; ment., IV.281, 324, 345

Bowles, William (the younger), of Heale House, III.245 and *n*4; SJ plans to visit, IV.177 and *n*4, 182–83, 188, 190, 191, 267–68; SJ gives account of his testicular sarcocele, IV.201–2, 210, 218–19, 230–31; on Stonehenge, IV.221*n*11, 222; political life, IV.289 and *n*5

– LETTERS: IV.176–77, 182–83, 188, 201–2, 210, 218–19, 230–31, 267–68, 273–74, 280–81, 289, 307–8, 323–24, 344–45, 361, 402–3

Bow Street, London, I.26*n*1

Bowyer, William (the younger), printer, IV.66 and *n*2, 424

Boyd, Charles, brother of James, II.61 and *n*8

Boyd, James *see* Errol, 15th Earl of

Boyd's Inn (Edinburgh) *see* White Horse Inn

Boyle, Charles *see* Orrery, 4th Earl of

Boyle, John *see* Orrery, 5th Earl of

Boyle, Robert, philosopher, IV.54 and *n*4

Boylston, George, of Lichfield, I.260 and *n*7

Braganza (play, Jephson), II.175 and *n*6

Brahe, Tycho, astronomer, II.337*n*3

Brandt, Sebastian, satirist, I.89*n*3

Brandywine, Battle of, III.95*n*10

bravery, IV.294

Braxfield, Robert Macqueen, Lord, Lord of Justiciary, III.255*n*2

Breachachadh Castle (Coll), II.101*n*4

Brent, Sir Nathaniel, translator, Warden of Merton College, Oxford, I.13*n*3

Breton language, I.152 and *n*6

Brewer, Father, II.336–37, 343

Brewse, John, Col., engineer, II.64 and *n*13

Bridge, Edward, steward, I.400 and *n*2, II.115 and *n*27

Bridgen, Edward, merchant, I.206*n*9

Bridgen, Martha Richardson (Mrs. Edward), I.206 and *n*9

Bright, Rev. Henry, headmaster: and George Strahan, I.209–10 and *nn*3,4, 217, 218; SJ dines with, II.217

— LETTERS: I.209–10, 332, 333–34, 338

Brighton (Brighthelmston): and the Thrales, I.249*n*2, 250*n*2; SJ joins Thrales in 1769, I.327*n*7; SJ on, I.349 and *n*1, II.361, III.193; R. Thrale sent to, II.207*n*5; SJ inquires if he and Thrales will visit in autumn of 1775, II.241 and *n*4, 255; SJ's trip to in 1776 ment., II.347*n*6; Thrales visit several times during 1777, III.15*n*2, 58, 73 and *n*9, 87 and *n*2; SJ's ment. of plans for and visit to Thrales in Nov. 1777,

III.55 and *n*4, 60, 75 and *n*4, 77, 78, 87 and *n*2, 94 and *n*2, 96 and *n*3, 97, 99; Thrales in temporary quarters in, III.80–81 and *n*4; principal meeting places in, III.81*n*7; ment., III.139 and *n*8; "The Steine," III.144 and *n*7; Thrales visit in 1779, III.165 and *n*2; SJ accompanies Thrales to in 1780, III.264*n*3, 317*nn*3,4, 318; unrest in Bath in 1780 causes Thrales to leave for, III.273*n*8, 274, 279*n*1; on news of husband's death, Hester Thrale leaves for, III.329*n*1, 331*n*3; SJ goes to in Oct. 1782, IV.77 and *n*8

Bristol, H.M.S., IV.49*n*1, 56

British Enchanters (Granville), III.246 and *nn*1,2

British Museum: and SJ's request concerning Swinton letter, IV.445 and *n*4

British Synonymy (H. L. Piozzi), IV.19*n*1

Broadhurst, Walter, watchmaker, III.166 and *n*2

Brochel Castle (Raasay), II.88 and *n*6

Brocklesby, Richard, M.D.: ment. in regard to SJ's health, IV.152, 155, 159, 160, 164, 211, 216, 261, 286*n*6, 291, 302, 438; and Juvenal, IV.155 and *n*6; SJ praises, IV.168; on A. Williams's death, IV.198; and W. G. Hamilton, IV.241 and *n*4, 243; and Essex Head Club, IV.257; SJ dines with, IV.325, 335; SJ gives account of his health to, IV.351–53, 355–56, 359, 364–65, 368, 376–78, 381–82, 415–16, 428, 436; accompanies SJ to Royal Academy, IV.418

— LETTERS: IV.192–93, 351–53, 355–56, 359–60, 364–66, 368, 370–71, 372–73, 376–78, 381–82, 386–87, 400–401, 405, 408–9, 415–16, 421–22, 428, 436

Brodaeus, IV.318*n*11

Broderic, Mr., V.23–24 and *n*2

Broglie, François Marie (Maréchal de

Broglie), Maréchal of France, I.29–30 and *n*19

Brolas (estate), II.105*n*17

Bromfield, Robert, M.D., I.368 and *n*2, 370; and Henry Thrale's stroke, III.168 and *n*2

Brooke, Francis, attorney, III.53 and *n*8

Brookes, Mrs., I.137

Broome, William, poet: and *Lives of the Poets*, III.233*n*5, 257, 278 and *n*1; and Pope's translation of the *Odyssey*, III.259 and *n*1

Brown, John, father of Mrs. John Hawkesworth, I.130*n*8

Browne, Isaac Hawkins, poet and M.P., IV.182 and *nn*4,5

Browne, Mrs. (of Bath), III.236 and *n*6

Browne, Sir Thomas, Kt., I.132 and *n*3, 133

Bruce, James, explorer and travel writer, II.193 and *n*1

Bruce, Mrs. (of St. Andrews), II.55–56 and *n*8

Bryant, Jacob, classical scholar, III.3 and *n*4

Buchan (Aberdeenshire) *see* Buller of Buchan

Buchanan, George, poet and scholar, I.58*n*6, II.126 and *n*4, III.306*n*6

Buller, Francis, jurist, III.249*n*10

Buller, Susanna Yarde (Mrs. Francis), III.249–50 and *n*10

Buller of Buchan, Aberdeenshire, II.61–62

Bunbury, Catherine Horneck (Mrs. Henry William), III.277*n*8

Bunbury, Henry William, caricaturist, III.277*n*8

Bunbury, Sir Thomas Charles, 6th Bt., II.128 and *n*4

Bunker Hill, Battle of, II.259 and *n*5

Burgoyne, Miss, godmother of Ralph Thrale, v.31 and *n*2

Burgoyne, Sir Roger, 6th Bt., IV.35*n*3, v.31*n*2

Burke, Edmund, I.218*n*1, 257*n*1, 259*n*3, 265*nn*12,13, 339*n*1, IV.62 and *n*3, 398*n*4; and Stamp Act repeal, I.264–65 and *nn*6,7; proposes A. Vesey for Club membership, II.26*n*3; proposes C. Fox for Club membership, II.128*n*3; ment., III.14*n*1, 258, v.25; SJ asks help of for J. Rann, III.161 and *n*2; SJ directs F. Reynolds to buy engraving of, III.192 and *n*2; on H. Croft's memoir of E. Young, III.322*n*5; and JB's political hopes, IV.27*n*4, 262*n*1; resignation of, IV.59 and *n*1; ment. as Club member, IV.96; and G. Crabbe, IV.116*n*1; tours southwestern England, IV.195 and *n*7, 196*n*2, 221; and East India Bill, IV.277 and *n*4; and P. Stockdale, v.21

– LETTERS: I.340, III.161

Burke, Jane Mary Nugent (Mrs. Edmund), I.340 and *n*2, IV.195*n*7, 196*n*2; ment., I.352, III.14 and *n*1; SJ's condolences on death of her father, II.277

– LETTER: II.277

Burke, Richard, Jr., son of Edmund, IV.62*n*3, 398 and *nn*4,5

Burke, Richard, Sr., brother of Edmund, IV.62*n*3, 195 and *n*7, 196*n*2

Burnet, Gilbert, Bishop of Salisbury: *History of His Own Time* ment., IV.89 and *n*2

Burnett, James *see* Monboddo, Lord

Burney, Charles (the younger): marriage of, IV.185 and *n*7

Burney, Charles, MUS.D.: ment., I.74*n*5, III.14 and *n*4, 85, 140, 143, 205, 244, 310; stays at Streatham Park, III.77 and *n*7; stepdaughter's elopement, III.85*n*2, 91; robbed, III.127; writes music history, III.135–36 and *n*3, 136–37, 140, 196 and *nn*15,16, 205, IV.21; and Baretti's musical scheme, III.144; and Henry Thrale's stroke, III.171; on his daughter's Latin les-

Burney, Charles (*cont.*)

sons, III.173*n*6; gives music lessons, III.238, 244; and Mrs. Ord, III.242 and *n*2; trip to Winchester, III.260*n*2; SJ requests research assistance from, III.293; and proofs for A. Pope's "Life," III.323*n*2; SJ revises passage in *General History of Music*, IV.21; SJ returns book belonging to, IV.242; and *An Account of the . . . Commemoration of Handel*, IV.357 and *n*1, 384–85 and *nn*1,14, 392, 431

— LETTERS: I.102–3, 157–58, 159–60, 256, III.135, 171, 242, 293, IV.21, 173, 199–200, 357–58, 379–80, 384–86, 392–93, 430–31, 437

Burney, Charlotte Ann (Sophy), daughter of Charles, the elder, III.310 and *n*2, IV.242 and *n*3; ment., III.86 and *n*3, 91

Burney, Elizabeth Allen (2d wife of Charles, the elder): and daughter's elopement, III.85–86 and *nn*2,3, 91–92; robbed, III.127; health ment., III.135, 288 and *n*1, IV.358 and *n*3, 380, 431; ment., III.310

— LETTER: IV.173

Burney, Esther, daughter of Charles, the elder, III.59 and *n*2; ment., III.86 and *n*3, 91

Burney, Esther Sleepe (1st wife of Charles, the elder), I.158 and *n*8, 160, 256*n*4, III.310*nn*2,4

Burney, Frances: ment., I.158*n*8; III.133–34, 135, 205 and *n*1, 211, 219 and *n*4, 228*n*1, 229, 236 and *n*3, 238, 244, 249 and *n*10, 252, 257, 270, 273, 276, 281, 282*n*6, 310, 364 and *n*6, IV.245; first meets SJ, III.14*n*4; relationship with stepmother, III.86 and *n*3, 91; becomes protégée of SJ and Hester Thrale, III.130*n*4; godmother of, III.133*n*4; Latin lessons, III.173*n*6, 195 and *n*6; travels with Thrales to Brighton, III.186*n*3; ment. as "young-

ling," III.188 and *n*3, 199, 202; and R. Cumberland, III.196 and *n*12, 209; and J. Delap, III.196 and *n*13; *Evelina* discussed, III.213 and *n*6; fears during Gordon riots, III.273 and *nn*8,9, 279 and *n*3; receives advance copy of *Prefaces*, III.289*n*1; and proofs for SJ's "Life" of Pope, III.323 and *n*2; leaves Brighton, IV.88*n*1; and S. Dobson, IV.147 and *n*6; dines with SJ, IV.317, 319; and Thrale-Piozzi affair, IV.322*n*7, 328*n*1; frugal in sending her letter to SJ, IV.430*n*1, 431; SJ requests copy of *Cecilia*, V.3

— LETTERS: III.353, IV.48–49, 173, 432, V.3

Burney, James, son of Charles, the elder, the elder, III.317 and *n*5, 373 and *n*2, 378 and *nn*2,3, IV.56; and John Mara's employment, IV.48–49 and *n*1, 56

— LETTER: IV.56

Burney, Richard Thomas, son of Charles, the elder, IV.161 and *n*4; trip to Winchester, III.260*n*2

Burney, Sarah, daughter of Charles, the elder, III.86*n*3, 91

Burney, Sarah Rose (Mrs. Charles, the younger), IV.185*n*7

Burney, Susanna Elizabeth, daughter of Charles, the elder, III.310 and *nn*2,4; ment., III.86 and *n*3, 91

Burney family: SJ's love for, III.373

Burton, Catherine Kennedy (Mrs. John), III.371 and *n*5

Burton, John, of Ashbourne, III.371 and *n*5

Burton, Richard or Robert *see* Crouch, Nathaniel

Burton, Robert: *Anatomy of Melancholy* quoted, II.118 and *n*3, III.201

Bute, 3rd Earl of (John Stuart), I.199*n*7, 207–8, 212; resignation of, I.231*nn*1,3

— LETTERS: I.207–8, 212

Butler, Samuel, poet: and *Lives of the Poets*, III.122 and *n*2

Butter, Mrs., wife of Dr. William, III.70*n*4

Butter, William, M.D., I.395 and *n*4; and J. Taylor, II.40, III.155, 344–45

Byrkes, Robert (Robin of Doncaster), II.47 and *n*5

Byron, Augusta (later Mrs. Christopher Parker), III.144 and *n*6

Byron, Capt. George Anson, III.241*n*8

Byron, Charlotte Henrietta Dallas (Mrs. George), III.241*n*8

Byron, John, Vice Admiral, III.133*n*5, 208 and *n*1, 241*n*8, 372*n*4

Byron, Sophia Trevannion (Mrs. John), III.133 and *nn*5,6, 144, 204, 208 and *n*1, 211–12, 216, 241 and *n*8, 251*n*4, 372; ment., IV.41

C

Cadell, Thomas, bookseller: and G. Baretti's book, II.190; trade practices, II.306 and *n*6, 307 and *n*7; ment., II.354*n*1, III.23*n*1, 137 and *n*1, 325; and SJ's *Prefaces*, III.159 and *n*4; publishes J. Cook's *Voyages*, IV.332*n*2; requested to send SJ's books to Oxford, IV.440–41; SJ requests copy of Xenophon's *Hellenica* from, V.3

— LETTERS: III.104–5, 158, 159, 324–25, IV.113–14, 123, 440–41, V.3

Caesar, Gaius Julius, I.12

Calder, Rev. John, literary scholar: and Chambers's *Cyclæpedia*, II.4*n*3, 297; firing of, II.293–94 and *n*1, 297

— LETTER: II.297

Caldwell, Sir James, 4th Bt., diplomat, soldier, and author: ment., III.266 and *n*5

— LETTER: I.278–79

"Caldwell Minute" (Johnson), I.279 and *n*3

Callender, James Thomson, IV.28*n*6

Call to the Unconverted to Turn and Live (Baxter), II.150*n*7, IV.271 and *n*4

Calm Address to our American Colonies (Wesley), II.290 and *n*2

Calmet, Augustin, Benedictine writer, I.313 and *n*33, IV.318

Calvert, Felix, brewer, III.53 and *n*7

Calvert, Mrs., I.251, 253

Cambden, Hannah, III.48*n*3

Cambridge, Richard Owen, IV.100 and *n*5

Cambridge University, III.43 and *n*6; ment., III.257

Camden, William, IV.221 and *n*13

Campbell, Archibald, II.109*n*3

Campbell, Lady Elizabeth, daughter of 3d Earl of Loudoun, II.116 and *n*31

Campbell, Flora Macleod (Mrs. James) *see* Macleod, Flora

Campbell, James, of Treesbank, II.116 and *n*33

Campbell, James Mure (later 5th Earl of Loudoun), III.35*n*15

Campbell, John (1693–1770) *see* Argyll, 4th Duke of

Campbell, John (1723–1806) *see* Argyll, 5th Duke of

Campbell, John (1705–82) *see* Loudoun, 4th Earl of

Campbell, Mary Montgomerie (Mrs. James, of Treesbank), sister of Margaret Boswell, II.116 and *n*33

Campbell, Mr. (of Auchnaba), III.41 and *n*10

Campbell, Thomas, clergyman and antiquarian, III.23 and *n*1; and C. Congreve's sermon, II.163*n*4

camps, military *see* military camps

candlelight: helps drive off melancholy thoughts, II.179, 296

Canice, St. *see* Kenneth, St.

Canons of Criticism (Edwards), I.70*n*4

Canterbury, Archbishop of (1768–83) *see* Cornwallis, Frederick

Canterbury, Archbishop of (1758–68) *see* Secker, Thomas

Canynge, William, merchant of Bristol, II.336n9

Caogad (Synod of Argyle): McFarlane's version, II.150n8

captiousness, III.369–70

Carcass (ship), II.16 and n6

Carless, Ann Hector (Mrs. Walter), sister of E. Hector, I.343 and n11, 414, 416, III.362; ment., II.174 and n1, 275, 310, III.48, IV.26, 438, V.6, 7; SJ happy to see brother and sister live together, II.301–2

Carless, Rev. Walter, I.343n11

Carlisle, Cumberland, III.215nn7,8

Carlisle, Dean of *see* Percy, Rev. Thomas

Carlisle, 5th Earl of (Frederick Howard), IV.266n4; SJ's comments on manuscript of *Father's Revenge*, IV.10 and n1, 245, 251–52 and nn5,7

Carlisle, Margaret Leveson-Gower Howard, Countess of, IV.266 and n4

Carmen seculare (Horace), III.144n9

Carmichael, Poll, protégée of SJ, II.3 and n1, 124, III.139, 140

Carnan, Anna Maria *see* Smart, Anna Maria Carnan

Caroline Matilda, Queen of Denmark: death of, II.208 and n9

Carr, Rev. John, I.28–29, 31 and n5

Carr, William (of Etall), II.61n11

Carte, Rev. Samuel, antiquarian, Prebendary of Lichfield, IV.104 and n3

Carter, son of Charles: illness and death of, II.162–63, 162n3, 189–90 and n8, 195n2

Carter, Charles: and projected riding school at Oxford, II.183 and n2, 187 and n2, 188, 189, 193, 194, 195, 211, 218, 219, 223, 233, 260, 268n1, 293, 300, 303, 308 and n1, 309; forced to sell his horses, II.236n4

Carter, Elizabeth, Bluestocking, I.17

and n8, 20n2, 68nn4,6; ment., III.55, 266, IV.31 and n6

– LETTER: I.126

Carter, Laura, daughter of Charles, II.195 and n2

Carteret, John *see* Granville, 1st Earl

Carwardine, Penelope, painter, I.216 and n8

Casaubon, Isaac, classical scholar, III.8n4

Castiglione and Solferino, Prince of (Luigi Gonzaga), III.16 and n4

Castle Ashby, I.190n2

Castle Inn (Birmingham), I.7n9, III.48n3

Castle Inn (Brighton), III.81n7

Castle Street (London), I.14n1, 17n9, 110n1

Catalogi Librorum Manscriptorum Angliæ et Hiberniæ, I.86–87 and n2

Catalogue of the Lords of Session (Hailes), II.139n3

Catalogue of the MSS. in the Cottonian Library, III.354n1

Catalogus Bibliothecæ Harleianæ, I.37n2, 308 and n3

Catalogus Bibliothecæ Thuanæ, I.65n1

Catcott, George Symes, pewterer, II.339 and n6

Cathedral of *see* under geographical designation, e.g., St. Andrews, Cathedral of

Catherine II, Empress of Russia, III.231n8

Catholicon (Balbi), II.257 and n3

Cato, Publius Valerius, IV.391n7

Cato (Addison): quoted, II.339 and n4, IV.191n6

Cator, John, timber merchant, III.50 and n3, 216n2, IV.96, 98, 163 and n3, 275, 276 and n5, 318; named trustee of Hester Thrale's estate, II.58n19, 253–54 and n8; and G. Baretti, II.366n16; as executor of Henry Thrale's will, III.330n6, 331 and n5,

334, 341 and *n*2; and brewery negotiations, III.339, 341 and *n*2, 345 and *n*1, 352–53; and election results, IV.316 and *n*3; ment. as guardian of Thrale children, IV.337 and *n*3, 339*n*1; H. M. Thrale lives with, IV.339*n*1, 391

Caulfeild, James *see* Charlemont, 1st Earl of

Caulfield, Miss, III.10 and *n*2

Cave, Edward, bookseller: and Sarpi project, I.12–13 and *n*4; ment., I.24*n*1, 25, 58 and *n*8, 143*n*1; and Mr. Urban, I.32–33, 33*n*6; and C. Lennox, I.47 and *n*5; death of, I.126 and *n*3; heirs, I.128*n*4

– LETTERS: I.5–7, 12–22, 34, V.3–4

Cave, Richard, printer, I.143*n*1, 144 and *n*3, 145, 146

– LETTER: I.127

Cave, William, printer, I.128 and *n*4, 131, 144 and *n*4, 145

– LETTER: I.127

Cavendish, Lord Frederick, III.25 and *n*3, 359; resignation of, IV.59 and *n*1; ment., IV.109*n*1

Cavendish, Lord George, II.152*n*6, III.25 and *n*3, 359, IV.62*n*1; resignation of, IV.59 and *n*1; ment., IV.109*n*1

Cavendish, Lord John, III.25 and *n*3, 359, IV.62 and *n*1; resignation of, IV.59 and *n*1; ment., IV.109*n*1

Cavendish, William (1640–1707) *see* Devonshire, 1st Duke of

Cavendish, William (?1698–1755) *see* Devonshire, 3d Duke of

Cavendish, William (1748–1811) *see* Devonshire, 5th Duke of

Cawdor Castle (Nairn), II.64*n*11

Cebes of Thebes, putative author of *Tabula*, I.11 and *n*3

Cecil, James *see* Cranbourne, Viscount

Cecilia (F. Burney), III.364*n*6, IV.96 and *n*6; SJ requests copy of, V.3 and *n*1

Celsus, Aulus Cornelius, II.34 and *n*2

Celtic language, I.152*n*6

Chamberlaine, Frances *see* Sheridan, Frances Chamberlaine

Chamberlayne, Edward, author, I.72*n*9

Chambers, Anne, mother of Robert, I.287 and *n*3, II.50*n*26, 68 and *n*4

Chambers, Catherine (Kitty), maid, I.175 and *n*2, 180, 181, 182 and *n*1, 183–84, 185; and house in Lichfield, I.182 and *n*1, 263; ment., I.187, 196, 209, 222–23, 241; SJ visits during final illness of, I.241*n*3, 275 and *n*4, 282*n*2; description of disease of, I.282–84; death of, I.283*n*5, 293, 316*n*4

Chambers, Ephraim, lexicographer, I.21 and *n*2, II.4 and *n*2, IV.393 and *n*4

Chambers, Frances Wilton, Lady (wife of Sir Robert), III.203, V.8–9 and *n*1; marriage of, II.127 and *n*2; letter from, ment., II.236, 244, 245; and G. Baretti, II.244 and *n*4; and death of son, IV.215 and *n*7

Chambers, Hannah, sister of Robert, I.287 and *n*3

Chambers, Richard, banker, brother of Robert, II.68 and *n*4, IV.57–58

– LETTER: IV.57–58

Chambers, Sir Robert, Kt., jurist: and Vinerian professorship and Vinerian lectures, I.160–62, 164–65, 276–77, 282*n*1, 288, 288*n*1, 293*n*1, 320 and *n*2, 322*n*3, 333*n*1, 413; ment., I.205–6, 245*n*3, 303, 304, 305 and *n*3, 337, II.125, III.5*n*5, 112*n*1, IV.445, V.9*n*1; and East India Company, I.277–78; and P. Carmichael, II.3 and *n*2, 6, 124; trip to India ment., II.41 and *nn*4,5, 86 and *nn*2–4, 147; travels with SJ, II.45, 46–47 and *n*2, 50*n*26; II.120–21, 138, III.5*n*5, 203, IV.124–29, 214–16; SJ's intention to visit, II.120*n*1; and The Club, II.126*n*1; marriage of, II.127 and *n*2; brings SJ's letter to W. Hastings, II.135–36, 137; in Calcutta,

Chambers, Sir Robert (*cont.*)
II.236; politics and, IV.57–58 and
*nn*1–3,5, 62–63 and *n*8; sent revised
set of *Lives of the Poets* for distribution,
IV.123 and *n*1; as President of the
Asiatic Society, IV.127*n*23; and SJ's
proposals for Langton's estate,
IV.128–29; death of son, IV.215*n*7,
227–28; and Reynolds portrait of,
IV.227 and *n*5
— LETTERS: I.86–87, 112, 113–14, 138–
39, 160–62, 164–65, 190, 192, 195,
210–11, 218, 275–78, 287–88, 336,
358, 390, II.67–68, 85–86, 98–99,
120–21, 138, III.203, IV.124–29, 214–
16

Chambers, Thomas Fitzmaurice, son of
Sir Robert: death of, IV.215*n*7, 228

Chambers, Sir William, architect,
III.250*n*14

Chambers's *Cyclopædia* see *Cyclopædia, or
an Universal Dictionary*

Chamier, Anthony, financier and M.P.,
I.352 and *n*5, II.171 and *n*2, 329*n*9,
III.27*n*2, 34; and anticipated Franco-
Spanish invasion, III.180; SJ visits,
III.182*n*7

Chandler, Richard, D.D., author, II.209
and *n*9

Chapel of St. Moluag (Raasay), II.89
and *n*12

Chaplin, Charles, of Lincolnshire, III.59
and *n*4, 86

Chapone, Hester Mulso (Mrs. John),
poet and essayist, III.240 and *n*2; and
Lord Carlisle's manuscript, IV.10,
251–52; ment., IV.242 and *n*4
— LETTERS: IV.10, 245, 251–52

Chapone, John (husband of Hester),
III.240*n*2

"Character of a Good Parson, The"
(Dryden), IV.325*n*1

Characters Historical and Panegyrical (Perrault), III.61*n*6

Charlemont, 1st Earl of (James Caulfeild), Irish statesman, III.10*n*2

Charles II, King of England, I.192*n*2

Charles Edward Stuart, the Young Pretender, II.80 and *n*48, 83, 90 and *n*16

Charles, J.A.C., balloonist, IV.204*n*1

Charleton, Walter, M.D.: on Stonehenge, IV.221 and *n*14

Charlotte Sophia, Queen (wife of
George III), I.382 and *n*6, II.164*n*1,
III.15*n*1; reaction to *Journey*, II.166
and *n*2; and C. Lennox's *Proposals*,
II.201*n*1, 202 and *n*3; and M.
Knowles's needlework, II.332*n*8;
ment. of doctor to, IV.377*n*2; and C.
Burney's *History of Music*, IV.379 and
*n*3

Charterhouse, Aldersgate, London, I.10
and *n*14; and Isaac De Groot, III.36
and *n*2, 39

Chatham, 1st Earl of (William Pitt),
I.264 and *n*7, 277*n*2

Chatsworth (estate), I.411 and *nn*3,4; SJ
visits, I.411, 416, IV.397 and *n*1, 409
and *n*3; JB visits, III.79 and *n*17

Chatterton, Thomas, poet: and "Rowley" manuscripts, II.332 and *n*9, 336
and *n*9, 339*n*6, IV.14 and *n*1

chess (game), V.24 and *n*3

Chessington, III.364*n*6

Chester: JB visits, III.191 and *n*11,
214*n*1

Chester, Bishop of (1771–77) see Markham, William

Chester, Bishop of (1776–87) see Porteus, Beilby

Chesterfield, 4th Earl of (Philip Dormer
Stanhope), I.28 and *n*5, III.230 and
*n*1; SJ on patronage of, I.94–97
— LETTER: I.94–97

Chesterfield, 5th Earl of (Philip
Stanhope): and Dodd case, III.25*n*3

Chetwood, William Rufus, author and
prompter at Drury Lane Theatre,
I.23–24 and *n*15

Cheyne, George, M.D., II.118 and n2, 257–58 and n9, 348 and n2, III.304n1

child-rearing, I.325; see also parents and parental authority

"Chloe Jealous" (Prior), II.249 and n1

Cholmondeley, George James (later 1st Marquess of Cholmondeley), III.87 and n1

Cholmondeley, Mary Woffington (Mrs. Robert): ment., III.87n1, IV.41, 217; recommends artist T. Hickey, III.282 and n1, 283; SJ dines with, III.290; proposed move to Wales, IV.211–12

– LETTER: III.22–23

Cholmondeley, Rev. Robert, III.22n1

Cholmondeley, Robert Francis, son of Mary and Rev. Robert: death of, III.22 and n4

Chotusitz, Battle of see Czaslau, Battle of

Christ Church, Oxford, I.7nn1,8,9

Christianity: I.269; see also religion

Christian Morals (Browne), I.132 and n3, 133

Christ's Hospital (London), III.112–13 and nn2,3; and charity for blind, II.152–53 and n1

Chronicle, or Customs of London (Arnold), III.293n1

Chudleigh, Elizabeth see Kingston, Dowager Duchess of

Churchill, Charles, poet, I.173n13

Cicero, Marcus Tullius (Tully), I.12, 221 and n4, 310 and nn10,12; quoted, I.372n2, II.335n7, III.308n5, IV.360n2; ment., IV.352 and n3

Cirillo, Domenico, physician and botanist, IV.32 and n4

Clandestine Marriage, The (Colman and Garrick), I.285n1

Clapp, Rev. Joseph, I.315n1

Clapp, Mary (Mrs. Joseph), I.315 and nn1,2, 334, 353, 385; ment., I.350

Clare, Viscount (Robert Nugent), I.356 and n6

Clarendon, 1st Earl of (Edward Hyde), I.77 and n1, II.183n2, III.110 and n4

Clarendon Press, I.246n10, II.305n3

Clarissa (Richardson), I.70n4, 75n10, II.328 and n5; SJ on need for index, I.47–48 and nn1,2, 75; translations of, I.93 and n6; SJ alludes to, III.138 and n2

Clark, Richard, attorney: and P. Carmichael, II.3 and n3, 6, 124; and Essex Head Club, IV.257n2, 258, 278

– LETTERS: II.5–6, 124, III.112–13, 120–21, IV.92–93, 258, 278

Clarke, Godfrey Bagnall, II.152n6

Clarke, John, brother of Samuel, I.63n9

Clarke, John, of Sandford, Somerset, III.14n2

Clarke, John, schoolmaster, I.217n6

Clarke, Rev. Samuel, I.63 and n9

Clement IX (Pope), IV.239n9

Cleone (Dodsley), I.172–73 and nn8–12

Cleonice, Princess of Bithynia (Hoole), II.159–60 and nn1–3, 172–73 and nn2,3, 175

Clerke, Sir Philip Jennings see Jennings Clerke, Sir Philip

Clive, Catherine ("Kitty"), actress, I.111n3

Club, The (Essex Head Club) see Essex Head Club

Club, The (Ivy Lane Club) see Ivy Lane Club

Club, The (Literary Club): founding of and membership expansion, I.251 and n2; attendance of Burke, I.264; SJ on various members' attendance, I.265; SJ on its holding together well, I.267 and n8; ment., I.352, II.26, 27, 156, III.6, 42, 99, 116 and n2, 329n1; SJ attends, I.356, II.175, 195, IV.96, 138, 164 and n4, 166, 167, 335 and n2; seeking new members, II.126–27 and n1; new members added, II.128, III.12 and nn7,8; and Goldsmith's epitaph, II.330 and nn1–4; session to

Club, The (*cont.*)

commence with session of Parliament, III.132, 142; SJ on its heterogeneity, IV.126*n*19

— MEMBERS: Althorp, Viscount, IV.96; Banks, J., I.386*n*1, III.132*n*5, 142; Barnard, T., III.6*n*1; Beauclerk, T., I.192*n*2; Bingham, C. (1st Baron Lucan), III.84*n*2; Boswell, J., II.27 and *n*1; Bunbury, Sir C., II.128 and *n*4; Burke, E., II.26*n*3, 128*n*3, IV.96; Burney, C., I.102*n*1; Chambers, R., I.86*n*1; Chamier, A., I.352*n*5; Charlemont, 1st Earl of (J. Caulfeild), III.10*n*2; Dunning, J., (1st Baron Ashburton), II.286*n*2, III.42; Dyer, S., I.265 and *n*11; Eliot, E., III.198*n*4; Farmer, R., I.335*n*1; Fordyce, G., II.128 and *n*5; Fox, C., II.128 and *n*3; Gibbon, E., II.129*n*1; Goldsmith, O., I.251*n*2, 265, II.126*n*1, 129*n*1; Hawkins, Sir J., I.265 and *n*12; Jones, Sir W., IV.126; Langton, B., I.251*n*2; Macartney, G., III.213 and *n*4; Malone, E., IV.13*n*1; Nugent, C., I.265 and *n*13; Palmerston, Viscount, IV.164 and *n*4; Percy, T., I.190*n*1; Reynolds, Sir J., I.251*n*2, 265, II.330 and *n*2; Shipley, J., II.335 and *n*3; Steevens, G., I.254*n*3, II.126–27, 128, 129; Vesey, A., II.26 and *n*3; Windham, W., IV.140*n*1

Cobb, Mary Hammond (Mrs. Thomas), sister of Felicia Adey: ment., I.301 and *n*4, 317, 343, 364, II.224, 229, 230, 231, 263 and *n*1, 282, III.149, 160, 166, 365, IV.15, 22, 167, 294, 357

Cobb, Thomas, Lichfield mercer, I.301*n*4

Cocker, Edward, mathematician, II.67*n*30

Cocker's Arithmetick, II.67 and *n*30

Coffey, Charles, II.81*n*2

Coirechatachen (Skye), II.79–80 and *n*44, 81*n*52, IV.73*n*6, 215*n*12

Colebrooke, Sir George, 2d Bt., M.P., director and chairman of the East India Company, I.357 and *n*5

Colet, John, Dean of St. Paul's, IV.131*n*1

"Colin's Complaint" (Rowe): quoted, III.67 and *n*10; ment., III.235, 237

Coll, Isle of, II.98, 99 and *n*2; arrival on, II.100; description of, II.101

Collection of the Moral and Instructive Sentiments, Maxims, Cautions, and Reflexions, Contained in the Histories of Pamela, Clarissa, and Sir Charles Grandison (Richardson), I.75*n*9

Collet, Matthew, SJ's barber, IV.92–93 and *n*2

Collier, Arthur, lawyer and classicist: epitaph for, III.126 and *n*2; ment., III.127*n*4

Collier, George, R.N., I.246–47 and *n*2

Collier, Mary, relative of SJ: dispute over division of her mother's estate, IV.16*n*1, 53, 56, 60, 62, 64, 74*nn*3,4, 75, 76, 93, 94, 101, 105–7*nn*4–6, 141

Collier, Mary Dunn *see* Flint, Mary Dunn Collier

Collier, Sophia, relative of SJ: dispute over division of her mother's estate, IV.16*n*1, 53, 56, 60, 62, 64, 74*nn*3,4, 75, 76, 93, 94, 101, 105–7*nn*4–6, 141

Collins, Rev. John, Shakespearean commentator, IV.308 and *n*5

Collins, William, poet, I.77–78*nn*3–5, 88, 89, 91, II.214 and *n*9, III.227 and *nn*1,2; and *Lives of the Poets*, III.233*n*5, 254, 301

Colman, George, playwright, I.199*n*10; concern over *She Stoops to Conquer*, II.25 and *n*5; and S. Foote, II.366 and *n*19

— LETTERS: I.285–86, 320–21

Colquhoun, Sir James, Bt. (25th of the Colquhouns), II.109*n*1, 110 and *n*2

Colquhoun, Ludovick, son of Sir James, II.110 and *n*3

Columba, St., II.106*n*23

Colville, John, servant, iv.112 and n1

Colyear, Charles *see* Portmore, 2d Earl of

Commemoration of Handel (C. Burney) see *Account of the . . . Commemoration of Handel*

Commentaire (de Crousaz): SJ's translation of, 1.20–21 and n2

Commentary on the Four Evangelists (Pearce), iii.131n8

Commentary on the Psalms (Horne), ii.138n1

Companion for the Festivals and Fasts of the Church of England (Nelson), iii.158 and n3, 159 and n2

Companion to the Play House (Baker), 1.290n5

Compleat Angler, The (Walton), ii.139 and n5

Complete System of Astronomical Chronology (Kennedy), iii.169n5

Compton, Rev. James, librarian: admission into Church of England, iv.77–78; and dedication of his book, iv.82, 85; SJ recommends for position at St. Paul's School, iv.131 and n2

– LETTERS: iv.77–78, 82, 85

Comus (Milton), iv.178n1

Confession of Faith . . . Translated into the Irish by the Synod of Argyle, ii.150n7

Congreve, Rev. Charles, 1.8n14, 115; ill health and drinking, ii.163–64 and nn3,4, 198, 301, 302; ment., ii.167, 204; SJ on death of, iii.345

Congreve, John, father of Charles and Richard, 1.8n14

Congreve, Richard, friend of SJ, 1.8 and n14, iii.357n3

– LETTERS: 1.9–11, 114–15

Congreve, William, playwright, 1.374n7, iii.110n2; and *Lives of the Poets*, iii.233n5, 254, 262

Conquest of Granada (Dryden), iv.275 and n2

"Considerations on Corn" (Johnson), 1.276n4

Considerations touching the Usefulness of Experimental Natural Philosophy (Boyle), iv.54n4

controversies and quarrels: method of solving "vexatious affair" between E. Cave, T. Warren and Dr. R. James, 1.25–27; "an agreement can only be made by a communication of your thoughts," 1.27; on reconciling variances and interposing in controversies, 1.27; and W. Huggins, 1.85–86, 215; between D. Garrick and R. Dodsley, 1.172 and n9; between G. Colman and D. Garrick, 1.285n1; and E. Langton, 1.359, 373–74; involving P. Carmichael, ii.3n1, 124, iii.139, 140; G. Baretti and T. Davies "have had a furious quarrel," ii.9 and n7; between A. Murphy and D. Garrick, ii.23–24 and n4, 25; and O. Goldsmith and G. Colman, ii.25 and n5; and T. Johnson, ii.158 and n3, iii.100; and Rev. J. Coulson, ii.217 and n2; between W. Langley and J. Taylor, ii.244; between JB and his father, ii.364–65, iii.215; involving SJ, T. Percy, and T. Pennant, iii.113–14 and n1; between SJ and W. Strahan, iii.123 and n1; involving R. Levet, iii.127, 139, 140, 189, 209–10; involving A. Williams, iii.134, 139, 140, 191, 391, iv.137 and n8, 139 and n9; involving E. Desmoulins, iii.134, 140, 189, 191, 209–10, iv.137 and n8, 139 and n9; between C. Lennox and J. Dodsley, iii.138 and n1; between G. and W. Strahan, iv.79–80, 111; and T. Davies, v.4–5 and n1

conversation, ii.238–39 and n5

Conway, Francis Seymour *see* Hertford, 1st Earl of

Cook, Capt. James, explorer, 1.386n1, iii.50 and n5, iv.332n2; and J. Burney, iii.317n5

Cooke, Elizabeth Anne *see* Way, Elizabeth Anne Cooke

Cooke, William, biographer, III.93*n*11, IV.40*n*4

Cooke, William, D.D., Provost of King's College, Cambridge, III.3*n*2

Cooper, Anthony Ashley *see* Shaftesbury, 3d Earl of

Cooper, Grey, politician, II.186 and *n*7

Coote, Sir Eyre, Kt., II.64 and *n*14

copyright, II.125 and *n*4, 129–31 and *n*1

Copyright Act of 1709, II.125*n*4

Corbet, Andrew, brother of John, I.4*n*2

Corbet, Sir Corbet, Bt., IV.261*n*3

Corbet, John, schoolmate of SJ, I.4 and *n*2

Cork, Earl of *see* Orrery, 5th Earl of

Cornbury, Viscount (Henry Hyde), II.183*n*2, 303 and *n*1, 305

Cornwallis, Frederick, Archbishop of Canterbury, III.39 and *nn*2,6, 321

Correggio (Antonio Allegri da Correggio), painter, III.89*n*1

Correspondence of John Hughes (ed. Duncombe), III.224 and *n*2

correspondence *see* letter writing

Corsica: and JB, I.262*n*5, 273 and *n*11, 298 and *nn*2,3, 328

Cotterell, Charles, admiral, I.110*n*1

Cotterell, Charlotte *see* Lewis, Charlotte Cotterell

Cotterell, Frances ("Calamity"), daughter of Charles, I.205 and *n*3, 214, III.245 and *n*6, IV.145 and *n*4, 229 and *n*3, 321 and *n*6

— LETTER: I.110–11

Cotton, Elizabeth Aston (Mrs. Rowland), I.414*n*2

Cotton, Sir Lynch Salusbury, 4th Bt.: death of, II.259–60 and *n*7; ment., IV.239 and *n*6

Cotton, Philadelphia, cousin of Hester Thrale, III.80*n*23

Cotton, Sir Robert Salusbury, 5th Bt.,

cousin of Hester Thrale, II.148*n*1; as colonel in army, III.128*n*8, 129; and Thrale estate, III.251*n*6

Cotton, Rowland, admiral, cousin of Hester Thrale, I.414*n*2

Cotton, Sidney Arabella, aunt of Hester Thrale, II.332 and *n*6, III.73 and *n*9, 236, 238; ment., III.80, 83, 229; F. Burney on, III.228 and *n*4

Coulson, Rev. John, I.245*n*3, 336 and *n*2, III.46; ment., II.216, 217, 220, 268 and *n*1

Council of the Royal Academy, IV.112*n*2

Course of Lectures on Natural Philosophy (Helsham), I.72 and *n*8

Covent Garden Theatre, I.172*n*10, 285*nn*1,3, 320*n*3, II.24*n*4, III.201*n*5

Coventry: SJ at, III.165

Cowley, Abraham, poet, I.101*n*6, 374*n*4; and *Lives of the Poets*, III.81*n*13, 83*n*2, 122 and *n*2; quoted, III.308*n*3, IV.72 and *n*3

Cowley, Father William, II.272*n*5, 336, IV.304 and *n*1, 346 and *n*6

Cowpar (Fife), II.55

Coxeter, Elizabeth, daughter of Thomas (the elder): I.357 and *n*3, II.363

Coxeter, Thomas (the elder), writer, I.357 and *n*4; ment., II.362

Coxeter, Thomas (the younger), I.357; SJ seeks medical help for, II.362 and *n*4, 363.

Coxheath Camp, Kent, III.128 and *n*8, 129; George III visits, III.132*n*6

Crabbe, Rev. George, poet, IV.116–17 and *nn*1–4, 117 and *n*1, 118

Cradock, Joseph, man of letters, IV.107–8

Craggs, James (the elder), financier, I.37 and *n*5

Craggs, James (the younger), friend of Pope, I.37 and *n*5

Cranbourne, Viscount (James Cecil) (later 7th Earl of Salisbury), III.258*n*5

Cranbourne, Viscountess (Mary Amelia Hill), III.258 and n5

Crane, Edward, Prebendary of Westminster, II.335 and n4

Craven, 6th Baron (William Craven), III.241n10, 291 and n9

Craven, Baroness (Elizabeth Berkeley) (wife of 6th Baron) (later Margravine of Anspach), III.241 and n10, 258; SJ to dine with, III.253

Creation, The (Blackmore), v.32 and n3

Crescimbeni, Giovanni Mario, author, I.92 and n4

Crewe, Frances Anne, IV.239n9

Crichley, Jeremiah *see* Crutchley, Jeremiah

Crisp, Samuel ("Daddy"), dramatist and critic, III.310 and n3; death of, IV.199 and n1

Critical Pronouncing Dictionary (Walker), IV.100n4

Critical Review: founder of, I.72 and n3; and C. Lennox, I.136 and n1

Criticism on the Elegy written in a Country Churchyard (Young), IV.168 and n3

Croft, George, schoolmaster and Oxford don, I.297 and n4

Croft, Herbert, barrister: and "Life" of Young, III.322 and nn2,4,5; ment., IV.136–37

– LETTER: IV.113

Croker, Rev. Temple Henry, miscellaneous writer, I.84 and n5, 86

Crosbie, Andrew, advocate, II.53n14

Crouch, Anna Maria Phillips *see* Phillips, Anna Maria

Crouch, Nathaniel, writer and publisher, IV.271n2

Crouch, Rawlings Edward, naval officer, IV.140n3

Crousaz, Jean Pierre de, Swiss theologian, I.20n2

Crowmarsh (estate), Oxfordshire, III.201 and n2

Crown Office Row, II.195n3

Cruikshank, William Cumberland, surgeon: and Royal Academy, IV.135–36 and n1; SJ's request for medical attention from, IV.183; SJ presents *Lives of the Poets* to, IV.184; and SJ's testicular sarcocele, IV.196–97, 206, 207–8, 220, 226, 233; ment., IV.216

– LETTERS: IV.183, 184, 207–8, 213–14, 256, 286–87, 393–94

Crutchley, Jeremiah, M.P., II.184 and n3; legal negotiations for brewery sale, III.216n2, 334, 345 and n1, 352–53; as executor of Henry Thrale's will, III.330n6; and H. M. Thrale, III.372 and n7; health ment., IV.147; ment. as member of Parliament, IV.316; Hester Thrale borrows money from, IV.318 and n8; ment. as guardian of Thrale children, IV.337 and n3, 339 and n1

Cullen, Robert, II.53nn13,14

Cullen, William, M.D., II.53n14, IV.286n6

Cumberland, Duchess of (Anne): ment., III.283n2

Cumberland, Duke of (Henry Frederick): ment., III.283n2

Cumberland, Richard, playwright, II.318 and n7, III.195, 201–2, 204; and F. Burney, III.196 and n12, 209; alleged financial loss of, III.205 and n2, 210; *The Walloons*, IV.33 and n4

Cumming, Thomas, Quaker merchant, II.140–41

Cummins, Mr., creditor of Henry Thrale's estate, III.366 and n1

Cummins, Mrs. *see* Cumyns, Elizabeth Thornton

Cumyns, Elizabeth Thornton (Betsy), schoolmistress, II.326n1, III.280, 366n1, 367; and L. Carter, II.195n2, 209

Cursory Observations on the Poems attributed to Thomas Rowley (Malone), IV.14n1

Curzon, Sir Nathaniel, 5th Bt. *see* Scarsdale, 1st Baron

Cust, Richard, D.D., III.359*n*1

Cyclopædia, or an Universal Dictionary (Chambers), I.21*n*2, II.4 and *nn*2,3, 293*n*1; dedication, IV.393*n*4

Cymbeline (Shakespeare), IV.205*n*6

"Cymon and Iphigenia" (Dryden), III.82*n*15

Czaslau, Battle of, I.30 and *n*19

D

Dagge, James, London solicitor, I.320*n*3

Daily Advertiser, v.8 and *n*1

Dale, Mrs., II.244 and *n*6

Dale, Robert, II.244*n*6

Dalling, Sir John, Bt., Governor of Jamaica, III.291*n*9

Dalrymple, Alexander, IV.227*n*4

Dalrymple, Sir David *see* Hailes, Lord

Daman, Mary *see* Warton, Mary Daman

Darcy, Robert *see* Holdernesse, 4th Earl of

Darlington, Durham, II.48–49 and *n*17

Darnley, Lord (Henry Stewart): ment., II.52*n*8

Dartmouth, 2d Earl of (William Legge), III.30 and *n*3

— LETTER: IV.132

D'Aubigné, Theodore Agrippa, IV.147 and *n*6

D'Audiguer, Vital, author, translator, I.136*n*2

D'Avenant, Corbet *see* Corbet, Sir Corbet

D'Avenant, Hester Salusbury Cotton (Mrs. Corbet), cousin of Hester Thrale, III.134 and *n*12, IV.239, 261*n*3, 321; plans trip with Hester Thrale, II.222*n*7, 224*n*5, 226 and *n*7

Davenport, William: SJ secures job for,

II.161 and *n*2, 180, 197, 199; ment., IV.141 and *n*5

Daventry: SJ at, III.165

David I (of Scotland), II.52*n*8

Davies, Mrs. Thomas: ment., IV.150, 369

Davies, Thomas, actor and bookseller, I.285 and *n*2, III.62 and *n*1, 94, 104 and *nn*2,3; and G. Baretti, II.9 and *n*7; SJ to dine with, II.195; appointed Printer to Royal Academy, II.225*n*2, 227; theatre benefit for, III.110 and *n*2, 111; success as author, III.302 and *n*5; ment., IV.54 and *n*4, 82, 326, 374; SJ's affection for, v.4–5

— LETTERS: IV.150, 368–69, v.4–5

Davis, Mrs., companion to A. Williams, I.279 and *n*8, IV.199

De Anima Medica (Nicholls), IV.335*n*1

De Arte Graphica (du Fresnoy): and W. Mason's translation, IV.115*n*1

death, I.200, 300–301, 316, 404 and *n*1, II.20–21, 28; on mourning and on death of R. Elphinston, I.45–46; religion and, I.46, 301 and *n*2; "hears not supplications, nor pays any regard to the convenience of mortals," I.110; SJ on report of his own death, I.118; on death of E. Cave, I.126 and *n*3; difference between death by war and death by disease, I.167; on loss of his mother, I.176, 179–80, 181–82, 183, 184; SJ hopes that a good life will end in a contented death, I.200; "we are subject to the general law of mortality, and shall soon be where our doom will be fixed for ever," I.215; SJ on loss of various friends, I.215, III.48, 49, 51; and L. Porter's brother, I.220; "on Death we cannot be always thinking," I.296 and *n*4; on death of C. Hardinge, II.296–97; on death of Harry Thrale, II.311–12, 313–14; SJ consoles M. Cholmondeley on loss of son, III.22–23 and *nn*4,5,7; on death of

Mrs. C. Elphinston, III.121–22; on death of Mrs. Adey, III.163; hovering over us, III.169; SJ on death of a spouse (to T. Lawrence), III.223; on death of Henry Thrale, III.330 and *n*2, 331, 332, 334, 335; and mortality, ment., III.336; a minute between health and, IV.15, 23; pleasures of happy death compared to longest life, IV.26; and suicide, IV.40–41 and *nn*3,7,8, 43; "to die is the fate of man, but to die with lingering anguish is generally his folly," IV.40*n*7; "we are perpetually within the reach of," IV.138; when comes would excite less horror, IV.151; passing into another world, IV.168; thoughts on A. Williams's death, IV.187; on death of a friend, IV.236; must prepare ourselves for, IV.236, 290, 406; frequency of, IV.239–40; on consolations and condolences, IV.252–53; "a sinner approaching the grave is not likely to be very cheerful," IV.289; SJ's thoughts of his own, IV.289, 290; SJ's fear of, IV.312; pass life with attention fixed on eternity, IV.340; "who can run the race with?" IV.358

"Debates in the Senate of Magna Lilliputia," I.18*n*3

Debates Relative to the Affairs of Ireland (Caldwell), I.278*n*1

Decision of the Court of Session upon the Question of Literary Property (Boswell), II.125*n*4

"Declaration of Rights" (manifesto), II.170*n*3

deforestation, II.63 and *n*2, III.41 and *n*11

Deformities of Dr. Samuel Johnson (Callender), IV.28 and *n*6

De Groot, Isaac, great-grandson of Hugo Grotius, III.36–37 and *n*3, 39, 44

De jure belli ac pacis (Grotius), III.39*n*5

Delap, Rev. John, D.D., poet and playwright, II.241 and *n*6, III.196 and *n*13, 206

Delle arti del disegno (Reynolds, trans. Baretti), II.366 and *n*17

Deluge, The (painting, M. Lowe), IV.121–22, 121 and *n*2

De l'universalité de la langue française (Rivarol), I.321*n*1

De Medicina (Celsus), II.34*n*2

Denbigh, Wales, II.149 and *n*3

Denham, Sir John, Kt.: and *Lives of the Poets*, III.83*n*2, 122 and *n*2

Dennis, John, literary critic, I.52–53 and *n*8, III.225 and *nn*3–5

De officiis (Cicero), I.221 and *n*4, 310*nn*10,12, III.308*n*5

De Origine Moribus et Rebus Gestis Scotorum (Lesley), II.126 and *n*2

De placitis philosophorum (Plutarch), I.363*n*2

depression *see* melancholy and depression

Derby: ment., III.68; JB and SJ visit, III.70–71 and *n*4; on china made in, III.70–71 and *n*6

Derby, Rev. John, Rector of Southfleet, III.131 and *n*8

Derbyshire, I.347*n*2, 349*n*3, 363, II.11, III.20

Derbyshire china, III.70–71 and *n*6

De satisfactione Christi (Grotius), III.39*n*5

Descartes, René, I.118 and *n*7

Description géographique . . . de la Chine (Du Halde), I.19 and *n*6

De Senectute (Cicero), I.372*n*2

"Deserted Village" (Goldsmith), III.230*n*1

Desmoulins, Elizabeth Swynfen, member of SJ's household, I.125 and *nn*4,6, III.78, 190; and L. Paul's Birmingham mill, I.124*n*1, 125 and *n*6; ment., III.120, 131*n*6, 134, 139, 252, 376, IV.199, 250, 426, 433; and C. Lennox, III.138; relationship with R.

Desmoulins, Elizabeth (*cont.*)
Levet, III.140, 189, 209–10; SJ on daughter of, III.190; relationship with A. Williams, III.191, IV.137 and *n*8, 139 and *n*9; health ment., III.290 and *nn*6–8, 296, 300, IV.9 and *n*2, 15, 23; SJ recommends for Charterhouse position, III.321 and *n*5; departure of ment., IV.139, 145, 167
– LETTER: II.262

Desmoulins, John (Jack), son of Elizabeth: and employment at Drury Lane, III.131 and *n*6, 139, 140, 144; SJ attempts to find employment for, IV.132 and *n*1; ment., IV.145

Desmoulins, Mr. (husband of Elizabeth), writing master, I.125 and *n*5

Desormeaux, J.-L. Ripault, I.150*n*2

De Studiis Theologicis (Bentham), II.196*n*1

De Temperamentis (Lawrence), IV.9 and *n*2

De Thou, Jacques-Auguste, historian, diplomat and bibliophile, I.65*n*1

De Tranquillitate Animi (Seneca), III.354*n*1

Devonshire: SJ and Reynolds trip to, I.206*n*12, 215*n*1; Sir J. Reynolds in, III.308 and *n*4

Devonshire, Duchess of (Georgiana Spencer) (wife of 5th Duke), III.24*n*1, 26 and *n*4, 130 and *n*2; ment., IV.33; SJ visits at Chatsworth, IV.397, 398 and *n*5, 409*n*3

Devonshire, 1st Duke of (1640–1707) (William Cavendish), I.411*nn*3,4

Devonshire, 3d Duke of (?1698–1755) (William Cavendish), I.28*n*5, 29 and *n*10, 31 and *n*2, III.25*n*3

Devonshire, 5th Duke of (1748–1811) (William Cavendish), III.24 and *n*1, 25–26, 130*n*2, 359; ment., IV.62 and *n*2; SJ visits at Chatsworth, IV.397, 398, 399*n*6, 409*n*3; and J. Taylor, V.24*n*1

Dialogus de Oratoribus (Tacitus), III.79*n*12

Diary and Letters of Henry, Second Earl of Clarendon, II.300*n*1

Dicey, Cluer, printer and bookseller, I.141 and *n*2

Dick, Sir Alexander, 3d Bt., M.D., III.41 and *n*11, IV.286 and *n*7, 291*n*1; presented with 2d edition of *Journey*, II.180*n*1, 364*nn*2,3; cultivates rhubarb, IV.292 and *n*3

Dickens, Mrs., friend of Hester Thrale, III.204 and *n*1

Dictionariolum Trilingue (Ray), II.200 and *n*4

Dictionarium Saxonico-et Gothico-Latinum (Lye), I.231 and *nn*2,4, 250–51*nn*2,3; proposals for, I.252–53 and *nn*2,3; subscribers, I.252–53 and *nn*2,3, 265

Dictionary in Englyshe and Welshe (Salesbury), I.310*n*13

Dictionary of Ancient Geography (Macbean): SJ writes preface, I.21 and *n*2

Dictionary of the English Language (Johnson): and A. Macbean, I.21*n*2; partners in contract for, I.40 and *n*4, 41; SJ works on, I.42*n*3, 43*n*1, 82*n*1; partners "blockade," I.50–51 and *nn*1,2,4; culling of quotations completed, I.65*n*2; manuscript copy, I.73 and *nn*1,6; completion of first two volumes, I.81 and *n*5; plan for Oxford M.A. in time for inclusion on title page, I.88 and *n*3, 89, 90; Lord Chesterfield's advance publicity for, I.95–97; publication of, I.100 and *n*5, 109*n*8; SJ on reviews, I.101 and *n*7; C. Burney on, I.102–3*nn*1–5, 157 and *n*3; and S. Johnson, I.104 and *n*4; SJ on making of, I.105, 106; 2d edition, I.109 and *n*8; co-publisher, I.129*n*5; F. Greville on, I.129–30*n*5; critics of, I.157 and *n*5; and D. Garrick, I.274 and *n*1; 4th edition, I.382 and *n*3, 390 and *n*1, 392, 393*n*1, 396–97, II.8–9 and *n*6, 14, 30 and *n*2; printing of 1st edition, V.22 and *n*1

Dictionary of Trade and Commerce (Rolt), I.360*n*1

Dilly, Charles, bookseller: ment., II.30*n*1, 210*n*13, III.324–25; SJ to dine with, II.194, 330*n*4, 331*n*3; and trade practices, II.306 and *n*6, 307–8 and *n*7; SJ dines with, IV.325

— LETTERS: III.177, 355, IV.270–71

Dilly, Edward, bookseller, II.30*n*1, 192 and *n*3, 210*n*13, 330*n*4, 331*n*3; ment., II.200

disappointment, II.234

Discourses on Art (Reynolds): and Baretti translation, II.366 and *n*17

Dissenters Bill (1773), II.13 and *n*8

Dissertation on the Prophecies (Newton), I.216*n*6, II.6

Dissertations on the Ancient History of Ireland (O'Conor), I.151 and *nn*1,4; revised edition, III.23*n*3

Dixie, Willoughby, son of Sir Wolstan, IV.62*n*2, 64

Dixie, Sir Wolstan, 4th Bt., I.4 and *n*6, 31, IV.62*n*2

Dobson, Matthew, M.D., IV.147*n*6, 249 and *n*2, 250

Dobson, Susannah (Mrs. Matthew), writer, IV.147 and *n*6

Docksey, Merrial (later Mrs. James Patton), niece of David Garrick, III.215 and *n*3

Doctrines of a Middle State (Campbell), II.109*n*3

Dodd, Rev. William, LL.D.: forgery case of, III.25 and *n*3, 27–28*nn*1–3, 29*n*1, 30, 31–32 and *nn*1,2, 49, 58, 128, 283*n*2; death sentence, III.33–34 and *n*3

— LETTERS: III.30, 32–33

Doddy *see* Dodsley, Robert

Dodsley, Catherine Iserloo (Mrs. Robert): death of, I.90 and *n*6

Dodsley, James, bookseller, brother of Robert, IV.277*n*4; offer for T. Percy's *Reliques*, I.191*n*4; and C. Lennox, III.138*n*1; and *Irene*, IV.441

Dodsley, Robert, bookseller, I.15 and *nn*2,6, 16, 17–18, 40*n*4, 109 and *n*7, 150–51, 172*nn*8,9, 178*n*5; death of wife, I.90 and *n*6; and T. Percy's *Reliques*, I.190–91 and *n*4, 195*n*3; SJ requests "sheets" of edition of *Shakespeare*, V.5 and *n*1

— LETTERS: I.40–41, V.5

Dolben, Sir William, 3d Bt., M.P., III.254*n*9

Dolphin (ship), I.386*n*3

Donaldson, Alexander, II.125*n*4

Don Quixote: Baretti's translation, II.9*n*7

Dorset, 3d Duke of (John Frederick Sackville), I.372*n*2

Double Falsehood (Theobald), III.166*n*4

Douglas, Duchess of (Margaret Douglas) (wife of 1st Duke), II.53 and *n*10

Douglas, 1st Duke of (Archibald Douglas), II.53*n*10

Douglas, John: and establishment of Oxford riding school, II.300, 303–4, 305

— LETTERS: II.300, 303–4

Douglas Cause, III.76*n*3

Dovedale, Derbyshire, I.349 and *n*3

Drake, Sir Francis, Kt., soldier and explorer, I.348 and *n*7

Dramatic Works of Shakespeare, with Notes (Rann), III.100*n*1

Dromore, Bishop of *see* Percy, Rev. Thomas

Drummer, The (Addison), III.226 and *n*2

Drummond, Alexander Monro, physician, I.168 and *n*4, 169*nn*7,8, 281, II.350 and *nn*4,6

Drummond, Robert Hay, Archbishop of York, II.193 and *n*4, 215 and *n*5, 219

Drummond, William, Edinburgh book-

Drummond, William (*cont.*)
seller: ment., II.51, 350 and *n*5
— LETTERS: I.168–69, 268–71, 280–81, 289–90
Drury Lane Theatre, I.17*n*2, 23*nn*11,13, 80*n*9, 124*n*3, 252*n*2, 285*n*1, 320*n*3, II.24*n*4; and J. Desmoulins, III.131*n*6, 139, 144; R. B. Sheridan sells his share of, IV.33 and *n*6
Dryden, John, I.374*n*3, 375*n*1, III.8*n*4; quoted, II.231–32 and *n*6, III.79*n*15, 82 and *n*15, 90*n*2, 205*n*6, 218 and *n*10, 276*n*7, IV.251 and *n*3, 275*n*2, 325*n*1; and controversy with E. Settle, III.120–21 and *n*1; and *Lives of the Poets*, III.120–21, 122, 124 and *nn*1–4, 143*n*7; Lord Hailes's description of, III.182 and *n*6
Dublin, Ireland, I.170
Dublin, University of: SJ's degree from, I.257 and *n*2
Du Fresnoy, Charles Alphonse, painter and poet, IV.115*n*1
Du Halde, Jean Baptiste, author, I.19 and *n*6
Duke, Richard, poet: and *Lives of the Poets*, III.146 and *n*1
Dunbar, James, Professor of Philosophy, III.282 and *n*5, 304, 328*n*3
Dunbuy, Aberdeenshire, II.61
Duncan, William: and Ossian controversy, II.168*n*3
Dunciad, The (Pope), III.166*n*4
Duncombe, John, miscellaneous writer, III.224*n*2
Dundee, Scotland, II.56–57
Dunk, George Montagu *see* Halifax, 2d Earl of
Dunn, John, innkeeper, father of Mary Dunn Collier Flint, IV.74 and *n*4, 76
Dunning, John *see* Ashburton, 1st Baron
Dunvegan, House of: and SJ's mistaken statement concerning clan supremacy, II.203, 206

Dunvegan (Skye): arrival and stay at, II.71 and *n*3, 91–92, 114*n*20
Du Puy, Jacques, Parisian bookseller, I.65*n*1
Du Puy, Pierre, Parisian bookseller, I.65*n*1
Durham, II.49 and *nn*18,19
Durham Cathedral, II.49*nn*19,20
Durham Yard, London, I.26*n*1
Dury, Maj. Gen. Alexander, I.166–67 and *n*1
Dury, Mrs. Alexander (wife of Major-General), I.166*n*1
Dyer, John, poet: and *Lives of the Poets*, III.224*n*2
Dyer, Samuel, classical scholar, I.265 and *n*11; SJ directs F. Reynolds to buy engraving of, III.192 and *n*2; death of, IV.126 and *n*16; death ment., IV.259*n*6, 317
Dyott, Catherine Herrick (Mrs. Richard), II.238 and *n*3, 244 and *n*6, III.60 and *n*3
Dyott, Richard, of Lichfield, II.238*n*3, 244 and *n*6, III.60 and *n*3

E

Earl of Somerset (Lucas), III.21 and *n*3
East India Bill, IV.248*n*1, 277*n*4, 291*n*2
East India Company, I.277–78 and *n*2, 357 and *n*5, 392*n*3, IV.58*n*2; and J. Hoole, III.323*n*2, 324 and *n*6; and S. Dyer's investments, IV.126 and *n*16; and politics, IV.248 and *n*1
Easy Phraseology for the Use of Young Ladies (Baretti), II.339*n*5
Eclogues (Virgil): quoted, II.228*n*5, III.77*n*6, IV.139*n*11
Ecole des femmes, L' (Molière), III.88*n*3
Edgar and Emmeline (Hawkesworth), II.356*n*1

Edgcumbe, 3d Baron (George Edgcumbe) (later 1st Earl of Mt. Edgcumbe), III.213*n*5

Edgcumbe, Baroness (Emma Gilbert) (wife of 3d Baron), III.213 and *n*5

Edial Academy, I.10*n*11, 23*nn*4,11

Edinburgh: SJ visits in 1773, II.41 and *nn*5,7, 43, 46, 51, 52–53; food in, II.96; SJ ment. he soon hopes to get to, II.99, 100; and JB, III.214*n*1

Edinburgh, University of, II.52*n*6

Edinburgh Gazette, IV.28*n*7

education: on drawing up a plan of education for use in teaching, I.10; advises S. Ford to read classics and study Latin, I.11–12; on J. Elphinston's scheme for education, I.168–69; advice to G. Strahan, I.217–18, 219, 220–21, 234–35, 248; on learning to write by writing, I.220–21; advice to JB, I.238–40; advice to W. Strahan concerning his son George, I.244–46; cost in 1764 of Oxford education, I.245–46; and knowledge of Christian doctrine, I.269; "he that voluntarily continues ignorance is guilty of all the crimes which ignorance produces," I.269; importance of language study, I.269–71, IV.127; "you can never be wise unless you love reading," I.350; advice to JB "our minds cannot be empty," I.363; on St. Andrews University, II.56; on King's College, Aberdeen, II.59; on A. Macaulay's — "send him to an English school," II.213 and *n*6; on necessity of providing "innocent amusement," II.223; on intellectual growth and mind's need for "new subjects of meditation," II.261; on experience v. youth, II.263–64; on early childhood education — "let the child alone," II.327 and *n*8; importance of religious education, III.211; advice to R. Chambers on Asiatic study, IV.127 and *n*23; and arithme-

tic, IV.133, 138, 142–43, 176; take all opportunities, IV.302; *see also* knowledge; reading

Edwards, Edward, classical scholar, Vice-Principal of Jesus College, Oxford: kindness shown during SJ's stay in Oxford, IV.51, 52, 55–56 and *n*3; death ment., IV.214, 329; and edition of Xenophon's *Memorabilia*, IV.304 and *nn*2,3, 345–46 and *nn*4,5
 – LETTER: III.135–36

Edwards, Rev. Thomas, curate, II.190*n*2

Edwards, Thomas, literary critic, I.70*nn*3,4

Eglinton, Countess of (Susanna Kennedy), II.116 and *n*35

Eglinton, 11th Earl of (Archibald Montgomerie), III.12*n*3, 102 and *nn*3,4

Egremont, 2d Earl of (Sir Charles Wyndham), I.231*n*1

Eld, John, I.29 and *n*9

Elegy to the Memory of an Unfortunate Lady (Pope), IV.187*n*6

Elements of Criticism (Kames), V.14 and *n*1

Elements of Elocution (Walker), IV.100*n*4

Elgin, Morayshire, II.63 and *nn*7,8

Elgin Cathedral, II.63 and *n*7

Elibank, 5th Baron (Patrick Murray), lawyer and army officer, I.363 and *n*6
 – LETTER: II.68–69

Eliot, Edward (later 1st Baron Eliot), III.198 and *n*4

Eliza *see* Carter, Elizabeth

Ellis, Rev. William, headmaster, I.350 and *n*3, 353

Eloisa to Abelard (Pope), II.106*n*19

Elphinston, Clementina (Mrs. James): death of, III.121 and *n*1

Elphinston, James, translator and schoolmaster: ment., I.168*n*4, 169*nn*7,8, 281, II.25 and *n*4; SJ's condolences on death of wife, III.121–22

Elphinston, James (*cont.*)
— LETTERS: I.42, 45–46, 57–58, III.121 –22, v.5
Elphinston, Margaret Penelope *see* Strahan, Margaret Penelope Elphinston
Elphinston, Rachel Honeyman (wife of Rev. William), mother of James, I.45 and *n*2
Elphinston, Rev. William, I.45*n*2
Emmanuel College, Cambridge, I.11*n*1
Enchiridion Militis Christiani (Erasmus), III.82 and *n*18
Endeavour (ship), I.386*nn*3,4
English Chapel (Edinburgh), II.52 and *n*3
English Malady, or a Treatise of Nervous Disease of All Kinds (Cheyne), II.348 and *n*2
English proverbs: quoted, III.199*n*9, 290 and *n*4
Enquiry Concerning the Principles of Taste, and of the Origin of Our Ideas of Beauty, etc. (F. Reynolds), IV.116*n*1, 311 and *n*1; SJ's criticism of, III.355–56 and *nn*1,2, IV.30–31 and *nn*2–4; cost of publishing, and SJ's suggestions, IV.323; decision not to print, IV.327
Epigrams (Martial), III.92*n*3
Epilogue to the Satires (Pope): quoted, IV.423*n*5
Epimetheus (Greek myth), I.413*n*1
Epistles (Horace): quoted, I.358*n*1, II.71*n*5, III.48*n*5, 104*n*6, 202*n*8, 215*n*2, IV.347 and *n*2, 370 and *n*2
Epistle to Cobham (Pope), IV.153*n*21
"Epistle to Dr. Arbuthnot" (Pope), III.258*n*2
Epistolae Ho-elianae (Howell), III.72*n*12
epitaph: on Hogarth's by Garrick, I.383–85
Epitaphs (Pope), III.324 and *n*2
Epsom, Surrey: SJ visits, III.182*n*7
Erasmus, humanist, III.82 and *n*18; quoted, IV.360*n*2
Ercilla, Alonso de, poet, v.16*n*3

Ernest Augustus, Prince: birth of, I.382*n*6
Errol, Countess of (Isabella Carr) (wife of 15th Earl), II.61*n*11
Errol, 15th Earl of (James Boyd), II.61 and *nn*8,11, 63
Erse language (Scots Gaelic), I.269 and *n*2, 270*n*7, II.266
Erskine, Sir Henry, 5th Bt., soldier, I.208*n*3
Essay of Health and Long Life (Cheyne), II.118*n*2
Essay on Man (Pope): quoted, III.363*n*3, 374*n*4, IV.12*n*1, 192*n*1, 321*n*4
Essay on Mr. Hume's Essay on Miracles (Adams), I.80*n*6
Essay on the Learning of Shakespeare (Farmer), I.335*n*1
Essay on the Nature and Immutability of Truth, An (Beattie), I.382*n*1
Essay on the Origin, Progress, and Establishment of National Society (Shebbeare), v.27*n*2
Essay on the Writings and Genius of Pope (J. Warton), I.133–34 and *n*1
Essay on the Writings and Genius of Shakespear (Montagu), I.185*n*1
Essay on Truth (Beattie), I.393 and *n*1
Essays on the History of Mankind (Dunbar), III.282*n*5
Essays Upon Several Subjects (Blackmore), III.260 and *n*3
Essay towards a Real Character and a Philosophical Language (Wilkins), IV.176 and *nn*3,4
Essay upon Unatural Flights in Poetry (Granville), III.246 and *n*2
Essex Head Club, IV.284–85, 308, 317, 332 and *n*3, 335 and *n*1, 345 and *n*3, 351 and *n*4, 390 and *n*4, 395 and *n*3, 401 and *n*2, 416 and *n*1; establishment of, IV.256–57; absentee fine, IV.257, 278, 308, 324, 378, 404, 406; SJ's poor health prevents his attendance,

IV.279–80 and *n*7, 319; rules of, IV.280 and *n*7

— MEMBERS: Barrington, D., IV.240*n*2; Barry, J., IV.120*n*1; Boswell, J., IV.257*n*2, 345; Bowles, W., III.245*n*4, IV.289 and *n*2; Brocklesby, R., IV.257; Clark, R., IV.257*n*2, 258, 278; Hoole, J., IV.278, 395 and *n*3; Jodrell, R. P., III.229*n*8, IV.257*n*2; Murphy, A., IV.257*n*2; Nichols, J., IV.257*n*2; Paradise, J., II.194*n*12, IV.257*n*2; Ryland, J., IV.351 and *n*4, 416 and *n*1; Sastres, F., IV.3*n*1; Strahan, W., IV.345 and *n*4; Windham, W., IV.140*n*1, 257*n*2

Estaing, Comte d' (Jean-Baptiste-Charles-Henri d'Estaing), III.213 and *n*2

Eugenio, or, Virtuous and Happy Life (Beach), I.16 and *n*2

Eunuchus (Terence): quoted, III.4*n*1, IV.372*n*4

Euripides, I.12; quoted, IV.360*n*2

European Magazine, I.205*n*1

Eutropius, Roman historian, I.221*n*6

Evans, Rev. James, II.35 and *n*6, 326 and *n*3, III.244; ment., III.253, 288

Evans, Mr., apothecary, II.189–90 and *n*8, III.49*n*3

Evans, Mr., unidentified: ment., IV.326

Evelina (F. Burney), III.140, 196 and *n*14, 213 and *n*6, 236 and *nn*3,4, 370; and A. Wedderburn, III.130*n*5; and E. Montagu, III.130*n*4

Evelyn, John, diarist, I.327 and *n*5

Examen (de Crousaz), I.20 and *n*2

Exercises to the Accidence (Turner), I.217*n*4

Exeter Street, London, I.12*n*1

expectation, I.203–4

experience: and learning, II.263–64

Experiments and Observations on Different Kinds of Air (Priestley), IV.218*n*3

Experiments and Observations on the Mal-

vern Waters (Wall), I.361 and *nn*1,2, 366*n*5

Explanatory Notes upon the New Testament (Wesley), II.290 and *n*1

Explanatory Notes upon the Old Testament (Wesley), II.290 and *n*1

Eyles, Mr., II.17*n*5, 20, 22 and *n*3

F

Fables for the Female Sex (Moore), III.249*n*7

Fabricius, Johann Albert, classical scholar, I.312*n*28

Fairfax, Edward, poet, III.116–17 and *n*2

Falconer, James, D.D., Prebendary of Lichfield, IV.29–30 and *n*5

Falkland Islands, I.392*n*3

False Alarm, The (pamphlet, Johnson), I.333*n*2, II.325*n*2

family, I.171–72; on "discordant" families and "the pleasure of peace," II.365; *see also* parents and parental authority

fancy and imagination, II.134

Farmer, Richard, D.D., Cambridge don: ment. I.417, IV.14; and *Lives of the Poets*, III.257

— LETTERS: I.335–36, 355, III.43, 257

fatality, II.31

Father's Revenge, The (Earl of Carlisle), IV.10*n*1, 251–52 and *nn*5,7

Faulkner, George, printer and bookseller, I.30 and *n*22, 63, 75*n*10, 80 and *n*8, 151, 279; ment., II.205

Fauques, Mademoiselle de (Marianne Agnès Pillement), I.178*n*4

Female Quixote (Lennox), I.46*n*1, 56*n*3, 58–59 and *n*3

Fennici Lexici Tentamen ("Finnick Dictionary"), I.88*n*5, 97, 157*n*6

Fenton, Elijah, poet: and *Lives of the*

Fenton, Elijah (*cont.*)
Poets, III.233*n*5, 247–48 and *nn*1,2, 254; and Pope's translation of the *Odyssey*, III.259 and *n*1

Ferguson, Adam, II.53*n*14

Fermor, Arabella, II.272*n*4

feudalism, I.311 and *n*16, 394, III.200

Fielding, Henry: quoted, I.380*n*3; death in Lisbon, IV.285 and *n*4

Fielding, Sir John, Kt.: and Gordon Riots, III.268 and *n*4

Fingal. An Ancient Epic Poem (Macpherson), II.168*n*1, 170 and *n*2

Finnick Dictionary see *Fennici Lexici Tentamen*

Firebrace, Bridget Bacon, Lady (wife of Sir Cordell), I.18–19 and *n*5

Firebrace, Sir Cordell, 3d Bt., of Ipswich, I.19*n*5

Firmian, Graf Karl Joseph von, Governor of Lombardy, I.213*n*5

Fisher, Philip, II.218–19

Fitzherbert, Selina, friend of SJ, protégée of H. Boothby, I.121 and *n*8

Fitzherbert, William, father of Selina, I.118 and *n*5, 121*n*8, 198–99 and *n*6

Fitzmaurice, John see Kirkwall, Viscount

Fitzmaurice, Mary see Shelburne, Dowager Countess of

Fitzmaurice, Thomas, M.P., III.251 and *n*6
– LETTER: III.146–47

Fitzmaurice, William Petty see Shelburne, 2d Earl of

Fitzroy, Lady Caroline see Harrington, Countess of

Flavius Eutropius see Eutropius

Fleetwood, Charles, patentee of Drury Lane Theatre, I.17*n*2, 23 and *n*13

Fletcher, Mrs., friend of J. Taylor, IV.18 and *nn*1,2, 60

Fleury, André Hercule de, Cardinal, first minister of France, I.29 and *n*14, 30*n*19

Flint, Louise (later Mrs. Antoine Rivarol), friend of F. Reynolds, I.321–22

Flint, Martha, daughter of Mary and Thomas, II.246 and *n*10, IV.141 and *n*3

Flint, Mary Dunn Collier (Mrs. Thomas), cousin of SJ, III.59 and *n*9, IV.16*n*1, 106 and *nn*3,6

Flint, Thomas (b. 1724) clerk, I.233 and *n*5, II.246 and *n*10, III.59 and *n*9; dispute with daughters over inheritance, IV.16 and *n*1, 53–54, 74*n*3, 76, 106 and *nn*5,6, 107

Flint, Thomas (b. 1769), son of Mary and Thomas, IV.141 and *n*3

Floyer, Sir John, Kt., physician, I.6 and *n*5, IV.303 and *n*6, 353 and *nn*7,8

"Fly, An Anacreontick, The" (Oldys), II.148*n*7

food: on gluttony, IV.181–82; *see also* Johnson, Samuel–health

Foote, Samuel, actor and playwright, II.366 and *n*19, III.92–93 and *nn*6,8–11

Forbes, Sir William, Bt.: ment., II.53*n*13
– LETTER: IV.361–63

Ford, Benjamin, uncle of SJ, II.191*n*4

Ford, Rev. Cornelius, cousin of SJ, I.3*n*1, 369 and *n*5, II.191*n*3

Ford, Cornelius, grandfather of SJ, II.190–91 and *nn*3,4

Ford, Joseph, uncle of SJ, II.191 and *n*4

Ford, Mary, aunt of SJ, II.191*n*4

Ford, Mary, maternal great-grandmother of SJ, II.191*n*3

Ford, Nathaniel, uncle of SJ, II.191 and *n*4

Ford, Phoebe, aunt of SJ, II.191*n*4

Ford, Samuel, cousin of SJ, I.11–12

Ford, Samuel, uncle of SJ, II.191*n*4

Ford, Sarah, mother of SJ see Johnson, Sarah Ford

Fordyce, Alexander, banker, I.392 and *n*3, II.49–50 and *n*22

Fordyce, Elizabeth *see* Spence, Elizabeth Fordyce

Fordyce, George, M.D., II.49n21; elected to The Club, II.128 and n5

Fordyce, James, II.49n21

Forres, Morayshire, II.64

Fort Augustus, II.66nn23,24

Fort George, II.64 and n12

Fothergill, Thomas, Vice Chancellor, Oxford: and Oxford riding school, II.188 and n2, 193, 215 and n2, 216, 218, 219 and n4, 223, 246 and n8, 293; and SJ's honorary degree from Oxford, II.194n7, 196
− LETTER: II.196

Foulis, Andrew, printer, II.214n7

Foulis, Robert, printer, II.214n7

Foulis Press, I.393 and nn3,4, II.214 and nn7−9, V.3n1

Fowke, Francis, brother of Joseph, II.350−52

Fowke, Francis, son of Joseph, II.350n1

Fowke, Joseph, East India Company official, II.350n1, 351 and n2, III.203; sends packet from Portugal, IV.110n1; sent revised set of *Lives of the Poets*, IV.123 and n1, 129; ment., IV.128, 215; and "Nandakuma" trial, IV.129−30 and n3
− LETTER: IV.129−31

Fowler, Rev. Robert, headmaster, I.315 and n3

Fox, Charles James: and politics, II.128 and n3, IV.68n2, 263n3, 277nn1,4, 299n2, 306 and n4; and The Club, II.128 and nn3,4, III.12n8, IV.96; resignation of, IV.59 and n1; and East India Company, IV.248n1

Fragments of Ancient Poetry collected in the Highlands of Scotland (Macpherson), II.168n1

France: SJ's trip to, II.271 and nn1,4,6,7,9, 272−73, 301; proposed invasion of Isle of Wight and Portsmouth, III.180−81 and n2, 183, 184−85, 191, 193, 197, 207

Frankland, Sir Thomas, Bt., IV.177 and n5

Fraser, Alexander, II.63 and n3, 72n9

Fraser, Dr., dinner guest of Alexander Fraser, II.72n9

Frederick II (Frederick the Great), King of Prussia, I.29−30 and n19

Frederick, Prince of Wales, I.307n1

Frederick William (of Prussia), IV.279 and n3

French language, I.129−30 and n5

Frey, Thomas, president of St. John's College, Oxford, I.300n7

friendship: on friends long separated, I.9−10; "the greatest benefit which one friend can confer upon another, is to guard, and excite and elevate his virtues," I.45; on separation (death) as "incitement to virtuous friendship," I.46; "I think scarce any temporal good equally to be desired with the regard and familiarity of worthy men," I.57; and J. Elphinston, I.57; and T. and J. Warton, I.90; and C. Burney, I.102−3; and E. Hector, I.104, 107−8, 142−43, 146−47, 153, V.7; friendships of youth, I.104, 114, 146, 148, II.296−97, III.57, V.7; on "old" friend as opposed to "new," I.104, 114−15, 142n3, 146−47, 148, 153, II.277, III.228, 309−10, 345, IV.238−39; and R. and C. Congreve, I.114, 115; on earthly friendship, I.118; and H. Boothby, I.118; and J. Taylor, I.140, 148, II.277; and letter writing, I.140; "form and exercise of friendship varies," I.142; one of the "few states of which it is reasonable to wish the continuance through life," I.142 and n3; on having family members "born to friends," I.171; and G. Strahan, I.224−25; "to take friends such as we can find them, not as we would make

friendship (*cont.*)

them," 1.225; and Sir J. Reynolds, 1.244; on value of JB's, 1.261–62, 11.43, 280, 111.63–64; "he promises himself too much, who enters life with the expectation of finding many friends," 1.262; on high value put on friendship, 1.262; on acquiring new friends in old age as "uncommon instances of happiness," 11.40; SJ hopes his friends (the Thrales) will never forget him, 11.71–72 and *n*5; on a "common friend" caught between adversaries, 11.351; on acquisition of the Thrales' friendship, 111.83; on Henry Thrale's friendship, 111.83, 174, 175; "one of the greatest comforts of this weary pilgrimage," iv.22–23; "fortuitous friendships of inclination or vanity are at the mercy of a thousand accidents," iv.134; on friend lost and found, iv.238–39; and "incommunicative taciturnity," iv.246; "a friend at once cheerful and serious is a great acquisition," iv.383; true use of, iv.389; at time when weakness of body or mind loses pride, iv.434–35; on falling out and falling in again, v.10–11

Frisick language, 1.240 and *n*11

Frome, Somersetshire, 111.298 and *n*7

Fuentes, Don Remigo, friend of Baretti, 1.214*n*6

Fuentes, Rosina, inamorata of Baretti, 1.213, 214 and *n*6

Fust, Johann, printer, 1.310 and *nn*10,11, 313–14 and *n*29

G

Gaelic language, 1.269

Gage, Viscountess (Elizabeth Gideon), 111.15*n*1

"Galatea" (Walsh), 111.276*n*4

Galba, Servius Sulpicius, Roman emperor, 11.259*n*8

Galbraith Castle, 11.110 and *n*4

Galen, physician, 111.299 and *n*5

Galick and English Vocabulary (M'Donald), 11.150*n*7

Galliff, Elizabeth Taylor, sister of John Taylor, 1.148–49 and *n*7

Gardiner, Ann, wife of a tallow chandler, 1.330*n*1; health ment., 11.206; ment., 111.3, 272, iv.199, 330

Garrick, David, 1.17*n*2, 23 and *n*11, 26*n*1; ment., 1.31, 80*n*9, 172 and *n*9, 173 and *n*22, 264*n*7, 302*n*4, 11.311*n*4, 111.124*n*3, 215 and *n*3; and SJ's *Shakespeare*, 1.247–48; and G. Colman, 1.285*n*1; and Hogarth's epitaph, 1.383–85; A. Murphy's attack on, 11.23–24 and *n*4, 25; and *Zaphira*, 11.172*n*1; and J. Hawkesworth's works, 11.262 and *n*1; SJ on death of, 111.93*n*8, 150*n*1, 152–53; assists M. Lowe, 111.115 and *n*5; epitaph, 111.150*n*1; and Walpole's drama, 111.225*n*1; terms of will of, 111.365*n*5; funeral costs and payment, iv.33 and *n*7; sells share of Drury Lane Theatre, iv.33*n*6; SJ requests theater reservations for W. Bell, v.6

— LETTERS: 1.247–48, 251–52, 274, 383–85, v.55

Garrick, Eva Maria Veigel (Mrs. David): ment., 1.252 and *n*4, 274, iv.33, 35, v.14; and Nollekens's bust of SJ, 111.108; SJ's condolences to, 111.150; and H. More, 111.335 and *nn*1,3; SJ dines with, iv.31, 325

— LETTERS: 111.150, iv.296–97, 412

Garrick, George, brother of David, 111.365*n*5; and D. Garrick's dispute with A. Murphy, 11.23–24 and *n*4

Garrick, Merial, sister of David, 111.365*n*5

Garrick, Peter, wine merchant, brother

of David, I.17n2, 23n11, 247n2, II.311 and n4, IV.412; and SJ's visit to Lichfield, III.51, 166, 365

Gassendi, Pierre, II.337n3

Gastrell, Jane (Mrs. Francis): ment., II.222 and n5, III.11, 13, 56, 97, 148, 149, 152, 153, 197, 208, 364, 368, IV.384

– LETTERS: III.101, IV.29–30, 202, 296, 437

Gawler, Mr., of Putney, III.290

Gay, John, poet: *Lives of the Poets* ment., III.301; and Spaulding Society, IV.84 and n2

Gell, Dorothy Milnes (Mrs. Philip, the elder), II.244n7

Gell, Philip (the elder) of Hopton Hall, Derbyshire, II.244 and n7, III.60n3, 316 and n1

Gell, Philip (the younger), II.244 and n7

General History of Music (C. Burney), III.135–36 and n3, 136, 196nn15,16, 205, IV.20; keeps journal to collect material for, II.7 and n6; SJ revises passage in, IV.21 and n1; and SJ's dedication, IV.379n3

General History of the Science and Practice of Music (Hawkins), IV.18 and n2, 20

genius, III.284

Genoa stone see *Sententia Minuciorum*

Gentleman's Magazine, I.5n1, III.227 and nn1,2; SJ's suggestions for, I.6nn4–7, 18–20; SJ's first contribution to, I.14 and n2; SJ's epigrams to "Eliza" (E. Carter) published in, I.17 and n8; reporting of parliamentary proceedings, I.18 and n3; and Du Halde's *Description géographique . . . de la Chine*, I.19 and n6; co-printer, I.143n1; and Hawkesworth, III.17–18 and nn5,6

Genuine Account of the Behavior and Dying Words of William Dodd (Villette), III.35 and n12

"Geographical Dictionary": SJ's proposal for, I.68–69 and n2

George II, King of England, I.198 and n5; ment., IV.393n4

George III, King of England, I.198 and n5, 279 and n3, 305–6, 382n6, III.15n1; coronation of, I.201 and n1, 207n13; grants SJ's pension, I.208 and n6, 222; and Lord Bute, I.231n3; and J. Beattie's pension, II.42n8; and *Journey*, II.159, 164, 166; ment. of sister's death, II.208n9; dismissal of Prince of Wales's preceptors, II.347 n10; and Dodd case, III.25n3, 27n1, 30 and n1, 32 and n4, 33n3, 34; ment., III.116n2, 181; visits Warley Camp, III.132 and n6; and *Lives of the Poets*, III.156 and n5, 348; and Gordon Riots, III.269n13, 271, 275; and contemporary politics, IV.59n1, 263n3, 291 and n2, 305n2, 306; and SJ's request for pension increase, IV.342n3, 398n1; and dedication of C. Burney's *An Account of the . . . Commemoration of Handel*, IV.357n1, 392 and n2; Sir J. Reynolds appointed painter to, IV.375 and n5; ment. of doctor to, IV.377n2

George Augustus, Prince of Wales (later George IV of England): ment., II.347 and n10, IV.321, 407n2

George Wichers' Almshouses (Westminster), IV.269 and n3

Georgics (Virgil), III.124n2; quoted, III.15n2

Germain, Lord George, politician: and P. Stockdale, III.286n3, 291

Germantown, Battle of, III.95n10

Germany: ment. in SJ's advice on creation of Royal Library, I.308, 309

Gerusalemme Liberata see *Jerusalem Delivered*

Getcliffe *see* Galliff, Elizabeth Taylor

Gibbon, Edward: rejected but later elected to The Club, II.129 and n1, III.12n8

Gibbons, Rev. Thomas, III.38n3

Gillespie, Thomas, M.D., IV.286n6, 291n1

Gill, Mr., printer, I.246n10

Glasgow: SJ's visit to and impression of, II.102 and n3, 115

Glenelg, Inverness-shire, II.76

Glenmoriston (Glenmorrison), II.67, 72

gluttony, IV.181–82

GM see *Gentleman's Magazine*

Golden, Robert, architect, III.81n7

Goldsmith, Henry, brother of Oliver, III.10n1

Goldsmith, Mrs. Henry, III.10 and n1

Goldsmith, Oliver: and The Club, I.251n2, 265, II.126n1, 129n1; and the Hornecks, I.339n1, 340nn2,3, 352 and n4; ment., I.356 and n6, II.128n5, III.6n1, 192 and n2, 230n1, 269n9; and *She Stoops to Conquer*, II.9 and n8, 14, and n10; and G. Colman's campaign against *She Stoops to Conquer*, II.25 and n5; and JB's candidacy for membership in The Club, II.27; and J. Oglethorpe, II.124n2; death of, II.146 and n6, 147; SJ's Greek verses on, II.148 and n8; quoted, II.229 and n8; epitaph, II.330–31 and nn1–5, 344 and n3, 345–46 and n2, 366–67 and n2, III.44n2; biography of, III.10 and n1; death of ment., IV.126

— LETTER: II.27

Gongora, Luis de, poet, v.16 and n2

Gonzaga, Luigi *see* Castiglione and Solferino, Prince of

goodness, IV.294–95

Gordon, Sir Alexander, 7th Bt. of Lismore, II.59–60 and n29, 72 and n7, 120 and n3, III.9

Gordon, 4th Duke of (Alexander Gordon), III.274 and n11

Gordon, Lord George, President of the Protestant Association, III.267 and n1, 270 and n3, 272n2, 274n11

Gordon, Thomas, Professor of Philosophy, II.59 and n26

Gordon Riots, III.263n12, 267–69 and nn1–3,6–10,12–15, 270–71 and nn2–4,7, 272–74 and nn1,2, 274–75, 303; and A. Williams, III.288n2; and Streatham, III.303

Gosnell, Thomas R., IV.11 and n5

Gough Square, London, I.43n1, 160n5

government: SJ on absolute governments, I.29; on fault of British Constitution, I.161; on equal representation in, IV.109; "operations of government have little influence upon the private happiness of private men," IV.124; *see also* politics and the contemporary political situation; self-government

Graevius, Johann Georg, classical scholar, I.310 and n12

Graham, George: and *Telemachus*, II.214n8, III.9

Grandison (Richardson) see *History of Sir Charles Grandison*

Granger, James, collector and historian, I.416–17

Grant, Colquhoun, II.181 and n6

Grant, Gregory, M.D., II.181 and n6

Grantham, Lincolnshire, II.47

Granville, 1st Earl (John Carteret), I.28n5, 29–30 and n19

Granville, George, poet: and *Lives of the Poets*, III.233n5, 246 and nn1,2, 254, 296; and preface to *British Enchanters*, III.246 and n1

Gray, Stephen, experimenter, I.79n2

Gray, Thomas: SJ on letters of, II.206 and n11; and *Lives of the Poets*, III.233n5, 257, IV.70 and n3

Gray's Inn, I.184n1, 187n2

Gray's Inn Journal, I.160 and n5

greatness, I.213

Greaves, Samuel, footman to Henry Thrale, IV.257 and n1

Greek language, I.11–12, III.136

Greene, Richard, surgeon, apothecary, and antiquarian, I.318 and n2, 345, 346, 380, III.162, 163–64, 166, 167;

SJ lends artifacts to, possibly for museum of, II.11; ment., II.224, III.48, 51, 92, 164; visits SJ, II.244; SJ and JB visit, II.311; ment. of Taylor-Wood case, II.335n6, 355; museum of, III.51 and n8; and epitaph and gravestones for SJ's family, IV.443–44
— LETTER: IV.443–44

Greene, Thomas Webb, son of Richard, II.335 and n6; ment. of Taylor-Wood case, II.355

Green Hill (Lichfield), II.263 and n1

Greenwich, I.12n1

Gregory, James, M.D., III.31n2

Grenada, III.208n1

Grenville, George, politician, I.231n1, 356n3
— LETTER: I.221–22

Greville, Frances Macartney (Mrs. Richard Fulke), III.133 and n4

Greville, Richard Fulke, essayist and M.P., I.129–30nn2,4,5; ment., III.133n4

Gribon (Mull): Mackinnon's Cave, II.107 and n24

Grierson, George, printer and philologist, I.268 and nn1–3

Griffith, Thomas, Fellow of Pembroke College, Oxford, I.376–77 and n3, 377, 379

Grotius, Hugo, jurist and statesman, III.36n3, 39 and n5, 44

Gruterus, Janus, classical scholar, II.199–200 and n2

Guadaloupe, I.202 and nn1,2

Guarini, Giovanni Battista, poet, II.337n2

Guest, Jane Mary (later Mrs. A. A. Miles), musician, III.248 and n3

Gunning, Elizabeth see Argyll, Duchess of

Gutenberg, Johann, I.310n10, 313n32

Guthrie, William, miscellaneous writer, I.18n3

Gutteridge, Anne see Percy, Anne Gutteridge

Gutteridge, Barton, of Desborough, Northamptonshire, I.192n8

Gwynne, Nell, actress and mistress of Charles II, I.192n2

Gwynn, John, architect, I.201n1, III.45–46 and n2, 107–8

H

Hailes, Sir David Dalrymple, Lord, Scots judge, II.139 and nn3,4; and Walton's *Lives*, II.139 and nn3,4, 145–46, 150; and *Annals of Scotland*, II.150, 171, 213, 266, 269 and n1, 274 and n5, 280, 284 and n4, 295, 298n1, III.33 and n1, 104, 157 and n4; Ossian controversy, II.170 and n2; SJ's feelings for, II.171; SJ wishes opinion of concerning *Journey*, II.172; and Inchkenneth verses, II.178n9; and JB's controversy with his father over entail, II.285 and n2, 289, 291n1, 292, 294–95, 299; ment., II.304, III.325, IV.209; and *Journey* presentation copy, II.364n2; and Knight case, III.42 and n18, 104; compared with T. Percy, III.114; description of Dryden, III.182 and n6; sent set of *Lives of the Poets*, IV.91 and n5; sends gift to ailing SJ, IV.165

hair see wigs and hair

Halifax, 1st Earl of (George Montagu), IV.35n3

Halifax, 2d Earl of (George Montagu Dunk), I.231n1

Hall, Edward, chronicler, I.63 and n7

Hall, Martha Wesley (Mrs. Wesley), IV.234 and n2, 319; ment., II.290, V.35

Hall, Rev. Wesley, IV.234n2

Hamilton, Anthony, D.D., Vicar of St. Martin's in the Fields, IV.144, 286, 287–88, 330

Hamilton, Archibald, printer, I.72 and

Hamilton, Archibald (*cont.*)
*n*3; and firing of J. Calder, II.293*n*1, 297
— LETTER: II.293–94
Hamilton, 6th Duke of (James Hamilton), II.109*n*3
Hamilton, John, Archbishop of St. Andrews (1546–71), IV.343–44 and *n*5
Hamilton, W. G. (William Gerard) ("Single-Speech" Hamilton), M.P., I.259*n*3, 276*n*4; SJ to dine with, II.193 and *n*1, 194; SJ dines with, III.244; offers financial assistance to SJ, IV.241 and *n*4, 243, 266, 422*n*1; SJ gives account of his health to, IV.422–23; ment., V.25*n*1
— LETTERS: IV.243, 422–23
Hamlet (Shakespeare), IV.46*n*2; quoted, I.381*n*3, II.17*n*3, 229*n*11, 267*n*9, 333*n*11; Jennens's edition of, II.25 and *n*7
Hammond, Henry, Chaplain to Charles I, author of *Paraphrase and Annotations upon . . . the Psalms*, II.255–56 and *n*2, 269 and *n*1, III.358
Hammond, James, poet: and *Lives of the Poets*, III.233*n*5, 260 and *n*2
Hampton Court Palace: SJ requests grace-and-favor lodgings, II.319–20 and *nn*2,4
Handel, George Frederick: and C. Burney's *An Account of the . . . Commemoration of Handel*, IV.357*n*1, 384*n*1, 385 and *n*14, 431*n*4
handwriting *see* penmanship
Hannah, servant to J. Taylor, I.226–27 and *n*5, 233, 236
happiness: SJ on, I.111, III.119
Harborough, 3d Earl of (Bennet Sherard), I.218*n*1, IV.108*n*2
Harcourt, 1st Earl (Simon Harcourt), III.72 and *n*1
Hardestee, William, usher, I.4*n*3
Hardinge, Caleb, M.D., II.296 and *n*5

Hardinge, George, lawyer: and Walpole's drama, III.225 and *n*2, 226
Hardy, Sir Charles, Kt., admiral, II.154 and *n*2, III.180 and *n*12, 181
Hardy, Rev. Samuel, III.315–16
Harington, Henry, M.D., II.332 and *n*5, 336 and *n*10; ment., III.236
Harleian Catalogue see Catalogus Bibliothecæ Harleianæ
Harleian Miscellany, I.37*n*2
Harley, Thomas, politician, II.162 and *n*2
Harrington, Countess of (Caroline Fitzroy): and Dodd case, III.27*n*1, 31–32
— LETTER: III.31–32
Harrington, Henry *see* Harington, Henry
Harriot Stuart (Lennox) *see Life of Harriot Stuart*
Harris, Elizabeth Clarke (Mrs. James), III.14 and *n*2
Harris, James, classical scholar, III.14 and *n*2, 245
Harris, Thomas, soap manufacturer, I.320*n*3
Harrison, Rev. Cornelius, II.48–49 and *n*16
Harrison, John, saddler, uncle of SJ, I.7*n*9
Hartwell, John, dyer and woolen manufacturer, I.343 and *n*9
Harvest of 1775, II.226, 237–38, 245, 249–50, 251–52
Harvest of 1777, III.46 and *n*4, 48–49, 51, 52–53, 56, 59, 67, 69, 73
Harvest of 1783, IV.175
Hastie, John, schoolmaster, I.388*nn*1, 4,5, 390*n*4, 393
Hastings, Warren, Governor-General of India: asked to aid W. C. Lawrence, II.86*n*4, 161; and Fowke case, II.351 and *n*2; ment., III.5*n*5, IV.403 and *n*3; sent revised set of *Lives of the Poets*, IV.123 and *n*1, 124; and "Nandakuma" trial, IV.129*n*3

– LETTERS: II.135–37, 160–61, III.282–83, 323–24

Haunch Hall (estate), II.190–91 and *n*3

Havana: captured by England, I.211 and *n*2, 215

Hawkesworth, Honor *see* Ryland, Honor Hawkesworth

Hawkesworth, John, author, I.67*n*2, 68*n*6, 77 and *n*1, 128*n*4, 278 and *nn*1,2; and Chambers's *Cyclopædia*, II.4; and posthumous edition of his works, II.262 and *n*1, 356*n*1, 359; edition of Swift, III.17 and *n*3, 295 and *n*3; and Cook's voyages, III.50 and *n*6; and Ivy Lane Club, IV.247*n*1; death ment., IV.259 and *n*6, 317

– LETTERS: I.129–30, II.4

Hawkesworth, Mary Brown (Mrs. John), I.130 and *n*8, III.17, 18; health of, II.4; undertakes posthumous edition of her husband's works, II.356*n*1

Hawkins, Sir John, Kt.: on SJ's *Proposals*, I.5*n*1; and The Club, I.265 and *n*12; marriage of, II.3*n*5; and P. Carmichael, II.3, 6; and Walton's *Angler*, II.139 and *n*5; and his *History of Music*, IV.18 and *n*2, 20; ment., IV.92*n*1, 126*n*16, 336; and Ivy Lane Club, IV.246–47, 256; biographical project of, IV.308 and *n*6; and his son's manuscript, IV.310–11 and *n*1

– LETTERS: II.3, IV.246–47, 256, 351, 436

Hawkins, John Sidney, son of Sir John, IV.310–11 and *n*1

Hawkins, Laetitia Matilda, daughter of Sir John, IV.92 and *n*1

Hawkins, Sidney Storer, Lady (wife of Sir John), II.3 and *n*5

Hay, Charles, advocate, II.53*n*14

Hay, George, M.P.: ment., I.300*nn*7,9

– LETTER: I.187–88

Hay, John, servant, II.65 and *n*17

Haymarket Theatre: and Samuel Foote, II.366 and *n*19

Head, Mr. *see* Plunkett, Mr.

Heale House (Wiltshire), IV.177*nn*2,4, 194 and *n*3; SJ's visit to ment., IV.267, 268, 274

health (mental and physical): melancholy indisposition, I.143 and *n*8; effect of bad marriage on, I.236–37; "to preserve health is a moral and religious duty," I.359; advice to E. Aston, "gayety is a duty when health requires it," III.13; thankful for exemption of mind from disorder of body, III.64–65; keep an easy, free, quiet, open mind, III.154–55, 175, 265, IV.64, 66–67, 92, 94, 244, 254, 259, 262; ill health often the effect of intemperance, IV.40*n*7, 41*n*8; the body receives some help from a cheerful mind, IV.52; effect of constipation, IV.67; "upon your mind in my opinion your health will very much depend," IV.67; basis of all happiness, IV.74; importance of exercise, IV.86, 244, 247; difference between health at 30 years and at 70 years, IV.90; keep body open and mind quiet, IV.94; importance of change of environment, IV.191; "disease produces much selfishness," IV.200; effect of solitude on, IV.213; importance of diet, IV.244; use of milk, IV.247, 253, 254, 269; on effect of visitors when one is ill, IV.265; perverseness of sick men, IV.305; when one regains health, one regains peace of mind, IV.321–22; "let nothing vex you," IV.333; "with the health of mind and body a man may supply or bear the remainder of his wants," V.5; *see also* Johnson, Samuel—health; medicine; melancholy and depression

Heberden, William, M.D., II.40 and *n*4; and Henry Thrale's illness, III.169, 172 and *n*2, 179, 184 and *n*2, 221*n*6; ment., IV.42, 267, 352, 353, 355, 356; SJ wishes to see, IV.149, 152, 164; and

Heberden, William (*cont.*)
SJ's remarkable recovery, IV.155, 157, 275, 276–77, 291–92, 293, 295, 296, 300; and SJ's illness, IV.158, 159, 164; SJ praises, IV.168; and SJ's testicular sarcocele, IV.197n6, 207, 208, 226; recommends opiates for SJ, IV.265, 269; and H. Fielding, IV.285n4; on appetite as barometer of health, IV.318, 365; SJ gives account of his health to, IV.418–20; SJ disobeys, IV.436
— LETTERS: IV.282, 418–20
Hebridean journal (Boswell) see *Journal of a Tour to the Hebrides*
Hebridean tour: early ment. of, I.362n1, 363, 389n7; JB encourages SJ to plan, II.41 and nn1,3, 43n2, 45; SJ sets out on, II.45–46; beginning of, II.54; SJ describes, II.122; SJ wishes to send gifts to people who were hospitable to him, II.128; SJ pays expenses owed JB in books, II.348 and n3, 349; as most pleasant journey, II.361; delight in talking over, III.57; ment., III.65n3, 303 and n6; and Duke and Duchess of Argyll, III.76n3; *see also* Boswell, James — Hebridean trip; Scotland
Hector, Ann *see* Carless, Ann Hector
Hector, Edmund, surgeon and friend of SJ: SJ on long friendship with, I.42 and n3, 104, 153, 291, IV.312, V.6–7; ment., I.106n9, 343, II.11, 19, 175, 310, III.48, 141n13; visits SJ, II.343 and n4; on SJ's health, III.362, 373
— LETTERS: I.104–5, 107–8, 141–43, 146–47, 152–53, 259–61, 291, 414–16, II.174, 190–91, 274–75, 301–2, IV.25–27, 437–38, V.6–7
Hector, Mary Gibbons (Mrs. Edmund), I.291 and n4
Hector (dog), III.374 and n2
Heeley, Elizabeth Ford (Mrs. Humphrey), cousin of SJ, I.290 and n2, 316
Heeley (Heely), Humphrey, iron-

monger, I.290 and n3, 316, II.165 and n1, 309; and Wicher's Almshouses, IV.269–70 and n6; in need of money, IV.366
— LETTER: IV.366
Hellenica (Xenophon): SJ requests copy of, V.3n1
Helmont, J. B. van, author, IV.38n2
Helsham, Richard, mathematician and physicist, I.72 and n8
Henault, Charles Jean François, historian and playwright, II.266 and n7, 283, 295
Henderson, Mr., Henry Thrale's valet, III.26 and n2
Henley, II.310 and n1
Henry, David, bookseller and printer, I.143 and n1, 144
Henry IV Part I (Shakespeare): quoted, III.78n3, 212n9, 238 and n6, IV.97n1
Henry IV Part II (Shakespeare): quoted, III.77 and n5
Henry VI (Shakespeare): quoted, I.368n2
Henry VIII, King of England, I.10n15
Henry VIII (Shakespeare): II.34n2, quoted, II.95 and n44
"Henry and Emma" (Prior), III.293n1
Henry of Blois, Bishop of Winchester, papal legate, I.255n3
Herbert, George, poet, IV.308 and n5
Hercules Furens (Seneca): quoted, III.175n3
Hereford, Dean of *see* Wetherell, Nathan
Hereford Infirmary, II.210 and n16
Hermes, or a Philosophical Inquiry concerning Universal Grammar (Harris), III.14n2
Hermit of Warkworth. A Northumberland Ballad (Percy), I.356 and n5
Herne, Elizabeth (Phebe), cousin of SJ, III.297 and nn3,4, 320, IV.288 and n4
Heroides (Ovid): quoted, I.211n4, III.143n1

Herschel, William, musician and astronomer, IV.301–2 and n3

Hertford, 1st Earl of (Francis Seymour Conway), II.319–20

Hervey, Catherine Aston (Mrs. Henry), I.375 and n1; health ment., III.86; SJ to dine with, III.164, 310

Hervey, Henry see Aston, Henry Hervey

Hickey, Thomas, portrait painter, III.282–83 and n2, 283

Hickman, Dorothy, cousin of SJ, I.3n3, III.296n9

Hickman, Gregory, cousin of SJ: ment., III.296n9

– LETTER: I.3

Hinchingbrooke, Viscount (John Montagu) (later 5th Earl of Sandwich), IV.35n3

Hinchliffe, John, Bishop of Peterborough, III.258 and n4, 266 and n4

Hinckley, Blanche Pyott (Mrs. Thomas), of Lichfield, I.293 and n7

Hippolyte, Marie Charlotte see Boufflers-Rouverel, Comtesse de

Histoire de Charles XII (Voltaire), I.28n6

Histoire de la Marquise de Pompadour (Fauques), I.178n4

Histoire des Conjurations, Conspirations et Révolutions Célèbres (Tertre), I.150 and n2, 151n4

Historia del Concilio Tridentino (Sarpi), I.13 and n3

Historiae Romanae, I.221n6

Historiarum sui Temporis (De Thou), I.65n1

Historical and Philosophical Account of the Barometer (Saul), IV.218n3

Historie of Foure-Footed Beasts (Topsell), I.22 and n3

history: difference between history writing and journal writing, I.34, 329; "topography or local history prevail much in many parts of the Continent," I.311; and feudalism, I.311 and

n16, 394; SJ's dislike of stock conversations on history, "talk not of the Punic War," II.238 and n5; and chronology, III.61; "many falsehoods are passing into uncontradicted history," III.200; SJ's history "a narrative of misery," IV.383

History and Antiquities of Hinckley in the County of Leicester (Nichols), IV.104n1

History and Antiquities of the City of Bristol (Barrett), II.336n9

History of America (Robertson), II.357n3

History of Charles V (Robertson), II.357n3

History of English Poetry (T. Warton), III.255n3

History of his Own Times (Burnet), IV.89 and n2

History of Ireland (Leland), I.257n1, III.23 and n4

History of Music (C. Burney) see General History of Music

History of Music (Hawkins) see General History of the Science and Practice of Music

History of Scotland (Robertson), I.281n4

History of Sir Charles Grandison (Richardson), I.48n2, 56n1, 74 and n1, 75nn7,9,10, 79nn1,3–5; importance of an index for, I.48n2; quoted, III.79 and n10

History of the American Indians (Adair), II.210 and n13

History of the Council of Trent: SJ's proposals for, I.13 and n3, 19–20 and n8

History of the Life and Reign of Philip, King of Macedon (Leland), I.257n1

History of the Marchioness de Pompadour (trans. Johnson), I.178 and n4

History of the Rebellion (Clarendon), I.77 and n1, II.183n2

History of the Reign of Philip the Second, King of Spain (Watson), II.357 and n2

Hitch, Charles, bookseller, I.40n4, 129 and n5, 131

Hoadley, Benjamin, playwright, IV.393 and *n*4

Hoare, Sir Richard, Kt., banker, III.86*n*6

Hoare's Bank, III.86 and *n*6

Hodder's Arithmetick, IV.138 and *n*4

Hodgson, Brian, Ashbourne innkeeper, III.371 and *n*4

Hogarth, William, painter: epitaph for, I.383–85 and *nn*1,2,4,8; "Columbus Breaking an Egg," I.384 and *n*4

Holder, ?Robert, apothecary, IV.6 and *n*1, 34; ment., IV.359, 365, 368

Holdernesse, 4th Earl of (Robert Darcy), II.347 and *n*10

Holinshead, Raphael, author, I.63 and *n*7

Holland *see* Netherlands, The

Hollyer, John, cousin of SJ, II.157–58, IV.440

Home, Henry *see* Kames, Lord

Homer, I.12, 52 and *n*6, 92*n*3; quoted, I.404 and *n*1, IV.128*n*27; and Macpherson's translation of the *Iliad*, II.169 and *n*9

Hood, Samuel, Baron, IV.306*n*4

Hoole, John, dramatist and poet: SJ to dine with, II.26, 194; ment., I.279 and *n*7, 334 and *n*1, II.142*n*1, III.115, 192*n*3, 282, IV.33, 238*n*3, 306, 309; and *Cleonice*, II.159–60, 172–73*nn*2,3, 175; translation of Ariosto's *Orlando Furioso*, III.323–24 and *nn*2,4,6; SJ dines with, IV.31, 100*n*1, 317, 319, 325; and Essex Head Club, IV.278, 395 and *n*3; and J. Scott's biography, IV.404*n*1; and SJ's last days, IV.441*n*1

– LETTERS: II.27–28, 159–60, 267, 358–59, III.283, IV.212, 240, 363–64, 394–95, 403–4, V.7

Hoole, Rev. Samuel, IV.238 and *n*3, 240*n*2, 395

Hoole, Susannah Smith (Mrs. John): ment., II.27 and *n*1, 267, IV.363–64,

395, V.7; illness and recovery, II.358–59; dines with SJ, IV.317, 319

hope, I.203, 207

Hope, John, M.D., IV.286*n*6

Hopkins, Benjamin, politician: and chamberlainship election, II.347 and *nn*8,9

Hopper, Ann Carless, niece of E. Hector, III.141 and *n*13

Horace, I.51–55; quoted, I.95*n*13, 299*n*2, 343*n*12, 345*n*4, 358 and *n*1, 363*nn*4,5, 381*n*4, II.13 and *n*4, 71*n*5, 100*n*2, 194*n*14, III.48*n*5, 104*n*6, 141 and *n*12, 143*n*5, 202 and *n*8, 215*n*2, IV.47*n*7, 347*n*2, 370*n*2, 387*n*6, V.29*n*2; Baretti's and Philidor's use of, III.144*n*9

Horne, George, Vice-Chancellor of Oxford, Bishop of Norwich, and Walton's *Lives*, II.138–39 and *n*1, 145–46

– LETTER: II.138–39

Horneck, Catherine, friend of Goldsmith, I.339*n*1, 340 and *n*2, 352 and *n*4; marriage of, III.277 and *n*8

Horneck, Hannah (Mrs. Kane), friend of Goldsmith: ment., II.239, III.14, 276, 277, 288, IV.41; SJ to give set of *Lives of the Poets* to, III.352

– LETTER: I.339–40

Horneck, Capt. Kane, Royal Engineers, I.339*n*1

Horneck, Mary, friend of Goldsmith, I.339*n*1, 340 and *nn*2,3, 352 and *n*4; ment., II.239

Hotham, Sir Richard, Kt., East India merchant and M.P., III.254 and *n*4, 276

Houssaye, Amelot de la, I.13*n*3

Howard, Charles, proctor, friend of SJ, I.180 and *n*3, 185, 229, 234

Howard, Frederick *see* Carlisle, 5th Earl of

Howard, John, philanthropist, IV.322 and *nn*8,9

Howe, Sir William, general: and American War, III.95n10

Howell, James, author, III.72 and n12

Huddesford, George, Vice-Chancellor of Oxford, President of Trinity College: ment., I.155

– LETTER: I.98–99

Hudson, Miss, embroiderer and seamstress, IV.145–46 and n5, 147, 172

Huggins, William, scholar of Italian literature: gold watch incident, I.83–86; death of ment., I.215

– LETTERS: I.83–86

Hughes, John, poet, I.81 and n4

Hughes, John, schoolmaster, I.3n2

Hume, David: ment., I.393n1, II.357n3; and copyright issue, II.129n1

Humphry, Ozias, portrait painter: and apprenticeship for SJ's godson, IV.309, 313, 328

– LETTERS: IV.309, 313, 328

Hunter, Elizabeth see Seward, Elizabeth Hunter

Hunter, Rev. John, I.185n1, 301n5

Hunter, John, M.D., III.117 and n1

Hunter, Lucy Porter Howard (Mrs. John), I.185 and n1, 301n1, 316n4

Hunter, William, M.D.: to present advance copy of *Journey* to King George III, II.164; ment., IV.32n4; discusses politics with SJ, IV.59; death of, IV.119 and n2, 136n1; and Royal Academy, IV.135–36 and n1

– LETTERS: II.164, III.117–18

Huntingford, Rev. George, III.259–60 and n2

Hussey, Rev. John, III.147–48

Hussey, William, politician, IV.289n5

Hutton, James, Moravian church leader, III.34n11, 273 and n7

Hyde, Edward see Clarendon, 1st Earl of

Hyde, Henry see Cornbury, Viscount

Hydrops (Lawrence), I.283 and n3

Hyett, Benjamin, IV.55n1

I

Iceland, I.170 and n5

Icolmkill (Iona), island, II.106 and n23, 107–8 and n27

idleness, I.147–48, 273; "few are so busy as not to find time to do, what they delight in doing," I.76; "be not solitary; be not idle," II.118, 313, III.201; "keep yourself busy, and you will in time grow cheerful," II.319; SJ now paying fine of idleness, III.308; "be always busy," III.142, 265; "never be without something to wish, and something to do," III.377; on not being idle, IV.180–81; on leisure as disease, IV.349; *see also* solitude

Idler, I.48n1, IV.441; reference to SJ's final essay in, III.84n4

Ignoramus (Ruggle): and J. S. Hawkins, IV.310n1

ignorance, I.269–71

Iliad, The (Homer): quoted, I.62 and n2, 404 and n1; and J. Macpherson's translation, II.169 and n9; Pope's translation, IV.66 and n2, 84n6

Il Palmerino d'Inghilterra, II.309 and n5

Il pastor fido (Guarini), II.337n2

imagination: *see* fancy and imagination

Impey, Sir Elijah, Kt., Chief Justice, IV.58 and n5

Improvement of the Mind, The (Watts), III.367 and n6

Inch Galbraith, II.110n4

Inchkeith, island, II.54–55 and n2

Inchkenneth, island, II.104–6, 171

Inchkenneth verses (Johnson) see *Insula Sancti Kennethi*

Inchlonaig, II.110n4, 111 and n8

India, IV.248, 277; and R. Chambers, II.86 and nn2–4, 120n1, IV.127, 215

indulgence, II.301

infidelity (religious), I.314

Inge, Henrietta Wrottesley (Mrs. Theodore William), IV.185 and n5

Inge, Theodore William, Staffordshire landowner, IV.185*n5*

Inge, William, scholar and antiquarian, IV.185*n6*

Inner Temple Lane, I.187*n2*

Inoculator, The (Sutton), I.282*n4*

Inquiry into the Causes of Infidelity and Scepticism (Ogilvie), IV.115*n1*

Inquiry into the Original of the Public Debt (Elibank), I.363*n6*

Inscriptiones Antiquae Totius Orbis Romani (Gruterus), II.199*n1*

Insula Sancti Kennethi (Johnson), II.106 and *n19*, 171, 178*n9*

intellect, intelligence (mind), I.363, IV.254; on powers of mind liable to change, I.134; on reaching the limit of one's intellectual potential, II.261–62 and *n1*; and learning, II.263–64; *see also* education; knowledge

Introduction to the Italian Language (Baretti), I.92*n4*

Introduction to the most useful European Languages (Baretti), II.190 and *n9*

Inverary Castle (Scotland), II.108 and *n2*, III.73*n3*

Inverness, II.65

Iona, island *see* Icolmkill

Ireland: SJ on, I.151–52, 170; SJ on need for history of, III.23–24; political situation and free trade, IV.64–65 and *n5*; reforms demanded, IV.217 and *n12*; *see also* Irish language; Irish literature

Irene (Johnson), I.12*n1*, 17 and *n2*, 23–24 and *n17*, 28; produced at Drury Lane, I.42*n3*; copy to be sent to Pembroke College, Oxford, IV.441

Irenicum, or the Importance of Unity in the Church of Christ Considered (Worthington), II.175 and *n3*

Irish language, I.152 and *n6*, III.23

Irish literature, I.152, III.23–24 and *nn1,3–5*

Isaacs, Isaac, neighbor of SJ, I.119*n3*

Isay (Isa) Island (Skye), II.71 and *n4*

Iserloo, Catherine *see* Dodsley, Catherine Iserloo

Islam (Ilam) Garden, Staffordshire: SJ and JB visit, III.73 and *n4*; ment., III.79

Isle of Wight: and threatened Franco-Spanish invasion, III.180*n2*; ment., III.279

Italian Library (Baretti), I.92*n4*

Italy: ment. in relation to creation of Royal Library, I.308, 309, 311; ment. of proposed 1774 trip with Thrales to, II.223 and *n12*; plans for, then postponement of, 1776 trip, II.299 and *n2*, 316, 317*n7*, 318 and *n1*, 319, 321, 322, III.299 and *n2*; SJ's proposed 1784 trip to, IV.342*n3*

Ivy Lane Club, IV.317; beginnings of, IV.246–47 and *n1*; plans for reunion, IV.246–47, 256; members reunion, IV.259; SJ gives dinner for remaining members, IV.316

—MEMBERS: Bathurst, R., I.68*n3*; Dyer, S., I.265*n11*; Hawkins, Sir J., IV.246–47 and *n1*, 256; Hawkesworth, J., I.67*n2*; Lawrence, T., I.116*n2*; Payne, J., I.47*n3*; Ryland, J., I.127*n1*, IV.246, 247*n1*, 256

J

Jack the Giantkiller, I.296 and *n5*

Jackson, Andrew, uncle of SJ, I.7*n9*

Jackson, Cyril, sub-preceptor to Prince of Wales: dismissed by King, II.347*n10*

Jackson, Harry, friend of SJ, I.291 and *n3*, II.297, 301; death of ment., III.48 and *n4*, 51, 57

Jackson, Humphrey, chemist, II.22–23 and *n5*, III.305*n4*

Jackson, Richard, government official, IV.237–38

Jackson's Oxford Journal, I.413n1

Jamaica: capture of by French, III.198 and n6, 212 and n12; and P. Stockdale, III.286n3, 287, 291 and n9

James IV (of Scotland), II.58n21

James V (of Scotland), II.52n8, 90 and n14

James VI (of Scotland), II.52 and n6

James, Robert, M.D., I.24n1, 25 and n2, 26–27 and n4, 125n6, 129; and Mrs. Salusbury's illness, II.16–17 and nn1,2, 18 and n1; SJ on medicines of, IV.372

Jealous Wife, The (Coleman), I.199 and n10

Jeans, John, II.72 and n10

Jebb, Sir Richard, 1st Bt., physician: ment., III.168n2, 248 and n1, IV.13, 19, 20, 42n1, 43; medical advice, IV.47 and nn4,6, 48

– LETTER: IV.50–51

Jeffries, Elizabeth, Maid of Honour, II.205 and n7

Jeffs, William, Reader at the Temple Church, IV.238n2

Jenkinson, Charles, M.P., politician (later Earl of Liverpool): ment. I.300 and n9, III.29; and Dodd case, III.29, 30

– LETTERS: I.258–59, III.29

Jennens, Charles, Shakespearean editor, II.25 and n7

Jennings Clerke, Sir Philip, 1st Bt., M.P., friend of the Thrales, III.168 and n3, 195, 206 and n6, 253, IV.161, 163n6; contractor's bill of, III.240–41 and nn4,5; and Gordon Riots, III.269n14

Jephson, Robert, II.175 and nn6,7

Jerusalem Delivered (Tasso): Hoole's translation, I.279n7; Fairfax's translation, III.117n2

Jervis, William, Warwickshire squire, I.22n1

Jessop, William, clergyman, I.268

Jewel, William, friend of S. Foote, III.93n10

Jodrell, Richard Paul, classicist and playwright: SJ dines with, III.229 and n8, IV.325; and Essex Head Club, IV.257n2

– LETTER: IV.122–23

Johnson, Elizabeth Jervis Porter (Tetty) (Mrs. Samuel): impending marriage to SJ, I.10n10, 11n16; SJ's concern over health of, I.22–24, 31, 32, 44 and n5, 59; financial problems inherited from first husband, I.39 and n1; death of, I.59n2, 61nn1,3, 90 and n7; E. Desmoulins and, I.125n4; ment., I.185n1; SJ's wish for Thrale child to be named for, I.302n4; funeral service for ment., II.29n1; lettering and placement of gravestone of, IV.348–49 and nn1,3; inscription on gravestone of, IV.444

– LETTER: I.22–24

Johnson, Elizabeth Reynolds (Mrs. William), sister of Sir J. Reynolds, I.215n1, 216 and n4, 376n2

Johnson, John, Vicar of Cranbrook, IV.178 and n5

Johnson, Maurice, IV.84n2

Johnson, Michael, father of SJ: ment., I.275n2, IV.104n3

SAMUEL JOHNSON

catalogue of his books, I.7–8 and n4; plans to keep boarding school, I.10; on failed cotton mill investment, I.24–26, 125 and n6; on proposed historical account of British Parliament, I.34–36 and n5, 36–37 and n3; moderator in gold watch dispute, I.83–86; and M.A. from Oxford, I.88 and n3, 89, 90, 94, 97, 98–100; on difference between real and ideal, I.165–66; on

Samuel Johnson (*cont.*)

"every man's" affairs, I.212; receives degree from University of Dublin, I.257 and *n*2; Spanish fluency ment., II.26 and *n*2; French letters, II.37–39, v.29–30; apologizes to J. Macleod of Raasay on statement of mistaken supremacy in *Journey*, II.203, 206, 265–66; named trustee of Hester Thrale's estate, II.253–54 and *n*8; and JB's controversy with his father over entail, II.286–89, 291–92, 294–95; on importance of method in life, II.361 and *nn*5,6; epitaph on monument in St. Paul's ment., III.7*n*1; Nollekens bust of, III.54 and *n*2, 98, 108–9; parodies politicians, III.72 and *nn*11,12; talk of another expedition with JB, III.74; lends JB money, III.74–75; on hair care, III.95–96; portraits of, III.127 and *nn*5,6, 278 and *n*1, IV.120*n*1; as executor of Henry Thrale's will, III.330 and *n*6; on the common course of life, IV.170; on use of initials, IV.233; on old animals, IV.264; on "speaking figure," IV.331; on Hester Thrale's marriage, IV.338, 339, 343–44 and *n*7, 351; on public opinion, IV.367; *see also* under the specific subject heading, such as death; medicine; politics and the contemporary political situation

– DIET: IV.47; abstinence (fasting), I.122–23, III.157–58, 186, 207, 234, 245, 248, 275; avoidance of meat, advocates a semivegetable or alternate diet, III.198, 202, 229*n*6, 241, 248, 266, 279, 283–84, 288, IV.136; potatoes and spinach, III.248; is thinner, the less we eat the better, III.290–91; eats little, IV.7; eats meat, IV.155; use of milk, IV.365, 397, 409

– FAMILY AND PERSONAL LIFE: on wife's illness, I.31, 32, 42–43 and *n*1, 59; response to his mother's sickness and death, I.43, 174–75, 176–77; on death of his wife, I.61–62 and *nn*1,3, 90 and *n*7; on rumor of his death, I.118; and death of H. Boothby, I.123*n*2; on being only child, I.171–72; attends theater, I.199–200; on return to his birthplace, I.206, 207; on rising early, I.265 and *n*9, 267; named godfather to Thrale child, I.302 and *n*4, 324–25, 326; wish for Thrale child to be named after "Tetty," I.302*n*4; first love, I.343*n*11; on his 64th birthday, II.75; cousin squanders borrowed money, II.157–58 and *n*3; receives D.C.L. from Oxford, II.193–94 and *n*7, 196; on death of longtime friend C. Hardinge, II.296–97; on death of Harry Thrale, II.311–12, 313–14; godfather to J. Langton, III.37 and *n*1; on being 68 years old, III.68, 73, 87, 88; ment. of 70th birthday, III.191, 202; reference to his 71st birthday, III.308; on his love of the Burneys, III.373; and Collier inheritance affair, IV.16 and *n*1, 53, 56, 60, 62, 74–75, 76–77, 93, 94, 101, 105–7, 141; plans for his birthday dinner in 1783, IV.199; makes his will, IV.288, 433*n*1, 442–43 and *n*2; on his wife's gravestone, IV.348, 430, 435, 444; on epitaph and gravestones for family, IV.443–44; love for his wife, IV.444

– FINANCIAL ISSUES: mortgage and finances, I.37–38 and *n*3, 43, 64, 153–54, v.12 and *n*3; financial problems, I.39 and *n*1, 48–49, 82, 158 and *n*2, 179 and *n*9; W. Strahan as SJ's agent, banker, and paymaster, I.50 and *n*1; under arrest for debt, I.132; pension issues, I.208*nn*4,6, 209, 212, 221–22, IV.398 and *nn*1,2, 399–400, 446; if he had enough money what he would do, II.243; on debts, III.40; profits from political tracts, III.137*n*1; expects Henry Thrale to be his personal banker, III.174 and n2; and F. Reynolds's German friend, III.177; overpayment and money from M. Prowse, III.344 and n4; *see also* money – HEALTH: I.317, 318 and n1, 324, 375, 410, II.5; on pain and illness, I.62, 117; on being near madness, I.91 and n2; bloodletting, I.116, II.40, III.4, 5 and n2, 7, 9, 158, 167 and n2, 234, 275, 277, IV.4–5, 16–17, 19 and n3, 29, 34–35, 38; cough, I.116, 118–19, 196, 216, II.5, 10–11, 14, 125, III.35, 209, 223, 234, 236, 275, IV.8, 12–13, 20, 37, 38, 42, 44, 46–47, 51, 309–10; restless and tedious nights, I.122, III.11, 21, 142, 162, 164, 290, IV.7, 39, 356; eye inflammation and other disorders, I.128 and n3, 132–33, 134, 222, II.35 and n1, 37, 40 and n3, 41, 45, 98; colds, I.196, II.5, 40, 125, 364, III.209, 212, 229, 234, 236, 275, IV.26; bloodletting ment., I.196, II.253, III.158, 223, IV.5, 6, 7, 20; rheumatism, I.336, 337, 339, 344, 345, 346–47, 349, 367, 373, 374, 375; lumbago, I.367; flatulence, I.410, II.238, 248, III.21; gout and foot problems, II.5, 268, 339, 342, 343, 346, 347, 350, III.185 and n3, 186–87, 189, 190, 191, 193 and n5, 204, 221 and n1, IV.17, 202, 205, 206, 208, 209, 244; SJ's comments on state of his health, II.9–10, 33, 34, 102, III.63, 92, 99, 108, 153, 154, 160, 367, 368; dejected and depressed, II.38n2, 39n6, IV.212, 279, 282; on importance of exercise, II.40, 45 and n3, III.175, 179; during Hebridean trip, II.98, 125; hearing disorder, II.113–14, 226; fainting fit, II.212; respiratory problems, III.4–5, 6–7, 9, 36, 52 and n2, 148, 162, 164, 179, IV.17, 34, 44, 83, 107n1; takes ipecacuanha, III.4 and n2, 52 and n2; illness leads to visit to Streatham, III.6n2; takes physic, III.21, 166, 167,

179, 186, 202, 207, 223, 234, 248, 275, 277; remedies, III.96 and n2, 97; lamed one of his knees, III.125; takes musk, III.125–26 and n1, 127–28; new medicine, III.131; takes valerian, III.140 and n3, 141; feeling better, improvement in, III.149, 197, 203, 207, 212, 233, 243 and n3, 275, 277, 279, 294, 302, 318, 327, 349, 372; takes opium and opiates, III.158, 186, 193, 233, 236, 275, IV.24–25, 42, 47, 48n2, 97n2, 136, 149, 151, 219, 265, 272, 274, 283, 297–98, 303, 353, 377, 381, 388–89, 419; told how well he looks, III.158, 190, 193, 198; to J. Taylor on, III.163; better than when in Scotland, III.181; JB says he looks well, III.189; grows light and airy, III.202, 221, 243 and n3, 280; "gravedo," III.364; hurt in leg grown better, III.373; bronchitis, or a chronic bronchial infection, IV.4 and n1; Latin letters to Thomas Lawrence on, IV.4–5, 7, 16–17, 20, 24–25, 34, 39; takes "poppy" for sleep, IV.119; "arthritical" complaints, IV.119; effect of illness of 1768, IV.125n5; mind unimpaired body given way to repeated shocks, IV.130; cathartics, IV.136, 353; "stroke of palsy," IV.148–49 and n1, 148 and n3; swollen legs, IV.149; on his loss of speech and problems with his voice, IV.149, 151–52 and n10, 162, 164, 167, 171, 174, 177, 179; stroke ment., IV.149, 150, 151, 157, 159, 164; and blistering, IV.153, 154–55 and nn3,4; stroke reported in newspapers, IV.159 and n1; use of cantharides, IV.161, 162, 163, 165, 167, 359, 364–65, 370; testicular sarcocele and ment. of possible surgery, IV.182, 183 and n2, 184, 196–97 and nn4,6, 200, 201, 205, 206–7, 208, 209, 210, 219–20, 226, 230, 210, 211, 213, 216, 218, 220, 223, 225, 230, 231,

SAMUEL JOHNSON (*cont.*)

235; tooth extracted, IV.211; being solitary, IV.232 and *n*3, 237; testicular sarcocele gone, IV.244, 246; dropsy, IV.268*n*3, 283, 285, 287, 290, 294, 296, 297, 300, 304, 312, 319, 334, 436; dreads effect of opiates, IV.280; asthma, IV.285, 296, 297, 300, 303, 304, 319, 334, 368, 372, 373, 376; diuretics, IV.289, 290 and *n*1, 293, 364–65, 382; thanks God for recovery, IV.319; on his miraculous recovery, IV.319–20; takes squills, IV.348, 356, 368, 370, 372, 373, 376–77, 381, 394, 401, 419, 428, 435, 436; gives account of his health to various individuals, IV.351–53, 355, 423; constipation, IV.353, 409, 415, 422, 428; diacodium, IV.365, 381; improvement and recovery, IV.368–70, 386–89, 393, 394, 396, 405; relapse of dropsy, IV.436; since his 20th year has seldom given him ease, V.7

– LITERARY WORKS *see* under the title of the individual work

– OPINIONS AND COMMENTS *see* under the specific topic, such as death; education; friendship

– RELIGION: "I cannot receive my religion from any human hand," I.119; prayer, "When my Eye was Restored to its Use," I.128 and *n*3; prayer on day of mother's funeral, I.179–80 and *n*1; on last day of Lent, I.391 and *n*1; Sarum Rite, I.396*n*8; prayer when sick, IV.151 and *n*3; on prayer and fasting as reason for recovery, IV.290 and *n*1; God has granted a reprieve, IV.292–93; receives holy sacrament at home, IV.312; thanks God for recovery, IV.319; first care is to please God, IV.367; *see also* religion

– RESIDENCES: Exeter Street, I.12*n*1; Castle Street, I.14*n*1, 17*n*9, 110*n*1; Bow Street, I.26*n*1; Durham Yard, I.26*n*1; Gough Square, I.43*n*1, 160*n*5; Staple Inn, I.184 and *n*1; Gray's Inn, I.187*n*2; Inner Temple Lane, I.187*n*2; Johnson's Court, I.252*n*1, II.316 and *n*1; home in Lichfield, I.263 and *n*3, 275 and *n*2, 346 and *n*6; constructs "new study," I.265 and *n*10; Sadler Street, I.346 and *n*6; move from Johnson Court to Bolt Court, II.316 and *n*1; Bolt Court, II.316 and *n*1, III.7–8 and *n*3; requests free accommodations at Hampton Court Palace, II.319–20 and *nn*2,4

Johnson, Samuel, nephew of Sir J. Reynolds, I.376–77 and *n*2

Johnson, Sarah Ford, mother of SJ: business and finances of, I.23*n*8, 24*n*18, 38, 154, 181, 182; SJ on eventual death of, I.43, 45; death of, I.45*n*3, 177*n*1; ment., I.61, II.191 and *n*4; and *Dictionary*, I.104 and *n*4; SJ's hope to visit, I.106*n*9, 114–15; SJ's concern she will hear rumor of his death, I.119; and subscriptions for SJ's *Shakespeare*, I.142, 147, 153; SJ on death of, I.179–80, 181–82, 183, 184; SJ's wish to settle debts of, I.182, 187

– LETTERS: I.174–75, 176, 177–78

Johnson, Thomas, currier and cousin of SJ: ment., I.326 and *n*1, 337, 339, III.165–66, IV.440 and *nn*1,2; squanders money lent by SJ, II.157–58 and *n*3

– LETTER: III.100

Johnson, William, mayor of Torrington, merchant, I.216 and *nn*4,7, 376*n*2, 377

Johnson, William Samuel, agent in London for Colony of Connecticut, II.14–16

Johnson's Court (London), I.252*n*1, II.316 and *n*1

Johnston, Arthur, poet, III.9 and *n*11, IV.299

Johnston, Margaret Penelope, granddaughter of W. Strahan, III.285 and *n*10

Johnston, Rachel Strahan, daughter of W. Strahan: ment., III.285*n*10

Johnston, William, bookseller, I.178 and *n*5, 390

Jones, Benjamin, prisoner, IV.363 and *n*1

Jones, Capt. Benjamin, of the East India Company, I.357 and *n*2

Jones, Griffith, printer, translator, and editor, V.8

Jones, John, prisoner, IV.363 and *n*1

Jones, Mary, poet, I.155 and *n*5

Jones, Mr., shoemaker, III.316–17

Jones, Rev. Oliver, chantor of Christ Church Cathedral, Oxford, I.155*n*5

Jones, Sir William, orientalist, II.137 *n*14; and politics, III.254 and *n*9, 266; ment. concerning The Club, IV.126

Jonson, Ben, poet: ment., III.120*n*4

Jopp, James, Lord Provost of Aberdeen, II.60 and *n*1

Jortin, Rev. John, D.D., classical scholar, IV.84 and *n*6

Joseph, JB's servant *see* Ritter, Joseph

journal-keeping, II.260–61 and *n*1, III.61, 107–8; difference between history writing and, I.34, 329

Journal of a Tour to the Hebrides (Hebridean journal) (Boswell), II.77*n*30, 95; MS given to Hester Thrale to read, II.206 and *n*13, 209 and *n*5; Hester Thrale's reaction to, II.209 and *n*5, 266; SJ inquires if Hester Thrale has read, II.223, 228–29; H. L. Piozzi's concealment of SJ's comments on JB, II.236*n*2; SJ glad Hester Thrale has read, II.239, 253

Journal to Stella (Swift), I.322 and *n*1

Journey from London to Genoa (Baretti), I.200*n*11, 348 and *n*6

"Journey, The" (Churchill), I.173*n*13

Journey to the Western Islands of Scotland (Johnson): and SJ's letters to Hester Thrale, II.54*n*1; deforestation ment., II.63*n*2, III.41*n*11; controversial statement on supremacy of clans, II.83*n*11; SJ gathers information for, II.120*n*5, 123*n*1; manuscript delivered to printer, II.134 and *n*5, 144 and *n*1; printing begins, II.144 and *n*3, 147; contrasts notion and fact, II.145 and *n*1; printing of 2d edition, II.145 and *n*2; JB supplies information for, II.146 and *n*11; SJ regrets having to neglect proofs to visit Wales, II.149; printing of and distribution plans, II.150, 151 and *n*5; number of pages printed, II.154; corrected last page of, II.155 and *n*1; canceled leaf in, II.156–57 and *nn*2,4,7; 1st edition and errata leaf, II.159 and *nn*3,4; JB receives copy of, II.166 and *nn*1,3; SJ sends in boards, II.167; and Macpherson-Johnson controversy, II.168*n*3, 181 and *n*5; to send JB parcel containing copies, II.170; divided opinion on, II.174 and *n*2; sales of, II.182; SJ apologizes to J. Macleod of Raasay for mistake concerning clan supremacy, II.203; theme of patriarchal authority, III.40 and *n*8, ment., III.137*n*1; financial contract for, III.325 and *n*2; copy sent to Oxford library, IV.441 and *n*3

– PRESENTATION COPIES: for certain people, II.144, 180 and *n*1, 364 and *n*2; sent to Hester Thrale, II.159 and *n*3; sent to W. Hastings, II.160–61; sent to W. Hunter to present to George III, II.164; and J. Taylor, II.167; SJ instructs JB regarding 2d edition for friends in Scotland, II.180 and *n*1

Jugemens des sçavans sur les principaux ouvrages des auteurs (Baillet), I.312 and *n*26

Julius Caesar (Shakespeare): and Jennens's edition of, II.25n7; quoted, III.77n9

Juslenius, Daniel, lexicographer, I.88n5

Juvenal (Decimus Junius Juvenalis), I.16 and n3; quoted, I.172 and n5, III.358n7, IV.155 and n6, 355n1, 401n1

K

Kam (dog), III.374 and n1

Kames, Henry Home, Lord, Scots jurist, III.31n2; and *Elements of Criticism*, V.14 and n1

Kearsley, George, bookseller: ment., III.361; and *The Beauties of Johnson*, III.361n1, IV.28n5, 40n4, 41

− LETTER: IV.41

Kedleston Hall, Derbyshire, I.392 and n2, 395

Keegan, Allen, balloonist, IV.279n2, 415n1

Keep, Mr., II.7 and nn8,9

Kelly, Hugh, playwright: SJ's prologue for benefit performance of *A Word to the Wise*, III.27nn6,7, 49

Kelly, Mrs. Hugh, III.27 and n7

Kemble, John Philip, actor, manager of Drury Lane Theatre, IV.228n8, 232−33 and n6

Kennedy, Catherine (?1700−1779) (Mrs. John), III.169 and n5

Kennedy, Catherine, daughter of Rev. John Kennedy *see* Burton, Catherine Kennedy

Kennedy, Rev. John, III.169n5, 371

Kenneth (Canice), St., II.104 and n9

Keppel, George *see* Albemarle, 3d Earl of

Kettell Hall (Oriel College), I.108n5

Kilmorey, 10th Viscount (John Needham), IV.239 and nn5,7,8

Kindersley, Jemima, author, IV.217 and n7

King, Rev. William, D.C.L., Principal of St. Mary's Hall, Oxford, I.98 and n1, 186 and n5

Kinghorn (Fife), II.55

King Lear (Shakespeare), I.351 and n2; quoted, III.368n3

Kingsburgh (Skye), II.90−91

King's College (Aberdeen), II.58 and n21, 59 and n29

Kings Norton parish, II.190−91 and n2

Kingston, Dowager Duchess of, Elizabeth Chudleigh, II.321n3

Kinsey, Peter, neighbor of SJ, I.119n3

Kippis, Rev. Andrew, clergyman and biographer, III.226n2

Kircaldy (Fife), II.55

Kirkwall, Viscount (John Fitzmaurice): birth of, III.147 and n3

Knapton, John, bookseller, I.40nn3,4, 41

Knapton, Paul, bookseller, I.40nn3,4, 41, 110 and n1

Knight, Joseph, former slave, III.42 and nn17,18, 104

Knightsbridge: Mrs. Langton visits baths at, III.245 and n7

knowledge, I.269−71; is always to be wished to those who can communicate it well, I.192; the most pleasing and valuable of all acquisitions, I.219; SJ's quest for, II.136−37; acquaintance with the world is, III.256; *see also* education; intellect; reading

Knowles, Mary Morris (Mrs. Thomas), II.332 and n8

Knowles, Rev. Thomas, II.332n8

Know Your Own Mind (Murphy), II.24n4

Knox, John, II.55 and n5, 56n9

L

La Bruyère, Jean de, moralist, I.380

Lade, Ann Thrale, Lady (wife of Sir John, 1st Bt.), sister of Henry Thrale, III.62–63, 65 and n1, 69, 91, 366; and brewery finances, II.245 and n10; ment., III.184n2; on Gordon Riots, III.272 and n4

Lade, Sir John, 2d Bt., nephew of Henry Thrale, II.98 and n51, III.62–63nn3,5, 65, 69, 73, 91, 272n4; SJ writes 21st birthday poem for, III.296 and n8

Ladies' Charity School, I.330 and n1, 360 and n2; A. Williams's bequest to, IV.205 and n7, 225

land tenure *see* feudalism

Langdon, Robert *see* Longdon, Robert

Langley, Mrs. William: ment., III.59

Langley, Rev. William, headmaster, Ashbourne Grammar School, IV.56–57, 141; controversy with J. Taylor, I.394 and n2, II.244, III.59, 69; and employment for W. Davenport, II.161 and n2; ment., II.231, III.155; makes improvements in his garden, II.249; and Collier-Flint inheritance controversy, IV.16 and n1, 56–57, 75, 101 and n2, 105–6 and n4, 141

– LETTERS: IV.56–57, 141

Langton, Algernon, son of Bennet, the younger, IV.24n6

Langton, Bennet (the elder), Lincolnshire gentleman, I.106 and n7, 107, 163 and n7, 193, 264, 267, 359 and n2; ment., IV.128

Langton, Bennet (the younger), friend of SJ: ment., I.157n5, 163, 218, 251n2, 319–20, 359, 361–62 and n2, II.42n10, 48n9, 194n12, 209, III.67n4, 112, 216, IV.43, 118–19, 313 and n1; height of ment., I.164 and n4; travels with T. Beauclerk, I.192n1, 213; offended by SJ, II.42 and n9; visits SJ,

II.170; SJ's advice for rheumatism, II.200–201; ment. of departure for Lincolnshire, II.209, 213; and possibility of stabling C. Carter's horse at estate of, II.236n4, 246; SJ dines with, II.326, 350, IV.138; SJ on mismanaged finances of, II.360; to dine with SJ and T. Percy at Chaplain's table, II.362; SJ plans to dine with, III.3, 4, 41n15, 245; family ment., III.9 and n7, 41 and n15, 47, 67nn5,6, 99, 118–19; at military camp, III.36 and n19, 47, 118, 124–25, 142, 182; SJ on, III.118–19 and n3; and T. Beauclerk's will, III.231 and n8; on leave from militia, engaged in engineering work, III.266 and n7; and *Prefaces*, III.278 and n2; financial problems, IV.126 and n14, 128–29 and n31, 383–84; pays SJ a sick call, IV.156; SJ to travel to Rochester with, IV.165 and n5, 168, 171, 172; SJ thanks for hospitality shown in Rochester, IV.200; and SJ's Latin poems, IV.318n11, 441n1; SJ has money on deposit with, IV.383 and n6; recipient of SJ's Polyglot Bible, IV.395n3; summoned to SJ's bedside, IV.441n1

– LETTERS: I.105–7, 165–67, 171–74, 192–94, 264–67, 351–52, 355–56, 381–82, 387, 391, II.147–48, 200–201, 208, 345, III.7–8, 36–37, 124–25, 131–32, 350–51, IV.22–24, 200, 208, 224–25, 302–3, 309–10, 314, 349–50, 382–84, 441

Langton, Diana, daughter of Bennet, the younger: ment., II.326 and n5, 345, 360, III.9n7, 47, 67 and n6, IV.174 and n4

Langton, Diana, sister of Bennet, the younger: ment., I.171 and n3, 193, 267, 356, II.42n10

Langton, Diana Turnor (Mrs. Bennet, the elder): ment., I.172 and n6, 193, 264, 267, 356, 387, III.74n2, 76–77,

Langton, Diana (*cont.*)
78 and *n*8, IV.314 and *n*6, 350; visits Knightsbridge, III.245*n*7

Langton, Elizabeth, daughter of Bennet, the younger: birth of, III.9 and *n*6; ment., IV.174 and *n*4

Langton, Elizabeth, sister of Bennet, the younger: ment., I.171 and *n*3, 193, 264 and *n*2, 267, 356, 375, II.42*n*10, III.78 and *n*9, IV.314 and *n*6; SJ comments on her claims of his "frigidity," I.373−74; health ment., I.387 and *n*2; SJ sends *Lives of the Poets* to, IV.303 and *n*11

− LETTER: I.358−59

Langton, George, son of Bennet, the younger: birth of, I.387 and *n*1; ment., I.391, II.148 and *n*9, 326 and *n*5, 345, 360, III.9*n*7, 47, IV.24, 314; SJ on education of, II.327 and *n*7

Langton, Isabella, daughter of Bennet, the younger: birth of, IV.31 and *n*5

Langton, Jane (Jenny), daughter of Bennet, the younger: birth of, II.345*n*2, 350 and *n*7; ment., II.360, III.9*n*7, 37 and *n*1, 47, 351, IV.24, 174 and *n*4, 314

− LETTER: IV.324−25

Langton, Juliet, sister of Bennet, the younger: ment., I.171 and *n*3, 193, 267, 356, II.42*n*10, III.74*n*2, 76−77

Langton, Mary (Mrs. Bennet, the younger) *see* Rothes, Mary, Dowager Countess of

Langton, Mary, daughter of Bennet, the younger: ment., II.148 and *n*9, 326 and *n*5, 345, 360, III.9*n*7, 47, IV.174 and *n*4, 303 and *n*9, 314

Langton, Peregrine, son of Bennet, the younger, IV.24*n*6

Langton, Peregrine, uncle of Bennet, the younger, I.266−67 and *nn*1−3,5

Langton, Lincolnshire, III.119*n*4

language: importance of Greek, I.11−12, III.136; on use of two languages,
I.197; and education, I.248; importance of, I.269−71; on speaking a language perfectly, II.271 and *n*9; *see also* under the names of the specific language such as French language; Irish language; Latin language

La Rochefoucauld, François de, Duc de: quoted, III.91−92 and *n*10

Latin language, I.12, 219, 220−21, 234−35, II.271*n*9, IV.318; SJ corrects JB's use of, I.272 and *nn*3−5

Latin poems (Johnson), IV.151 and *n*6, 318 and *n*11, 441*n*1

La Trobe, Rev. Benjamin, general director of the Moravian congregations in England, III.34 and *n*11

law: on professorship of the common law, I.161−62; and women, I.228

Law, William, theologian, I.72 and *n*7, 123*n*1

Lawrence, Charles, son of Thomas, III.310−13

Lawrence, Elizabeth, daughter of Thomas, IV.42, 50, 57, 61, 70−71, 111−12

Lawrence, Frances Chauncy (Mrs. Thomas), III.218 and *n*12; death of, III.223

Lawrence, John, son of Thomas: visits SJ, IV.61 and *n*2; death of, IV.147 and *n*5

Lawrence, Soulden, son of Thomas, II.172 and *n*1, III.44 and *n*1

Lawrence, Thomas, M.D.: and bloodletting, I.116 and *n*2, IV.4−5, 16−17, 19*n*3; ment., I.117, 119, 120, 122, II.11, 40, 206−7, III.36, 52, 131, 189, 310*n*1, 311, IV.6, 61*n*2, 128, 160, 219; medical advice, II.33; SJ wishes to assist son of, II.86 and *n*4, 161; and SJ's gout, II.268; and A. Williams's health, II.360; SJ to visit, II.363; SJ dines with, III.3, 229, 235, 290; treats SJ, III.4, 5, 7, 127−28, 131, 140, 221; SJ suggests Hester Thrale call on, III.184; wife's illness and death, III.218 and *n*12; SJ's condolences on wife's death, III.222–23; and *Evelina*, III.236 and *n*3; medical suggestions for Henry Thrale, III.261, 301*n*1, 309; on diet, III.294; SJ's Latin letters, IV.4–5, 7, 16–17, 20, 24–25, 34, 39; suffers stroke, IV.39 and *n*3; health ment., IV.42, 126; one of last medical directives, IV.47; SJ's concern for, IV.50, 57, 61, 71, 111–12, 123–24; health worsens, IV.65; death of, IV.147 and *n*5; death ment., IV.152, 214; use of Latin, IV.154 and *n*1

— LETTERS: I.282–84, II.154–55, 158, 172, 176, III.44, 125–26, 146, 178, 222–23, IV.4–5, 6–7, 8–9, 16–18, 19–20, 24–25, 34, 39, 123–24, V.8–9

Lawrence, Thomas, painter, II.328 and *n*8

Lawrence, William Chauncy, son of Thomas, II.86 and *n*4, 161, IV.128, 215, V.8–9 and *n*1

Layer, Christopher, Jacobite conspirator, V.4 and *n*5

Leake, James, bookseller, I.320*n*3

learning *see* education

Le Courayer, Pierre François, theologian, I.13 and *n*3

Lectures on Hebrew Poetry (Lowth), III.286*n*1

Lectures on the Truly Eminent English Poets (Stockdale), III.286*n*2

Ledbrooke, Rev. John, curate of Market Bosworth, III.170 and *n*1

Lee, Arthur, M.D., II.331 and *n*3

Lee, William, merchant and diplomat, II.331 and *n*3

Leedes, Edward, philologist, I.11 and *n*5

Leek, Staffordshire, III.86 and *n*8

Legge, William *see* Dartmouth, 2d Earl of

Leibnitz, Gottfried Wilhelm, philosopher, I.20

Leland, Thomas, historian: ment., II.205; and *History of Ireland*, III.23 and *n*4

— LETTER: I.257

Lennox, Alexander, husband of Charlotte, I.46*n*1, 66 and *n*2, 137, II.202, V.9; ment., III.280*n*7, 353

Lennox, Charlotte Ramsay (Mrs. Alexander), author: and S. Richardson, I.56 and *n*3; and Lord Orrery, I.63 and *nn*5,6; and G. Baretti, I.87*n*8; reviews of her translations, I.135–37; SJ on soliciting for edition of *Original Works*, II.201–2; copyright controversy with J. Dodsley, III.138 and *n*1; and R. Cumberland, III.201 and *n*5, 202; daughter ill, III.280 and *n*7; SJ seeks help for, III.353–54; SJ on her letters, V.10; SJ quarrels with, V.10–11

— LETTERS: I.46–47, 58–60, 66, 71, 135–37, 150–51, II.201–2, III.138, V.9–11

Lennox, Harriot Holles, daughter of Charlotte, III.280 and *n*7

Le Nôtre, André, landscape architect, I.411*n*4

Lescaro, Doge of Genoa, II.94 and *n*41, IV.321

Lesley, John, writer, II.126 and *n*2

Lester, Mr., II.257 and *n*8

Lettere familiari (Baretti), I.200*n*11

Letters from Italy (Miller), III.236*n*7

Letters from Italy (Sharp), I.193*n*6

Letters from the Island of Teneriffe . . . and the East Indies (Kindersley), IV.217 and *n*7

Letters of Sir Thomas Fitzosborne (Melmoth), III.249 and *n*6

Letters on the Study and Use of History (Bolingbroke), I.60*n*4

Letter to Lord Braxfield (pamphlet, Boswell), III.255*n*2

Letter to the People of Scotland, On the Present State of the Nation (Boswell), IV.285 and *n*5, 291 and *n*2, 299*n*3

letter writing, I.139–40, 142, 237–38,

letter writing (*cont.*)
II.256, 260 and *n*1; as mark of friendship, I.139–40, 200–201; short letter to distant friend is an insult, I.196; on unauthorized publication of, I.298 and *n*2; punctuality of correspondence is proof of great regard, I.301; ment. of "letters about nothing," II.237, III.64, 70, 299; SJ on "materials" for excelling in, II.256; intermission of is not decay of kindness, III.64; as duty, III.71–72; to Hester Thrale, "how small a part of our minds we have written," III.88; SJ on his letters to Hester Thrale, "in a man's letters his soul lies naked," III.89–90; SJ on dating fully, III.214; SJ on Hester Thrale's lapse, III.301; material for, IV.170; SJ's advice to C. Lennox, V.10

Lever, Sir Ashton, Kt., III.163 and *n*4

Levet, Robert: ment., I.105*n*1, 138 and *n*5, 252*n*1, II.100, 121, III.4, 68, 72, 120, 127, 139, 140, 189, 203, 209–10, 300; marriage of, I.205 and *n*6, 214; SJ asks Henry Thrale to lend money to, II.108; and T. Cumming's health, II.140–41; injures himself in fall, II.343; health ment., II.361; register searched for information on, III.68, 72, 75 and *n*5; quarrels with A. Williams, III.127, 139, 140; quarrels with E. Desmoulins, III.140, 189, 209–10; medical advice of, III.290; death of, IV.6 and *n*2, 8, 9 and *n*1; death of ment., and its effect on SJ, IV.8, 9, 15, 23, 126, 130, 160, 167, 186, 225, 265; question of heirs, IV.10–12 and *nn*1–6, 22

— LETTERS: II.148–49, 270–73, 356–57, 358

Levett, John, son of Theophilus: and SJ's finances and mortgage payment, I.60–61, 64, 153–54, V.12–13; ment., I.206 and *n*10

— LETTERS: I.60–61, 64, 153–54

Levett, Theophilus, Town Clerk of Lichfield: ment., I.23*n*8, 43, V.12 and *nn*1–3

— LETTERS: I.37–40

Levy, Mr., III.251

Lewes, Thomas, commander, R.N., III.113*n*3

Lewis, Catherine Villiers (Mrs. John, 1st wife), IV.172 and *n*1

Lewis, Charlotte Cotterell (Mrs. John, 2d wife): ment., I.110*n*1, 205 and *n*4, 214, III.245 and *n*6, IV.145 and *n*4, 172, 298 and *n*1, 302*n*3, 321; and estate of deceased husband, IV.160*n*3, 166

— LETTER: IV.307

Lewis, Erasmus, Under-Secretary of State, III.248 and *n*3

Lewis, Rev. John, Dean of Ossory: ment., I.205*n*4, 214, IV.172 and *n*1; death ment., IV.160*n*3; estate of, IV.166 and *n*4

Lewis, William, M.D., III.68 and *n*3, 140*n*3, 189

Leycester, George, cousin of T. Beauclerk, III.231 and *n*7

libraries: SJ on formation of Royal Library, I.307–14

Lichfield, I.106*n*11, 260*n*9, 361; Bishop's Palace, I.223–24 and *n*5; SJ's birthplace, I.275 and *n*2; SJ visits C. Chambers in 1767, I.282*n*2; George Lane, I.327 and *n*4; Borough-Cop Hill, I.344 and *n*5; Stow Hill and Pond, I.344 and *n*3; Sadler Street, I.346 and *n*6; SJ visits in 1771, I.364; on effect of Reynolds's portrait, I.372 and *n*2; SJ visits in 1772, I.397 and *n*2; SJ's plans for and visit to in 1775, II.217 and *nn*4,5, 221, 254, 255; box clubs in, II.224; JB visits, II.309*n*4, 311, 330 and *n*4, III.191 and *n*11, 199–200 and *n*2, 207 and *n*1; SJ visits in 1777, III.20*n*6, 46–47 and *n*8, 48;

barren of entertainment, III.49; work-houses in, III.51 and n7; races at Whittington Heath, III.53 and n9, 55–56; SJ on people in, III.55; SJ visits in 1779, III.160, 165–66 and n2; SJ visits in 1781, III.233n1, 327 and n3, 356 and n1, 360, 362, 377–78; omits visit in 1780, III.296, 303, 308, 327, 336, 345, 349; SJ en route to see E. Aston, III.361; Thrales' visit to, III.365n4; SJ's hopes to visit soon are not realized, IV.22 and n3; SJ's 1784 visit to, IV.167n6, 340 and n1, 352; considers visiting with JB, IV.335–36

Lichfield Cathedral, II.156 and n2

Lichfield Grammar School, I.8n14, 104n1

life, I.199, II.360, IV.254; on looking back upon, I.146; melancholy errands, such is the course of Life, III.361; compared to nature, IV.198

Life of Alexander Pope (Ruffhead), III.295 and n1

"Life of Ben Jonson" (anonymous, possibly Chambers), I.138 and n1

Life of Harriot Stuart (Lennox), I.47n5

Life of Samuel Johnson (Boswell): and J. Hussey, III.148n2

Life of Savage (Johnson), I.32–33 and nn1–6, 35–36 and nn8,9

Life of Swift (Hawkesworth), III.17 and n3, 295 and n3

Lincoln: deanery of, III.359n1, 374, 377

Lincoln Cathedral, II.48 and n9

Linley, Elizabeth Ann *see* Sheridan, Elizabeth Ann Linley

Linley, Thomas, composer, IV.33nn5,6

Lintot, Bernard, bookseller, III.247n1

Lisgow, Tom, II.7 and n8

Literary Club *see* Club, The (Literary Club)

literary critics and criticism, I.92, 149–50 and n2, III.249, IV.251–52; on reviewers, I.107

Literary Magazine, I.138 and nn1,2,4,

160 and nn5,9; and Lennox's works, I.137 and nn5,7

literature and literary scholarship: SJ praises T. Warton for promoting English literature, I.81; schemes of the writer are his property and revenue, I.156; "commentary must arise from the fortuitous discoveries of many men in devious walks of literature," I.162; "Whatever strikes strongly should be described while the first impression remains fresh upon the mind," I.166; establishment of Royal Library, I.307–14; on fundamental premise of theory of biography, I.345–46 and n5; "he who calls much for information will advance his work but slowly," II.127; on dedicating works, III.358, 375; and anonymous authors, III.372; evidence of SJ's interest in scholarship during his last days, IV.445 and n4; *see also* education

Little Hagley, Worcestershire, I.369 and nn3,6

Littleton, Sir Edward, 4th Bt., M.P., III.262–63 and n9

Lives (Walton): and Lord Hailes, II.139 and n3, 145–46; ment., II.150

Lives of the Poets (originally *Prefaces*): beginnings of, III.20 and n9; SJ continues to search for material for, III.43; SJ visits Oxford for information, III.45; SJ's request for *Biographia Britannica*, III.76n11, 93; SJ works on, III.81 and n13, 83 and n2, 93, 122–23, 152 and nn2–5, 228 and n2, 238, 254, 260 and n2, 264, 273, 278, 285, 286, 294–95, 297, 301, 303, 304; and J. Nichols's involvement with *Prefaces*, III.109n1, 319 and n3, 338; SJ requests advance copy of *Prefaces*, III.122 and n2; SJ wishes J. Reynolds to read, III.123; SJ hopes to send JB "Lives" to read, III.143 and n7; and index to, III.145 and n1; revises of

Lives of the Poets (cont.)

Prefaces, III.146 and *n*4; passage from "Life of Smith" included in D. Garrick's epitaph, III.150*n*1; installments of *Prefaces* sent to L. Porter, III.153 and *n*1; JB requests proof sheets of *Prefaces* from F. Barber, III.156 and *n*2; and SJ–Cadell controversy, III.159 and *n*1, 348; SJ refers to first installment of *Prefaces*, III.195 and *n*4; and C. Burney, III.196*n*16; controversy surrounding Milton *Preface*, III.199*n*10; SJ continues work on, III.224–25, 226 and *nn*1,2, 227; SJ objects to designation as "Johnson's Poets," III.226 and *n*1, V.32; *Prefaces* ment., III.229*n*7; remaining "Lives" to finish, III.233*n*5; SJ distracted from work on, III.233, 246; last biography to be finished, III.237*n*9; "I am seeking for something to say about Men of whom I know nothing but their verses," III.237; SJ on progress toward completing, III.254, 296, 297; SJ requests information from R. Farmer, III.257 and *n*1; possible reference to B. Langton's advance copy of *Prefaces*, III.278 and *n*2; SJ on finishing, III.280 and *n*5; and corrections to final proofs of *Prefaces*, III.319 and *nn*2,3; and help of I. Reed, III.319 and *n*3; financial arrangements made for, III.325 and *nn*1–4; second and final installment of *Prefaces* published, III.325 and *n*3, 338*n*1; finished, III.328; holograph manuscripts of *Prefaces*, III.328*n*3; SJ has "load of copy" of *Prefaces* for JB, III.328 and *n*3; officially rechristened, III.338*n*1; title chosen, III.347 and *n*2; set promised to L. Porter will receive one, III.349; SJ wishes to complete gifts to friends, III.350; SJ requests set from C. Dilly, III.355; "generally commended," IV.26; revised editions of, IV.65*n*1, 70, 84 and *nn*3,5, 91; and advertisement to 2d edition, IV.81*n*1; financial compensation for revised text, IV.84 and *n*3, 113–14*nn*1,2

– PRESENTATION COPIES: to George III, III.156 and *n*5; to various friends in Scotland, III.157; to Mrs. Boswell, III.157 and *n*3, 177 and *n*2, 304; dispute with T. Cadell over presentation copies, III.159 and *n*4; advance copies sent to friends, III.289 and *n*1; G. Steevens to receive complete set of, III.343; to M. Prowse, III.344 and *n*3; to F. A. Barnard, III.348; to B. Langton, III.350–51; to W. Bewley, III.353 and *n*1; to T. Wilson, IV.103 and *n*6; to Sir J. Reynolds, IV.115*n*3; to J. Fowke, IV.123 and *n*1; to R. Chambers, IV.123 and *n*1; to W. Hastings, IV.123 and *n*1, 124; revised copies sent to W. Langley and Langley's response, IV.141 and *n*5; to W. Cruikshank, IV.184; to Pembroke College, Oxford, IV.441 and *n*3; *see also* under the name of the specific poet listed below: Addison, J.; Akenside, M.; Blackmore, R.; Broome, W.; Butler, S.; Collins, W.; Congreve, W.; Cowley, A.; Denham, J.; Dryden, J.; Duke, R.; Fenton, E.; Gay, J.; Granville, G.; Gray, T.; Hammond, J.; Hughes, J.; Lyttleton, G.; Milton, J.; Philips, A.; Philips, J.; Pitt, C.; Pomfret, J.; Pope, A.; Prior, M.; Rowe, N.; Sheffield, J.; Smith, E.; Stepney, G.; Swift, J.; Thomson, J.; Waller, E.; Watts, I.; West, G.; Yalden, T.; Young, E.

Lleweney, Denbighshire: Thrale family estate at, II.148 and *n*1, III.251 and *n*6

Lloyd, Rachel (Mrs. Sampson), II.310 and *n*2

Lloyd, Sampson, banker: SJ and JB dine with, II.310 and *n*2; ment., IV.26 and *n*4

Lobo, Father Jerónimo, Jesuit missionary, author of *Voyage to Abyssinia*, 1.143n8

Loch Lomond, II.110

Locke, John, 1.293 and n5

Lockhart, Mr., physician, III.117

Lombe, Sir Thomas, Kt., III.70n4

London, III.90, 119; St. John's Gate, 1.5 and n2; Charterhouse, Aldersgate, 1.10 and n14; Westminster School, 1.10 and n15; Durham Yard, 1.26n1; Mitre Tavern, 1.279 and n6; riots in Oct. 1774, II.15 and n4; Lothbury Street, II.112 and n7; SJ dissuades JB from visiting, II.132–34nn1–4; Middlesex Hospital, II.363 and n3; Hockley in the Hole, Clerkenwell, III.66 and n5; Hoare's Bank, Fleet Street, III.86 and n6; Apothecaries Hall, III.126n3; fire near London Bridge, III.204 and n5; Somerset House, III.250n14; Gordon Riots, III.267–69 and nn1–3,6–10,12–15, 270–71 and nn2–4,7; Argyll Street, IV.91 and n7; Blackfriars Bridge, IV.92 and n3; booksellers shops on London Bridge, IV.271n1

London (Johnson), 1.14–15 and n3, 15 and n2, 16–17 and n3, 18 and n3, 172n5, III.365n6

London, Bishop of *see* Lowth, Robert

London Bridge: booksellers' shops on, IV.271n1

London Chronicle, II.284 and n3

loneliness *see* solitude

Longden, Mrs. Robert: ment., IV.421 and n1

Longden, Robert, II.316–17 and n6, III.81

"Longinus": *On the Sublime*, III.237n10

Longman, Thomas (1730–97), bookseller, 1.40n4

Longman, Thomas (d. 1755), bookseller, ment., 1.41, 110 and n1

— LETTER: 1.40

Lothair I (of Germany), III.3n1

Loudoun, 4th Earl of (John Campbell), II.115 and n29; ment., III.35n15

Loudoun, Dowager Countess of (Lady Margaret Dalrymple), II.116 and n30

Loughborough, II.316n3

Louisa (Seward), IV.412 and n3

Louis XIV, King of France, 1.305–6 and n3

Louis XV, King of France, 1.308 and n3

Louis Xavier Stanislas, (Monsieur) (later Louis XVIII of France): and H. M. Thrale, II.272 and n2

Love for Love (Congreve), 1.374n7

Love of Fame (Young), 1.364n4

Lowe, Mauritius, artist: illness, III.117 and n5; and Lord Southwell, III.313–14; allowance restored, IV.81nn1,2; submitted painting is rejected for Royal Academy's exhibition, IV.121–22, 121 and n2, 135; SJ's evaluation of, IV.213

— LETTERS: III.114–15, IV.1, 81, 154

Lowth, Robert, Bishop of London: ment., III.291 and n9, IV.77n1, 82 and n5

— LETTER: III.286–87

Lucan, 1st Baron (Sir Charles Bingham, 7th Bt.) (later 1st Earl of Lucan), III.84 and n2; ment., III.115, 116n4, 187, 195n3, 209, IV.266n5; trip to Italy, III.204 and n2; SJ dines with, III.213, 251, 253

Lucan, Baroness (Margaret Smith Bingham), III.116 and n4; ment., III.187, 195 and n3, 198, 209, 213, 240, 245, 254; trip to Italy, III.204 and n2; and H. M. Thrale, III.262

Lucan, 2d Earl of (Richard Bingham), III.204 and n2

Lucan (Marcus Annaeus Lucanus): quoted, 1.303 and n4

Lucas, Henry, lawyer and man of letters, III.21 and n3

Lucian, 1.11 and n5

Ludwell, Philip, plantation owner, IV.425*n*3

Lunardi, Vincenzo, balloonist, IV.204*n*1, 407*n*2, 408 and *n*3

Lye, Rev. Edward, etymologist: and his Saxon dictionary, I.231 and *nn*2,4, 250–51, 252–53, 265

– LETTERS: I.250–51, 252–53

Lysandre et Caliste (D'Audiguer), I.132*n*2

Lysons, Samuel, antiquarian and lawyer, IV.336 and *n*1

Lyttelton, 1st Baron (George Lyttelton), poet: death of, II.112 and *n*10; and *Lives of the Poets*, III.233*n*5, 291–92, 292 and *n*2, 294, 295, 300 and *n*4, 301

Lyttelton, Thomas, son of George, II.112*nn*10,11

Lyttelton, William Henry *see* Westcote, 1st Baron

M

Macaria (Delap), III.196*n*13

Macartney, 1st Baron (George Macartney), diplomat, III.213 and *nn*2–4

Macartney, Baroness (Jane Stuart), wife of 1st Baron, III.213*n*3

Macartney, Frances *see* Greville, Frances Macartney

Macaulay, Aulay, son of Rev. and Mrs. Kenneth, II.213 and *n*6, III.112 and *n*5

Macaulay, Rev. Kenneth, II.213*n*6, III.111–12 and *n*3

Macaulay, Penelope (Mrs. Kenneth), II.213 and *n*6, III.112 and *n*3

Macbean, Alexander, SJ's *Dictionary* assistant, I.21 and *n*2, 71–72 and *n*4, III.12, 140; financial plight of, II.207 and *n*7, 208 and *n*1; and index to *Lives of the Poets*, III.145 and *n*1; at Charterhouse, III.333 and *n*1; death of, IV.336–37

Macbeth (Shakespeare): quoted, I.380*n*4,

II.212*n*3; references to, II.64, 65 and *n*15; Jennens's edition of, II.25*n*7

Macclesfield, 1st Earl of (Thomas Parker): trial before House of Lords, V.4 and *n*7

McClure, Captain, sailor, II.104 and *n*5

Macdonald, Sir Alexander, 9th Bt., II.8*n*3, 62 and *n*1, 69–70 and *n*3, 77 and *n*29, 114 and *n*23; SJ and JB visit on Hebridean trip, II.62 and *n*1, 77, 79*n*44, 114

Macdonald, Mrs. Alexander, mother of Allan Macdonald, II.91 and *n*20

Macdonald, Allan, II.90 and *n*18

Macdonald, Elizabeth Diana Bosville, Lady, wife of Sir Alexander, II.8*n*3, 77 and *n*29

Macdonald, Flora Macdonald (Mrs. Allan), II.90 and *nn*16,18, 91*n*20

Macdonald, Florence (Mrs. Roderick), II.75 and *n*22

Macdonald, Ranald (of Egg), II.180*n*3

Macdonald, Roderick (of Sandaig), II.75*n*22

McFarlane, Alexander, II.150*n*8

McGhie, William: death ment., IV.259*n*6

Machiavelli, Niccolò, I.74–75 and *n*6

Mackinnon family of Coirechatachan, IV.73*n*6, 89 and *nn*1,4, 215*n*12

Mackinnon, John, II.80*n*48

Mackinnon, Lachlan, II.79*n*44, 80*n*46

Mackinnon's Cave (Mull), II.106–7 and *n*24

Maclaurin, John, Scots advocate: presented with 2d edition of *Journey*, II.180*n*1; involved with JB in law case, II.349 and *n*3

Maclean, Alexander (14th of Coll), II.278–79 and *n*2; visits SJ, II.278, 281 and *nn*5,6

Maclean, Sir Allan, 6th Bt., (22d of Maclean), II.104–5 and *nn*11,17, 106–7, 214, 365; and lawsuit against Duke of Argyll, III.35 and *n*16, 40 and *n*5

Maclean, Donald ("Young Coll"), ii.91, 93–94 and n37, 101 and n6, 103, 104 and n13, 278 and nn1,2; SJ and JB stay with on Coll, ii.99n2; dances, ii.106n22; SJ on sending gift to, ii.128; death of, ii.153–54 and n1

Maclean, Hector (4th of Muck), ii.92 and n30

Maclean, Hector (11th of Coll), ii.104n13

Maclean, Hugh (13th of Coll), ii.93n37, 101n4, 278n2

Maclean, Isabella Macleod (Lady Muck), ii.92 and n30

Maclean, Sir Lachlan, 1st Bt., ii.105n17

Maclean, Lauchlan (12th of Coll), ii.101 and n4

Maclean, Maria, daughter of Sir Allan Maclean, ii.105 and n15, 106 and n22

Maclean, Sibella, daughter of Sir Allan Maclean, ii.105 and n15, 106 and n22

Maclean, Una Maclean (of Coll), wife of Sir Allan, 6th Bt., ii.104 and n13

Maclellan (clan), ii.74n19

Macleod, Alexander (of Ullinish), ii.92 and n32

Macleod, Alexandra, daughter of Lady Macleod, ii.92 and n31

Macleod, Ann, daughter of Lady Macleod, ii.92 and n31

Macleod, Anne, daughter of 11th of Raasay, ii.70 and n7, 82

Macleod, Catherine, daughter of 11th of Raasay, ii.70 and n7, 82

Macleod, Christina, daughter of 11th of Raasay, ii.70 and n7, 82 and n8

Macleod, Clan of: and SJ's mistaken statement concerning clan supremacy, ii.83 and n11, 203, 206

Macleod, Elizabeth, daughter of Lady Macleod, ii.92 and n31

Macleod, Emilia Brodie, Lady (of Dunvegan), mother of 23d of Macleod, ii.70 and n6, 71, 72, 85, 92 and n31

Macleod, Flora ("The Princess"),

daughter of 11th of Raasay, ii.70 and nn7,8, 82, 84 and n20; marriage of, iii.35 and n15

Macleod, Isabella, daughter of Lady Macleod, ii.92 and n31

Macleod, Isabella-Rose, daughter of 11th of Raasay, ii.70 and n7, 82

Macleod, James, son of 11th of Raasay, ii.70 and n7, 80 and n50

Macleod, Jane Macqueen (Lady Raasay), wife of 11th of Raasay, ii.82 and n5, 84, 203

Macleod, Jane, daughter of 11th of Raasay, ii.70 and n7, 82

Macleod, Janet, daughter of 11th of Raasay, ii.70 and n7, 82

Macleod, John (11th of Raasay), ii.70 and n7, 82 and n5, 89, 90, iv.73 and n5; ment., ii.75n22, 80n48; meets SJ on arrival on Raasay, ii.80; controversy over SJ's mistake concerning clan supremacy, ii.83 and n11, 203, 206, 214, 228–29, 265–66, 281; SJ on sending gift to, ii.128; presented with 2d edition of *Journey*, ii.180n1
  — LETTER: ii.203

Macleod, John (4th of Talisker), ii.81–82 and n3, 93 and n35

Macleod, John, son of 11th of Raasay, ii.70 and n7

Macleod, Julia, daughter of 11th of Raasay, ii.70 and n7, 82

Macleod, Lady *see* Macleod, Emilia Brodie, Lady

Macleod, Malcolm (10th of Raasay) (Old Raasay), ii.83 and n13

Macleod, Malcolm (b. 1711): and Prince Charles Edward Stuart, ii.80 and n48, 83, 90 and n16; ment., ii.88, 203

Macleod, Malcolm, son of 11th of Raasay, ii.70 and n7, 82 and n9

Macleod, Margaret, daughter of 11th of Raasay, ii.70 and n7, 82

Macleod, Maria, daughter of Lady Macleod, ii.92 and n31, 113–14 and n20

Macleod, Mary Maclean, wife of 4th of Talisker, II.82n3, 93 and n35

Macleod, Mary, daughter of 11th of Raasay, II.70 and n7, 82

Macleod, Norman (22d of Macleod), II.75 and n21, 91 and n22

Macleod, Norman (23d of Macleod) (Macleod of Macleod): ment. as head of clan, II.69–70 and n3, 82n3, 84 and n19, 87, 91; SJ thanks for hospitality, II.85; SJ on education and manners of, II.87 and nn2,4; ment., II.92 and n31; SJ on sending gift to, II.128
—LETTER: II.85

Macpherson, Isabel, sister of Rev. Martin, II.80 and n46

Macpherson, James: Ossian controversy, II.168–69, 170, 176–78 and nn2–4,6, 180–81 and nn2,3,5,6
— LETTER: II.168–69

Macpherson, Rev. Martin, II.80n46, 87n1

Macquarrie, Lauchlan (16th of Ulva), II.104 and n7, 365, III.40–41 and nn6,7,10

Macqueen, Rev. Donald, Minister of Kilmuir, Skye, II.93 and n36, 266 and n4; ment., II.203

Macqueen, Lauchlan, II.67n29

Macqueen, Robert see Braxfield, Lord

Macraes (clan), II.74–75, 74 and n19

Maddox, John, lawyer, II.354–55 and n4, IV.76 and n5

Maintenon, Madame de, mistress of Louis XIV, III.277 and n9

Mainz Psalter, I.312–13 and n29

Mallet, David, poet: quoted, IV.188n8

Malone, Edmond: on A. Vesey's election to The Club, II.26n3; ment., II.129n2, III.182n6, 351n1, IV.443n2
— LETTERS: IV.13–14

Mam Ratagan (Ratiken), II.76, 77

Manilius: quoted, IV.308 and n2

Manners, Lord Robert: tribute to by G. Crabbe, IV.117n3

Manning, Rev. Owen, antiquarian, I.231n2

Mansfield, 1st Earl of (William Murray), Lord Chief Justice, II.193 and n3; and Somerset slave case, II.349 and n4; and Dodd case, III.25n3, 27n1; relationship to Sir T. Mills, III.211n4; and Gordon Riots, III.267 and n1, 268 and n7

Manucci, Conte (Giovanni Tommaso), II.325 and n3, 326; to travel to Bath, II.328, 333

Manuzio, Aldo, classical scholar and printer, I.312 and n27

Mara, John, sailor, IV.48–49 and n1, 56

Maria Theresa, Empress, Holy Roman Empire, Archduchess of Austria, Queen of Hungary, I.30n19

Marie Antoinette, II.272 and n2, 275

Marie Joséphine Louise of Savoy (Madame): and H. M. Thrale, II.272 and n2

Marie Stuart Reyne d'Escosse, Nouvelle Historique (Boisguillebert), IV.344n5

Marischal College, Aberdeen, I.389n6, II.58n23

Market Bosworth, Leicestershire, IV.61–62 and n2

Market Bosworth School, I.4n6

Markham, Rev. Robert, Chaplain to the King, III.136 and n1

Markham, William, Bishop of Chester (1771); Archbishop of York (1777), III.7, 136 and n1, 267n1; and Oxford riding school, II.193 and n5, 215 and n3, 300, 303, 304; dismissed by King George III, II.347n10; SJ to dine with, III.3; and SJ's request on behalf of I. De Groot, III.37

Markland, Jeremiah, classical philologist, IV.84 and n7

Marlborough, 4th Duke of (George Spencer): ment., III.3n4

Marmor Norfolciense (Johnson), I.22n3

marriage, I.214, 329, II.32, V.20; on unsuitable or unhappy, I.226–30; on alimony, I.229; advice to J. Taylor after separation, I.242; on an imprudent marriage, v.20

Marsili, Giovanni, poet, translator, botanist, I.155 and n1, 207, III.168

Martial, III.92n3

Martinelli, Vincenzo, Florentine man of letters, I.74 and n5

Mary, Queen of Scots, II.52 and n8, 54n2, 146 and n7, IV.343–44 and n5

Mary of Guise, II.54n2

Mason, Rev. William, poet, biographer: and T. Gray, II.206 and n11; and *Art of Painting*, IV.115 and n1

masquerades: in Scotland, II.8 and nn3,4

Massingberd, William Burrell, Lincolnshire squire: ment., IV.146n7

Materia Medica (Lewis), III.140n3

Mathias, James, London merchant, I.339 and n5, III.233, 336

Matlock, Derbyshire, I.347 and n4, 349 and n3

Maurice, Rev. Thomas, poet, classical scholar, and orientalist, III.170 and n2

Mawbey, Sir Joseph, Bt.: and 1775 by-election, II.212 and nn4,5, 227 and n8, 228 and n3

Maximes (La Rochefoucauld), III.91n10

Maxims, Characters, and Reflections (Greville), I.129–30 and nn4–7

Maxwell, Anne Massingberd (Mrs. William), IV.146 and n7

Maxwell, Rev. William, D.D., reader of the Temple, I.268n2, IV.146 and n7

Mayne, Sir William, Bt., II.44 and n1

Mayo, Rev. Henry, LL.D., clergyman, II.30 and n3

Mazarin Bible, I.313n32

M'Donald, Alexander, II.150n7

Medicinal Dictionary (James), I.25n2, 37n2

medicine: remedy for indigestion and lubricity of bowels, I.120–21; use of balsam of Peru, I.122 and n2; use of bark, I.174, IV.47, 48, 335; and cataracts, I.193; and mineral springs, I.361–62nn1–3, 370, 392n2; suggested treatments for Mrs. Salusbury's cancer, I.361–62nn1–3, 416 and n4, II.18 and n1, 19 and nn1,2, 19–20; use of mercury, I.416 and n4, III.193, 264–65; advice for T. Cumming, II.140–41; advice to B. Langton for rheumatism, II.200–201; diacodium, II.298, IV.12 and n1, 20, 37, 38, 353, 359; ipecacuanha, III.4 and n2, 52, IV.365; treatment for worms, III.49 and n3; musk, III.125–26 and n1, 127–28; valerian, III.140 and n3; bloodletting (phlebotomy) defined in SJ's *Dictionary*, III.167n2; advice on bloodletting for Henry Thrale's illness, III.185, 243, 261, 301n1, 304–5, 306, 307, IV.335 and n1; on nurses, III.194; importance of exercise for Henry Thrale, III.195, 206, 221, 261, 305; diet of whey, III.220–21; avoidance of meat, III.229 and n6, 266; and abstinence, III.243, 261, 263–64; cathartic, III.261; on use of purge (purgative), III.265, 301n1, 304–5, 306; and diet—"the less we eat the better," III.290–91; treatment for E. Desmoulins, III.290nn6–8; importance of sleep, III.305, 307; on drinking a great deal of water, III.371; laudanum, IV.20; and iatrochemical school, IV.38n2; influenza epidemic of 1782, IV.42n1, 43n2; opium, IV.47, 359; use of electricity, IV.71; avoid constipation "costiveness," IV.74; use of calomel, IV.136; use of blisters, IV.153; "blistering ointment," IV.153 and n22; use of salts of hartshorn, IV.153, 157; use of cantharides, IV.155 and n4, 156, 157, 359, 364–65; treatment of testicular sarcocele, IV.196–97 and nn4,6; a trocar, IV.196n3; use of milk, IV.247, 253, medicine (*cont.*)

254, 269; difference between hysteric and apoplectic fits, IV.250; use of carbon dioxide or "fixed air," IV.253 and *n*1; defensative, IV.287*n*1; Pix Burgundica, IV.287 and *n*2; use of *acetum scilliticum* (dried squills and vinegar), IV.292 and *n*2, 348, 352, 356, 359 and *n*1, 364, 365, 368*n*2, 373, 394; *gum ammoniacum*, IV.372 and *n*3; use of turpentine or oil of terebinth, IV.382 and *n*3; diuretics, IV.394; use of decoctions of bran, v.29*n*2; see also health (mental and physical)

Meeke, Elizabeth Allen (Mrs. Samuel), stepdaughter of Dr. C. Burney, III.85–86*n*2

Meeke, Samuel, husband of Elizabeth, III.85*n*2

Mei, C. M., translator, III.378 and *n*5

melancholy and depression: "a greater evil than a disobedient wife," I.229–30; SJ on his own suffering, I.287; advice to J. Taylor on, II.179, 180, 296; advice to JB on, II.265, 299, 348, 349, III.232; advice to Hester Thrale on sorrow and, III.128; reference to "black dog" of depression, III.133, 139, 141, 143, 200 and *n*3; a journey may bring suspense of, IV.191; see also health (mental and physical); Johnson, Samuel—health;

Melmoth, William, poet, essayist, translator, III.249 and *nn*4,6

Memis, John, II.171*n*1, 176 and *n*1, 178, 365

Mémoires du Comte de Comminges (Tencin), I.136*n*2

Memoirs (Stockdale), III.286*n*3

Memoirs for the History of Madame de Maintenon (Lennox), I.150 and *n*3

Memoirs of Maximilian de Bethune, Duke of Sully (trans. Lennox), I.137 and *nn*8,9, III.138*n*1

Memoirs of Miss Sidney Bidulph (F. Sheridan), I.194*n*14

Memoirs of Samuel Foote Esq. (Cooke), III.93*n*11

Memoirs of the Countess of Berci (trans., Lennox), I.136–37 and *nn*1–3,6

Memoirs of the Life and Writings of Samuel Foote (anonymous), III.93*n*9

Memoirs of the Life of David Garrick (Davies), I.285*n*2, III.302*n*5

Memoirs of Watts (Gibbons), III.38*n*3

Memorabilia (Xenophon), III.136*n*5; Edwards's edition, IV.304*nn*2,3, 345–46

memory: SJ on, II.268

Mentelin, Johann, printer, I.313*n*32

Menyies, Mr., tutor, I.168*n*6, 169*n*8

Mercer's Company, IV.131

Merope (Voltaire), I.124*n*3

Merry Wives of Windsor (Shakespeare): quoted, III.92*n*7, 125*n*3, 140 and *n*10

Metamorphoses (Ovid): quoted, I.405*n*1, II.50 and *n*24, 201 and *n*6, III.85 and *n*10, IV.191–92*n*2, 265 and *n*2, 400*n*1

Metaphysics (Aristotle), III.122*n*7

Metcalfe, Philip, brewer and friend of Sir J. Reynolds: ment., IV.86 and *n*1, 232, 316

– LETTERS: IV.75, 438

Meynell, Littleton Poyntz, of Bradley Park, Derbyshire, I.118*n*5

Michelgrove, Sussex: the Thrales' visit, III.306*n*8

Michell, John Henry, scholar, King's College, Cambridge, III.307*n*1

Middle Ages: SJ on, III.355

Middlesex Hospital (London), II.362 and *n*3

Middleton, Lady (Diana Grey Middleton), II.60–61 and *n*7

Milbourne, Luke, poet, III.124 and *n*2

Miles, Mrs. A. A. see Guest, Jane Mary

military camps, III.128–29, 132

Millar, Andrew, bookseller: ment., I.40*n*4, 60, 137 and *n*6; acts as SJ's banker, I.82 and *n*1, 132; and Percy's

Reliques, I.194–95 and *n*3; SJ requests Kames's *Elements of Criticism* from, v.14 and *n*1

– LETTERS: I.71–72, V.23

Miller, Anna Riggs, Lady (wife of Sir John), Bluestocking, III.236*n*7

Miller, Sir John, 1st Bt., III.236*n*7

Mills, Sir Thomas, Kt., III.211 and *n*1

Milton, John: quoted, I.71 and *n*2, III.119*n*6, 139*n*5, 217*n*3, 368 and *n*2, IV.178*nn*1,2, 191*n*4; and *Lives of the Poets*, III.122, 152 and *n*5; attacks on SJ's "Life," III.199 and *n*10

Miscellaneous Observations on the Tragedy of Macbeth (Johnson), I.33*n*6

Miscellanies in Prose and Verse (Jones), I.155*n*5

Miscellanies in Prose and Verse (Stockdale), III.286*n*2

Miscellanies in Prose and Verse (Williams), I.185–86 and *n*3, 279*n*5, III.9 and *n*12, 240*n*1

Miscellany (Lintot), III.247*n*1

Mistakes of a Night (Goldsmith) see *She Stoops to Conquer*

Mistress, The (Cowley), I.374 and *n*4

mistresses, I.213

Mitre Tavern, I.279 and *n*6, II.315 and *n*1

Moisey, Abel *see* Moysey, Abel

Molière (Jean Baptiste Poquelin), III.88*n*3

monastery of St. Edmund, II.272*n*5

monastic life, I.200

Monboddo, James Burnett, Lord, Scots judge, II.266 and *n*4, III.31*n*2, 42 and *n*18, 250; SJ and JB visit, II.57 and *nn*14,16; and *Journey* presentation copy, II.180*n*1, 364*n*2

Monckton, Mary (later Countess of Cork and Orrery), III.251 and *n*8, 258; ment., IV.33

money: on not borrowing, III.71, IV.45; on living within one's means, IV.28; power of, IV.45; SJ warns JB against

debts, IV.72, 362; "pain of borrowing," ment., V.13; on small versus great debts, V.20

Monro, Sir Alexander, Bt., M.D., III.285*n*10, IV.286*n*6

Montagu, Edward, husband of Elizabeth, II.205 and *n*5

Montagu, Elizabeth Robinson (Mrs. Edward), author, letter-writer: ment., II.195, 205 and *n*5, 293, III.3, 27*n*5, 55, 192*n*3, 237, 238, 240, 251 and *n*4, 253, 258, 295, IV.137 and *n*7, 138; and Harry Thrale's death, II.313–14, 315, 322; print of, III.126–27 and *n*3, 157; and *Evelina*, III.130–31 and *n*4; and Hester Thrale, III.228, 249 and *n*4; and G. Lyttelton, III.292*n*2; health of, III.302 and *n*4; informed of A. Williams's death, IV.203, 217

– LETTERS: I.185–86, 189, II.121, 278–79, III.110–11, IV.203

Montagu, Lady Frances (Lady Frances Burgoyne), IV.35 and *n*3

Montagu, George *see* Halifax, 1st Earl of

Montagu, John *see* Hinchingbrooke, Viscount

Montagu, John *see* Sandwich, 4th Earl of

Montagu, Lady Mary Wortley, I.371 and *n*2

Montgolfier brothers, balloonists, IV.204*n*1

Montgomerie, Archibald *see* Eglinton, 11th Earl of

Montgomerie, Margaret *see* Boswell, Margaret Montgomerie

Montgomerie, Mary *see* Campbell, Mary Montgomerie

Monthly Review: and C. Lennox, I.136 and *n*1

Montrose (Angus), II.57 and *n*13

Moore, Edward, playwright, editor, III.249 and *n*7

Moore, William, printer and publisher, III.270–71 and *n*4

Moraes, Francisco de, author, II.309*n*5

More, Hannah, writer and social reformer: ment., IV.33, 412; SJ dines with, IV.51–52 and *n*2, 54, 55; SJ's criticism of *Le Bas Bleu*, IV.297 and *n*1, 317

— LETTERS: III.335, IV.296–97, V.14–15

More, Sir Thomas, Kt., I.112–13

Moret, Chevalier de, balloonist, IV.279*n*2

Morning Chronicle, IV.40*n*3, 41*n*8

— LETTER: IV.43–44

Morrison, Rev. Thomas, I.216 and *n*5

mortality *see* death

Moser, George Michael, Keeper of the Royal Academy, IV.142 and *n*2

Mother's Catechism for the Young Child (Willison), II.150*n*7

Mountstuart, Viscount (John Stuart), eldest son of 3d Earl of Bute, I.271–72 and *n*2, II.328*n*7

Mouseley (Mousley), Mr., neighbor of J. Taylor, I.140, 148

Moysey, Abel, M.D., III.228–29 and *n*5, 235, 261*n*2, 266

Muck, Lady *see* Maclean, Isabella Macleod

Muck *see* Maclean, Hector (4th of Muck)

Mudge, Jane (Mrs. John), I.215*n*2

Mudge, John, M.D.: ment., I.215 and *n*2, 244, II.35 and *n*1; and SJ's testicular sarcocele, IV.196–97 and *n*6, 206, 207, 208, 216, 220, 223–24, 226, 233

— LETTERS: IV.196–97, 206, 223–24

Mudge, William, son of John, SJ's godson, I.215*n*2, IV.197 and *n*8

Mull, Isle of, II.99 and *n*2, 101, 103, 106–7 and *n*24

Mulso, Hester *see* Chapone, Hester Mulso

Murchison, Murdoch, factor, II.76 and *n*27

Murdoch, Archibald (of Gartincaber), II.153*n*1

Murphy, Arthur, I.173 and *n*22, 249*n*1, III.140, 209*n*3; on SJ's *Shakespeare*, I.160 and *nn*5,6; dispute with D. Garrick, II.24 and *n*4, 25; and P. Carmichael, II.124 and *n*1; and copyright case, II.125 and *n*4; ment., II.194 and *nn*8,9, 240; Harry Thrale attends play by, II.323 and *n*2; and S. Foote, III.93 and *nn*9,10; and Lennox-Dodsley dispute, III.138 and *n*1; visits SJ, IV.163; and Essex Head Club, IV.257*n*2

Murray, Alexander, II.315 and *n*1

Murray, David *see* Stormont, 7th Viscount

Murray, James, architect, II.52*n*5

Murray, John, publisher, II.284*n*4

Murray, Patrick *see* Elibank, 5th Baron

Murray, William *see* Mansfield, 1st Earl of

Musgrave, Sir Richard, 1st Bt., II.334 and *n*7, 336, IV.137, 146, 273*n*5

Myddelton, John, of Gwaynynog, Denbighshire, III.68–69 and *n*7, 279 and *n*4

Mysterious Mother (Walpole), III.225 and *nn*1,2

N

Nairn (Nairnshire), II.64

Nairne, Sir William, 5th Bt., of Dunsinnan, Scots judge, III.31*n*2

Narrenschiff, Das (Brandt), I.89*n*3

Natural Method of Curing the Diseases of the Body, and the Disorders of the Mind Depending on the Body (Cheyne), II.257–58 and *n*9

nature: experience of compared to life, IV.198

Naudé, Cardinal Gabriel (Naudaeus), I.313

Neander, Michael, II.129 and *n*2

Neaulme, Jean, I.75*n*6

Needham, John *see* Kilmorey, 10th Viscount

Needwood Forest, I.347 and *n*2

neighbors: importance of being on good terms with, I.140

Nelson, Robert, author, III.158 and *n*3, 159 and *n*2

Nepos, Cornelius, historian, I.12 and *n*6, 217

Nesbitt, Arnold, II.34*n*3; SJ on death of, III.371

Nesbitt, Susanna Thrale (Mrs. Arnold), II.34 and *n*3, 36 and *n*7, III.85, 94 and *n*3, 168*n*1

Netherlands, The, I.309; Seven Provinces, I.240 and *n*12

Newark, Nottinghamshire, II.47 and *n*3

Newbery, John, bookseller: ment., 144, 164, 169*n*1, 170*n*6, 187*n*3

— LETTERS: I.48–49

Newcastle, 1st Duke of (Thomas Pelham-Holles), politician, I.28*n*5, 198*n*6

Newcastle, 2d Duke of (Henry Fiennes Clinton): and Spence's manuscript, III.229*n*7

Newcastle (Newcastle on Tyne), II.41 and *n*5, 51, 68*n*2

Newdigate, Sir Roger, 5th Bt., M.P., I.299 and *n*4, 300 and *n*9, III.254 and *n*9

New Dispensatory (Lewis), III.68*n*3

Newgate Prison: and Gordon Riots, III.268 and *nn*6,9

New Grammar of the Latin Tongue (Clarke), I.217*n*6

newspapers, IV.40; SJ advises L. Porter not to pay attention to, III.181, 220; report SJ's stroke, IV.159; and JB's self-promotion in, IV.195 and *n*5; on robbery at Thrale brewery, IV.234 and *n*2, 235

Newton, Andrew, Lichfield wine merchant, III.51 and *n*5

Newton, Thomas, D.D., Bishop of Bristol (1761–82), I.216 and *n*6, II.6

Nezzy *see* Nesbitt, Susanna Thrale

Nicholls, Frank, M.D., IV.335 and *n*1

Nichols, John, author and printer: ment., I.44*n*5, III.237, IV.114, V.32*n*1; and index to *Lives of the Poets*, III.145; correction to proofs of *Lives of the Poets*, III.319 and *n*3; and revision of *Lives of the Poets*, IV.65–66, 81, 84; and Essex Head Club, IV.257*n*2; SJ hopes for visit from, IV.281, 282; invited for dinner, IV.282; and J. S. Hawkins's proposal for publication of *Ignoramus*, IV.310–11; SJ hopes to hear from, IV.403; entrusted with J. Swinton's letter of "literary intelligence," IV.445

— LETTERS: III.109–10, 116–17, 122–23, 124, 145–46, 152, 224–25, 226–27, 246–48, 260, 277–78, 295, 300, 318–19, 322–23, 324, 338, 343, 347, 350, 379, IV.65–66, 78–79, 81, 83–84, 104, 281, 282, 310–11, 423–24, 445, V.15

Nicholson, Jane, chaperone of Hester Thrale's daughters, IV.337*n*2, 339*n*1

Nicol, George, bookseller: and J. Cook's *Voyages*, IV.332–33*n*2

— LETTERS: IV.332–33, 373–74, 395–96

Nicolaides, Mr., II.213 and *n*3

Nollekens, Joseph, sculptor: and portrait bust of SJ, III.98, 108–9 and *n*3

— LETTERS: II.366–67, III.54

Nollekens, Mary Welch (Mrs. Joseph), II.366*n*1, 367 and *n*3; ment., III.54, 106

Nomenclator Classicus sive Dictionariolum Trilingue (Ray), II.200*n*4

Norfolk Marble see *Marmor Norfolciense*

Norris, Randall, attorney, III.340 and *n*1, IV.95

North, Frederick, Viscount North, politician: stops sale of SJ's pamphlet,

North, Frederick (*cont.*)

 I.356 and *n*2; ministry ment., II.137*n*13, 240*n*6, III.197*n*4; and SJ's *Taxation No Tyranny*, II.184*n*1; proposals concerning American colonies, II.186*n*3; proposes SJ for Oxford D.C.L., II.194*n*7; SJ supporter of, II.212*n*5; ment., III.30, IV.407*n*2; proposes tax increase, III.156*n*3; resignation of, IV.27*n*4, 29*n*4; and free trade to Ireland, IV.65*n*5; and the political situation, IV.68*n*2, 248*n*3

 — LETTER: II.183—84

Northallerton, Yorkshire, II.45, 48

Northamptonshire, I.232*n*7; SJ and A. Williams visit, I.243 and *n*1

Northumberland, 1st Duke of (Hugh Smithson), II.4*n*3, 362 and *n*2; SJ visits, II.45—46 and *nn*2,3, 51—52 and *n*1; and T. Percy, III.113*n*1, 114

Northumberland House: fire at, III.231*n*9

Norton, William, II.222 and *n*2, 227 and *n*8

Notes and Observations on the Empress of Morocco (Dryden), III.120*n*1

Nouvel Abrégé chronologique de l'histoire de France (Henault), II.266*n*7

Nugent, Christopher, M.D., I.265 and *n*13; death of, II.277 and *n*1

Nugent, Edmund, son of Viscount Clare, I.356*n*6

Nugent, Robert *see* Clare, Viscount

Nundocomar *see* Bahadur, Raja Nandakuma

nursery rhymes: quoted, III.92*n*5, 144*n*11

"Nut-brown Maid" (ballad), III.293 and *n*1

O

Observations on the Faerie Queen of Spenser (T. Warton), I.80 and *n*1, 109 and *n*6

Observations on the Statutes (Barrington), IV.240*n*2

Observations on the United Provinces of The Netherlands (Temple), IV.360*n*3

O'Conor, Charles, Irish antiquarian and historian, I.151—52, III.23—24

Odes (Anacreon), I.393 and *n*4

Odes (Horace): quoted, I.343*n*12, 345*n*4, 363*nn*4,5, 381*n*4, II.100*n*2, 194*n*14, III.141*n*12, 143*n*5, IV.47*n*7, 387*n*6

Ode to William Pulteney (Nugent), I.356*n*6

"Ode Upon Liberty" (Cowley), IV.72*n*3

Odyssey, The (Homer), I.92 and *n*3, III.259 and *n*1

Oeconomicus (Xenophon), II.361 and *n*5

Offley Place, Hertfordshire, I.400*n*1

Of Heroic Virtue (Temple), III.219*n*14

Of Popular Discontents (Temple), II.295 and *n*5

Of the Origin and Progress of Language (Burnett), II.57*n*14

Ogilvie, Rev. John, D.D., Scots homilist and poet, IV.115 and *n*1

Ogle, Mr., oboist, I.189*n*1

Ogle, Mrs., I.189 and *n*1

Oglethorpe, Gen. James Edward, II.124 and *n*2; SJ to dine with, II.325

Okeover, Edward Walhouse, II.244 and *n*8

Old and New Testament Connected (Prideaux), II.72 and *n*12

Old Arcadia (Sidney), III.57*n*2

Old Bailey Sessions House, III.268 and *n*9

Oldys, William, antiquarian, I.37*n*2, II.139*n*5, 148*n*7, III.76*n*11

Onslow, Middleton, M.P., II.184 and *n*2

Onslow, Thomas, M.P., II.184*n*2

"On the Death of Dr. Robert Levet" (Johnson), I.138*n*5

On the Principal Prophecies of the Old and New Testament (Hardy), III.315*n*1

On the Sublime ("Longinus"), III.237*n*10

Opie, John, painter: and portrait of SJ, IV.151*n*3, IV.193 and *n*1, III.*frontispiece*

opium: use of *see* Johnson, Samuel—health; medicine

Opus Aureum (Neander), II.129*n*2

Oratio Harvaeana (Lawrence), IV.154*n*1

Ord, Anne Dillingham, Bluestocking, III.242 and *n*2; ment., III.243, 244, 245, 249, 277, 282

Ord, Robert, M.P., Chief Baron of the Scots Exchequer, II.53*n*11

Oriatrike (van Helmont), IV.38*n*2

Origin and Progress of Writing (Astle), III.354*n*1

Original and Progress of Satire (Dryden), III.8*n*4

Original Works of William King (Duke), III.146*n*1

Orkney, Countess of (Mary), III.147 and *n*5

Orlando Furioso (Ariosto), I.83*nn*1,3; quoted, I.92 and *n*2; Hoole's translation, III.323–24 and *nn*4,6

Oronsay, Isle of: echo cave on, II.92–93 and *n*33

Oroonoko (Southerne), II.356*n*1

Orphan of China (Murphy), I.173 and *n*19

Orrery, 4th Earl of (Charles Boyle), III.247*n*2, 248

Orrery, 5th Earl of (John Boyle), biographer and antiquarian: ment., I.55–56*n*3, 80, III.247*n*2, 248, V.31 and *nn*2,3

— LETTERS: I.51–55, 62–64

Orvilliers, Louis Guillouet, Comte d', French naval officer, III.180*n*2

Osborne, Thomas, bookseller, I.37 and *n*2

Osmund, St., I.396*n*8

Ossian: and SJ–Macpherson controversy, II.168–69 and *nn*1,3,7, 170 and *n*2, 176–78 and *nn*2–4,6, 180–81 and *nn*2,3,5,6, 339*n*6; compared to T. Chatterton, IV.14

Ostaig (Skye), II.81*n*52

Othello (Shakespeare): Jennens's edition of, II.25*n*7

Otho, Marcus Salvius, Roman governor, II.259–60 and *n*8

O'Toole, Arthurus Severus Nonesuch, soldier, I.417 and *n*4

Ottonelli, Giulio, scholar, IV.426*n*2

Otway, young boy, II.25

Oughton, Sir James Adolphus Dickenson, II.53 and *n*12

Ovid: quoted, I.211*n*4, 286*n*1, 287*n*3, 405*n*1, II.50*n*24, 201*n*6, III.69*n*12, 85 and *n*10, 143*n*1, 280*n*6, IV.185*n*2, 191–92*n*7, 265*n*2, 400*n*1; banishment of, IV.402*n*3

Owen, Henry, M.D., IV.304 and *n*3, 346*n*5

Owen, John, brother of Margaret, III.326*n*1

Owen, Margaret, cousin of Hester Thrale: ment., III.3 and *n*5, 14 and *n*4, 85, 88, 284–85, 294; health of, III.281 and *n*4; SJ's advice to, III.326–27

— LETTER: III.326–27

Oxford, I.377, II.120 and *n*1, III.90; SJ's 1754 visit to, I.81–82 and *n*6, 82 and *n*1; SJ's 1755 visit to, I.100 and *n*7, 109; SJ's 1759 visit to, I.186 and *nn*1–5, 187; SJ's 1762 visit to, II.216; SJ's 1767 visit to, I.288 and *n*5, 289; SJ's 1768 visit to, I.294*n*2; JB at, I.298*n*4; politics, I.299–300 and *nn*3–5,7,9; SJ's 1770 visit to, I.336; SJ's 1772 visit to, I.413 and *n*2; SJ and JB visit in 1776, II.309*n*4; SJ's 1777 visit to, III.20 and *n*6, 45; SJ wishes to visit in 1778, III.137 and *n*4; and elections, III.254 and *n*9; SJ at Angel Inn, III.361–62; SJ's 1781 visit to, III.361–62; SJ's 1782 visit to, IV.46, 50, 51–52; SJ's 1784 visit to, IV.305 and *n*5, 329, 330 and *n*1, 332–33, 408 and *n*5; *see also* Oxford University

Oxford and Cambridge Miscellany Poems (ed., Fenton), III.247*n*1, 248

Oxford Dictionary of English Proverbs, III.199*n*9, 290 and *n*4

Oxford University, I.8, 156; Christ Church, I.7*n*1, 8 and *nn*8,14, III.136 and *nn*2,3; Peckwater Quadrangle, I.7*n*2; SJ granted M.A. degree from, I.88 and *n*3, 89, 90, 94, 97, 98–100; Oriel College, I.108*n*5, 296–97 and *nn*1,2,4; Charles Viner's bequest to, I.161*n*2; University College, I.244–46 and *nn*3,4,5,8, 297*n*2; Chambers-SJ collaboration on Vinerian lectures, I.276–77 and *n*1, 322*n*3; New Inn Hall, I.293*n*1, 333*n*1; SJ presents Baskerville's *Virgil* to Trinity College, I.323 and *n*5; and riding school affair, II.183 and *n*2, 188, 189, 193, 215, 219, 223, 236*n*4, 246, 260, 268 and *n*1, 293, 300, 303–4; Lord Cornbury's bequest to, II.183 and *n*2, 193; SJ wishes to present *Taxation No Tyranny* to friends at, II.187–88; SJ awarded D.C.L., II.193–94 and *n*7, 196–97; and the Macaulays, III.111–12 and *nn*3,4; Jesus College III.135*n*1; Bodleian Library stairs, IV.418–19 and *n*3; SJ sends his books to Pembroke College, IV.441 and *nn*2,3; *see also* Oxford; Trinity College

Oxford University Press, II.305*n*4, 306

P

Page, Francis, M.P., I.299 and *n*5, 300 and *n*9

Page, Miss: ment., I.218

Paine, James, architect, II.52*n*1

Palmer, Rev. Joseph, nephew of Sir J. Reynolds: and *Cleonice*, II.172–73

— LETTER: II.172–73

Palmer, Mary, niece of Sir J. Reynolds, (later Marchioness of Thomond), III.151*n*2

Palmer, Mary Reynolds (Mrs. John), sister of Sir J. Reynolds, I.215*n*1, II.172*n*1, III.151*n*2

Palmer, Theophila, niece of Sir J. Reynolds (later Mrs. Robert Gwatkin), III.151*n*2

Palmerston, 2d Viscount (Henry Temple): and The Club, IV.164 and *n*4

Pamela (Richardson): and G. Faulkner, I.75*nn*9,10

Pandora's box, I.413 and *n*1

Paoli, Pasquale, Corsican patriot, I.262*n*5; SJ dines with, II.204, 325; ment., II.206, III.9, 115, 115*n*4, 142, 189, 335 and *n*2, IV.134, 136

Paradise, John, F.R.S.: and Essex Head Club, II.194*n*12, IV.257*n*2; SJ dines with, II.194 and *n*12, III.3, 4, 16*n*4, IV.31, 325; ment., II.213*n*3, III.282, IV.122, 139, 156, 185, 186; SJ gives account of his health to, IV.424–25

— LETTER: IV.424–25

Paradise, Lucy, daughter of John, IV.425 and *n*3

Paradise, Lucy Ludwell (Mrs. John), IV.425 and *n*3

Paradise, Philippa, daughter of John, IV.425 and *n*3

Paradise Lost (Milton): quoted, III.119*n*6, 139*n*5, 217*n*3, IV.133*n*2, 191*n*4

"Parallel Betwixt Painting and Poetry" (Dryden), III.276*n*7

Paraphrase and Annotations on the New Testament (Hammond), II.269*n*1, 282

Paraphrase and Annotations upon . . . the Psalms (Hammond), II.255 and *n*2, III.358

parents and parental authority, I.262, 325, II.31–32 and *n*3, V.19–20, 28*n*1; *see also* controversies and quarrels

Paris, III.75; SJ on his trip to, II.271 and *nn*4,6, 272–73, 274–75, 276

Paris, Treaty of (1783), IV.277*n*2

Parker, Augusta Byron (Mrs. Christopher) *see* Byron, Augusta

Parker, Sackville, Oxford bookseller, III.362 and n6

Parker, Thomas *see* Macclesfield, 1st Earl of

Parliament, British: SJ's proposed history of, I.34 and n2

Parliamentary History, III.109–10

Parnell, Thomas, poet, II.73n18

Parr, Rev. Samuel, schoolmaster and classicist, III.7 and n1

Partney, Lincolnshire, I.266 and n2

Paterculus *see* Velleius Paterculus, Gaius

Paterson, Charles, SJ's godson, I.389n1, II.353 and nn1,2; SJ seeks opportunities for, IV.142 and n1, 309 and n2, 313; further requests to O. Humphry, IV.328

Paterson, Samuel, bookseller and auctioneer: ment., II.353 and n1

– LETTER: I.389–90

Patrick, Charles, Hull tradesman, IV.10–12

Patriot, The (Johnson), II.15n4, 155 and nn2,3, 325n2

patrons, I.96, 213–14

Patten, Thomas, D.D.: ment., IV.102

– LETTER: III.356–58

Patton, James, husband of Merrial Docksey, III.215n3

Paul, Lewis, inventor: ment., I.260

– LETTERS: I.24–27, 116, 123, 124–25, 128–29, 130–31, 141, 143–46, V.15

Payne, John, bookseller and accountant, I.47 and nn3,5, 88n6; and Ivy Lane Club, IV.247n1; and E. Johnson's gravestone, IV.350, 435; health ment., IV.380, 389–90, 410–11, 416, 435

Peace of Paris (1792), I.212n2

Pearce, Zachary, Bishop of Rochester, III.131n8

Pearson, Elizabeth (Mrs. John), III.191n9

Pearson, Rev. John Batteridge, III.153 and n2, 191 and n9; ment., III.233, 328, IV.15, 167, 253, 294, 357

Pelham-Holles, Thomas *see* Newcastle, 1st Duke of

Pellé, Mrs., IV.144 and n2; ment., IV.286, 288, 330

penmanship, IV.143, 261

Pennant, Thomas, naturalist and traveler, II.93n36, III.41 and n13, 113–14 and n1

Penneck, Rev. Richard, Keeper of the Reading Room, British Museum: ment., I.295

– LETTER: I.294

Pepys, Lucas, M.D. (later 1st Bt.), III.168n2, 188 and n1, 285, 306n8; and Spence manuscript, III.229n7; and SJ's illness, IV.107, 149, 168 and n1

Pepys, William Weller, grammarian, II.175 and n5, III.341n2; ment., III.213, 235, 258, 282, IV.156

Percy, Anne, daughter of T. Percy: death of, I.352 and n1, 353n3

Percy, Anne Gutteridge (Mrs. Thomas), I.192 and n8, 201 and n2, 231, 243, 253, III.71 and n8

Percy, Barbara, daughter of T. Percy, I.352n2

Percy, Charlotte, daughter of T. Percy, I.352n2

Percy, Elizabeth, daughter of T. Percy, I.352n2

Percy, Henry, son of T. Percy, I.352n2, III.215 and n6; death ment., IV.127

Percy, Rev. Thomas: ment., I.251n2, 411n5, II.50, V.33 and n1; and M. Rolt, I.360 and n1; and O. Goldsmith's epitaph, II.331; asked to help T. Coxeter, II.362–63; and O. Goldsmith's biography, III.10n1; and debate with SJ over T. Pennant, III.113–14 and n1; as Dean of Carlisle, III.132 and n4, 215 and nn4,5; and fire at

Percy, Rev. Thomas (*cont.*)
Northumberland House, III.231 and
*n*9; SJ gives R. Chambers news of,
IV.127

— LETTERS: I.190–92, 194–95, 201,
231–32, 243, 330–31, 352–53, II.45–
46, 362–63, v.16

Percy (More), III.335*n*1

Perkins, Amelia Bevan (2d wife of John,
the elder): ment., III.194*n*1, 334*n*1,
348*n*1, IV.257, 274, 315, 415, 429,
v.17

— LETTERS: IV.271, 276, 333

Perkins, Henry, son of John, III.194 and
*n*1

Perkins, John (the elder), clerk at
Thrale brewery: and Thrale brewery,
II.20 and *n*2, 333–34; and Hester
Thrale's inheritance of Welsh estate,
II.58 and *n*18, 113*n*17; informs SJ of
Harry Thrale's death, II.311*n*1;
ment., III.176, 294, 338; and the management of brewery and negotiations
for sale, III.216*n*2, 305, 331, 334*n*1,
339, 341, 345–46 and *n*1, 348 and *n*1,
352–53 and *n*1, 360; and Henry
Thrale's 1780 parliamentary campaign, III.244, 250–51; and Gordon
Riots, III.269*n*14, 276; health ment.,
III.371 and *n*2, 374; SJ requests coal
from, IV.36–37, 103–4; SJ's advice on
travel, IV.63–64; SJ on an unpleasant
incident involving, IV.163*n*6; SJ
apologizes for not receiving, IV.274;
and money due SJ, IV.315; as SJ's private banker, v.16 and *n*3

— LETTERS: II.152–53, III.15, 348, 352–
53, 356, 360, IV.8, 36–37, 63–64, 85–
86, 89, 103–4, 234, 257, 270, 271,
274, 276, 315, 333, 414–15, 429,
v.16–17

Perkins, John (the younger), III.194*n*1,
360 and *n*1

Perks, Thomas, attorney, I.39 and *n*1,
40*n*3

Perrault, Charles, author, III.61*n*6

Perreau, Daniel, II.334*n*6

Perreau, Robert, II.334*n*6

Perrone, Conte di (Carlo Francesco),
Sardinian diplomat, I.84 and *n*6

Persian Grammar (Jones), II.137 and *n*14

Persian Heroine (Jodrell), III.229*n*8

Persian language, II.136

Persius, Roman satirist, III.358*n*7

Peter the Great, tzar of Russia, II.101
and *n*5

Petrarch: and S. Dobson, IV.147 and *n*6;
ment., IV.390

Petty Fitzmaurice, William *see* Shelburne, 2d Earl of

Peyton, Mrs. V. J., II.207*n*7, 315

Peyton, V. J., clerk: financial plight of,
II.207 and *n*7, 208 and *n*1, 309, 315;
death of, II.315

Phaedrus, fabulist, I.12 and *n*8

Philidor, François, composer, III.144*n*9

Philipps, Sir John, 6th Bt., M.P., I.160
and *n*1, 195 and *nn*2,4

Philips, Ambrose, poet: and *Lives of the
Poets*, III.233*n*5, 257, 278; ment.,
IV.185 and *n*6

Philips, John, poet: and *Lives of the
Poets*, III.152*nn*2,3

Phillips, Anna Maria, singer and actress, IV.140 and *n*3; ment., IV.137*n*6

Phillips, Peregrine, attorney, IV.140 and
*n*2

Philosophical Survey of the South of Ireland
(Campbell), III.23*n*1

Phipps, Constantine John, II.16 and *n*6;
ment., II.118

phlebotomy (bloodletting) *see* Johnson,
Samuel—health; medicine

Phormio (Terence), III.206*n*4

Phraates IV, King of Parthia, I.54*n*12

Pierson, John Batteridge *see* Pearson,
Rev. John Batteridge

Piles, Roger de, artist, author, III.89*n*1

Pindar, I.393 and *n*3, II.8 and *n*1

Pindarick Ode on Painting Addressed to

Joshua Reynolds, Esq. (Morrison), 1.216*n*5

Pine, William, 11.290*n*1

Piozzi, Gabriel Mario, singer, composer, music teacher, 111.375 and *nn*4,5, 378 and *n*5, 1v.322*n*7, 331*n*2, 337*n*2; love lyric composed by, 1v.19*n*1; ment., 1v.32; Hester Thrale on parting from, 1v.175*n*6; Hester Thrale's love for ment., 1v.241*n*5; and Hester Thrale's nervous breakdown, 1v.255*n*1; Hester Thrale's daughters condemn her marriage to, 1v.331*n*2, 337*n*2; marriage to Hester Thrale, 1v.343 and *nn*1,3; effect of marriage on Hester Thrale, 1v.351 and *n*1

Piozzi, H. L., 1v.19*n*1, 54*n*4, 158*n*4; on Bach-y-Graig, 111.66*n*4; on SJ's opinion of Mrs. Langton, the elder, 111.78*n*8; on "Lilly Lolly," 111.79*n*21; on Henry Thrale's stroke and health, 111.168*n*1, 187*n*3; on the Kennedys, 111.169*n*5; on Mr. Head (Mr. Plunkett), 111.209*n*3; on Mrs. Browne of Bath, 111.236*n*6; on SJ's thoughts on remedies and stewed lampreys, 111.239*n*9; and Mr. Cummins, 111.366*n*1; on SJ recommending a "pinch of snuff," 111.375 and *n*3; on the "speaking figure," 1v.331*n*3; and S. Lysons, 1v.336*n*1; *see also* Thrale, Hester Lynch;

Pitches, Sir Abraham, Kt., 111.26*n*5

Pitches, Lady, wife of Sir Abraham, 111.26*n*5

Pitches, Sophia, daughter of Sir Abraham, 111.26 and *n*5

Pitt, Christopher, poet: and *Lives of the Poets*, 111.233*n*5, 254

Pitt, William (the elder) *see* Chatham, 1st Earl of

Pitt, William (the younger), 1v.263*n*3, 291*n*2, 299*nn*2,3, 305*n*2; proposed reforms of, 1v.109*n*1

Plan of a Dictionary (Johnson), 1.94*n*1, 102*n*1

Plato, 11.290 and *n*3, 111.157

Pleaides, The, 1.348 and *n*8

pleasure, 11.133

Pliny (the elder), quoted, 1.371*n*3

Plumbe, Frances (Fanny) *see* Rice, Frances Plumbe

Plumbe, Ralph, Henry Thrale's nephew, 1.209*n*1, 332 and *nn*1,2, 333–34 and *n*3, 338 and *n*1

Plumbe, Samuel, sugar refiner, Henry Thrale's brother-in-law, 1.332*n*1, 333–34, 407 and *n*5, 11.31*n*3, 34 and *n*4

Plunkett, Mr. (called Mr. Head by SJ), 111.209 and *n*3

Plutarch, 1.363*n*2, 111.284*n*4

Poemata Omnia (Johnston), 111.9 and *n*11

Poems (Johnson), 1v.151*n*6

Poems by Eminent Ladies, 1.155*n*5

Poems on Several Occasions (Rowe), 111.227*n*2

Poems Supposed to Have Been Written at Bristol, by Thomas Rowley, 11.332*n*9

Poetical Amusements at a Villa near Bath (Miller), 111.236*n*7

Poetical Works of Mr. William Collins, 11.214 and *n*9

Poetical Works of Nicholas Rowe, 111.227*n*2

poetry: SJ on writing of, 1.3; SJ on Hogarth's epitaph by Garrick, 1.383–85

Polhill, Nathaniel, tobacco merchant, M.P., 111.254 and *n*4

Politian: proposals for printing poems of, 1.5*n*1

Political Account of Ireland (Macartney), 111.213*n*4

Political Tracts (Johnson), 111.325 and *n*3

politicians: SJ parodies, 111.73 and *nn*11,12

politics and the contemporary political situation: "the good or ill success of battles and embassies extends itself to a very small part of domestic life,"

politics (*cont.*)

I.213; and Henry Thrale's campaigns, I.250*n*3, 294–96, 297–98, III.244, 250–51 and *nn*2,5, 252–54, 256, 257, 262, 280–81; SJ's involvement as "fact gatherer," I.259 and *n*3; conflicts in 1774, II.15 and *n*4; on imperial conquest, II.16 and *n*7; dissolution of Parliament, II.151 and *n*1, 240 and *n*6; new Parliament meets, II.156 and *n*1; relations with America, II.186; SJ's concern over stability of English government and success in America, II.250–51; SJ hopes to obtain grace-and-favor lodgings in Hampton Court since he has had "honour of vindicating his Majesty's government," II.319–20*nn*2–4; SJ parodies politicians, III.72 and *nn*11,12; decline in trade, increase in taxation, III.156 and *n*3, 207–8 and *n*4; proposed invasion by Franco-Spanish fleet, III.180–81 and *n*2, 183, 184–85, 191, 193, 197, 207; nation full of distress, III.197; "We who have no part of the nation's welfare entrusted to our management, have nothing to do but serve God," III.207; SJ on economic recession, III.213–14 and *n*8, 220, 221; Contractors' Bill, III.240–41 and *nn*4,5; SJ on honest votes, III.262; Gordon Riots, III.267–69 and *nn*1–3,6–10,12–15; fall of Lord North, IV.27 and *n*4; successor coalition to Lord North's ministry, IV.29 and *n*4; death of Rockingham causes changes and resignations, IV.59*n*1, 60; and Cavendishes and Fox-North coalition, IV.62 and *nn*1,3; Ireland and free trade, IV.64–65 and *n*5; disagreements between Rockingham-Shelburne coalition, IV.68 and *n*2; and Shelburne, IV.74; and W. Pitt's proposed reforms, IV.109 and *n*1; "the state of the Publick, and the opera-

tions of government have little influence upon the private happiness of private men," IV.124; situation in April 1783, IV.124; economic situation due to the American War, IV.217 and *n*10; East India Bill, IV.248 and *n*3, 277 and *n*4; W. Pitt appointed First Lord of the Treasury, IV.263*n*3; dismay and gloomy times in, IV.267; the deleterious effects of political corruption on government, IV.277; and W. Bowles, IV.289 and *nn*2,5; parliamentary tumults have begun to subside, IV.299 and *nn*2,3,6; and JB, IV.305 and *n*2, 306 and *n*3; advice to JB on parliamentary candidacy, IV.306; *see also* American War; government; and under the names of specific events and statesmen

Politics (Aristotle), II.59*n*28

Polly Honeycomb (Colman), I.285*n*1

Pomfret, John, poet: ment., V.32*n*4

Poole, Sir Ferdinando, 4th Bt., III.84–85 and *n*5

Poole, Harriott, daughter of Sir Ferdinando, III.84–85 and *n*6

Poole, Lady, wife of Sir Ferdinando, III.84–85 and *n*5

Pope, Alexander, I.20 and *n*2, and J. Craggs, I.37*n*5; quoted, I.53*n*8, II.106*n*19, III.166*n*4, 188*n*4, 258*n*2, 363*n*3, 374*n*4, IV.12*n*1, 153*n*21, 187*n*6, 192*n*1, 321*n*4, 423*n*5; ment., I.60*n*4, III.89*n*2, 91*n*3; works ment., I.356*n*6, II.272*n*4; and *Lives of the Poets*, III.225 and *nn*4,5, 233*n*5, 237*n*9, 284*n*3, 295 and *nn*1,2, 319 and *n*1, 323 and *nn*1,2, 324 and *n*2, 328*n*3; and Lintot's *Miscellany*, III.247 and *n*1; and translation of the *Odyssey*, III.259*n*1; proofs of SJ's "Life," III.323 and *nn*1,2; and *Iliad* translation, IV.66 and *n*2, 84*n*6; SJ revises biography of, IV.66 and *n*2, 84*n*6

Porter, Elizabeth *see* Johnson, Elizabeth Jervis Porter

Porter, Harry, mercer and wool draper, E. Johnson's first husband, I.22*n*1, IV.444

Porter, Jervis Henry, brother of L. Porter: death of, I.220 and *n*1

Porter, Joseph, brother of L. Porter, I.301 and *n*6, 337–38, 339 and *n*5; ment. as possible recipient of SJ's letters, I.341*n*1, 361*n*1; ment., II.282 and *n*4, III.233, 336; death of, IV.236 and *n*1, 240, 252

Porter, Joseph, uncle of L. Porter, I.43*n*3

Porter, Lucy, SJ's stepdaughter: ment., I.24 and *n*18, 39, 61, 154, 364, 367–68, 372*n*2, 404, II.367, III.45*n*2, 50, 91, 93, 176, 200, 243, 285, 362, 372, IV.240, V.20; and S. Johnson, I.174, 175–76, 177; and S. Johnson's death, I.179–85; "a little discoloured by hoary virginity," I.206 and *n*11, 285; death of her brother Jervis, I.220; and brother's legacy, I.222–24; receives diamond ring from SJ, I.241; SJ visits in Lichfield, I.285, 326–27, 372–73, 379, 380, 397, II.11, 231, 235–36, 254, 258–59, III.55–56, 166, 365, 367, 368; and SJ's portrait by Reynolds, I.372*n*2; has gout in her hand, II.221, 222, 224, 255, 257, 276 and *n*4; health ment., II.226, 229, 255, 269–70, III.48, 58, 60, 87, 167, 365, 367, 368, IV.356–57, 410 and *n*1, 412, 421; ment. of Hester Thrale's gift to, II.226, 257; attends church after long absence, II.234; on prologue for H. Kelly's play, III.49; and Nollekens's bust of SJ, III.54 and *n*2, 98, 108–9; requests investigation of family of J. Patton, III.215 and *n*3, 220 and *n*1; SJ gives account of his stroke to, IV.159; death of her brother Joseph, IV.236,

240, 252; SJ to visit, IV.341; and family gravestones, IV.443, 444

– LETTERS: I.43–44, 118–19, 179–85, 187, 196, 208–9, 263, 274–75, 300–302, 315–16, 317, 318, 337–38, 338–39, II.269–70, 275–76, 281–82, III.97–98, 108–9, 149–50, 153–54, 160, 162–63, 180–81, 190–91, 220, 233–34, 327–28, 335–36, 349, 360, IV.15, 21–22, 122, 159, 167–68, 236, 252–53, 290, 293–94, 320, 341, 356–57, 369, 401–2, 444, V.55–56

Porter, Mary, actress, I.111 and *n*3, 205 and *n*3, 214, IV.229

Porteus, Beilby, Bishop of Chester, II.210*n*14, III.370–71 and *n*4; SJ dines with, IV.31 and *n*3

Port family of Islam, Staffordshire, III.73*n*4

Portmore, 2d Earl of (Charles Colyear), IV.313

Portree, Skye, II.68*n*1, 90 and *n*16

Portsmouth, England, I.215–16*nn*2,3

Pott, Percivall, surgeon: and SJ's testicular sarcocele, IV.196 and *n*2, 201–2, 206, 217, 218, 220, 223, 224, 225, 226, 229, 233, 235; SJ wishes that he be called in again, IV.287

poverty, IV.28, 112, 347; as destroyer of independence and influence, IV.45; a great enemy to human happiness, IV.90

Povoleri, Giovanni, Italian tutor, IV.19 and *n*1

Powell, William, I.320 and *n*3

power: "strongly entwisted with human nature is the desire of exercising power, however that power be gained or given," IV.189

"Prayer for Indifference" (Grenville), III.133*n*4

prayer *see* Johnson, Samuel—religion; religion

Prayers and Meditations (Johnson): ment., I.209*n*3

Prediction of Merlin, the British Wizard (Swift), III.293 and *n*1

Prefaces, Biographical and Critical, to the Works of the English Poets (Johnson) see *Lives of the Poets*

Present State of Music in France and Italy: Or, The Journal of a Tour through those Countries, undertaken to collect Materials for a General History of Music (C. Burney), II.7 and *n*6

Prestwick, Ayrshire, II.123 and *n*2

Price, Rev. John, II.219 and *n*3

Prideaux, Humphrey, theologian, II.72 and *n*12

Priestley, Joseph, scientist, IV.218*n*3

Prince of Abissinia. A Tale see *Rasselas*

printing and publishing: importance of an index, I.48 and *n*2, 75 and *n*7; estimating costs, I.191 and *n*4, IV.323; advice to E. Lye on subscriptions for his *Dictionarium*, I.250–51, 252–53; SJ secures job and forecasts journeyman's wages for W. Davenport, II.197; principles as they relate to Oxford University Press, II.305–8; on organizing collected works, III.18; advice to J. Compton, IV.82; on dedication of books, IV.82 and *n*4; and E. Edwards's edition of Xenophon's *Memorabilia*, IV.304, 345–46; and terms for publication of J. S. Hawkins's edition of *Ignoramus*, IV.310–11 and *n*1; SJ's suggestions for publication of F. Reynolds's *Enquiry Concerning the Principles of Taste*, IV.323; on dictionaries and lexicographic projects, IV.378–79, 390, 425–26; and SJ's dedication for C. Burney's *Commemoration of Handel*, IV.384–85 and *nn*1,14; and Polyglot Bible, IV.395–96 and *nn*2–4; and SJ's *Dictionary*, V.22 and *n*2; see also books; and under the names of SJ's individual works

Prior, Matthew, II.249 and *n*1; quoted, III.195*n*7, IV.220*n*6; and *Lives of the Poets*, III.224*n*1, 224 and *n*2, 228, 254; and ballad of "Nut-brown Maid," III.293 and *n*1

Priory of St. John of Jerusalem, I.5*n*2

Priory of the Canons Regular of St. Augustine, II.55 and *n*6

Proby, Rev. Baptist, Dean of Lichfield Cathedral, III.55 and *n*2

Proby, Mary Russell (Mrs. Baptist), III.55 and *n*3

Progress of Discontent (T. Warton), I.100 and *n*4

"Prologue to *The Conquest of Granada*" (Dryden), III.218*n*10

Proposals For Printing, by Subscription, the Dramatick Works of William Shakespeare (Johnson) see *Shakespeare* (Johnson)

Proposals for Printing by Subscription, Dedicated to the Queen, A New and Elegant Edition, Enlarged and Corrected, of the Original Works of Mrs. Charlotte Lennox, II.201 and *n*1

Proposal . . . to Remove the Nuisance of Common Prostitutes (Welch), II.329*n*9

"Propositions for conciliating the Differences with America" (Lord North), II.186*n*3

Prowse, Elizabeth (Mrs. Thomas), III.297–98 and *nn*1,2,4,5, 320, 344

Prowse, Mary, daughter of Elizabeth and Thomas; see also Rogers, Mary Prowse

– LETTERS: III.297–98, 320, 343–44, IV.46

Prowse, Thomas, M.P., III.297 and *nn*1,2

Prujean, Sophia Aston (Mrs. William), III.148*n*1

Prujean, William, III.148 and *n*1

Public Advertiser: false report of Henry Thrale's death, III.16*n*2; and "Cinna," V.27*n*2

public opinion, IV.367

publishing see printing and publishing

Q

Quarles, Francis, poet, III.5n4, 121n4
quarrels *see* controversies and quarrels
Queeney *see* Thrale, Hester Maria
Queensberry, 3d Duke of (Charles Douglas), II.328n7
Quesnel, Joseph, I.65n1

R

Raasay, House of: and SJ's mistaken statement concerning clan supremacy, II.203, 206
Raasay, Isle of, II.69 and n2, 70, III.41; SJ sets out to visit, II.79; arrival and reception at, II.80, 82; description of, II.88–89
Raasay, Lady *see* Macleod, Jane Macqueen
Raasay *see* Macleod, John (11th of Raasay)
Racehorse (ship), II.16 and n6
Racine, Jean, I.305–6 and n3
Raleigh, Sir Walter, I.44
Rambler, I.57n3, 60nn1,2, IV.77n1, 134n4, 281n4; publisher of, I.47n3; SJ's payment for, I.49n2; SJ apologizes for "trouble" his revisions have caused, I.55n2; Edinburgh edition, I.57n5; SJ requests sets of, III.355; ment., IV.144; and Russian language, IV.284 and n3; quoted, IV.316n5; presentation copies sent to Pembroke College, Oxford, IV.441 and n3
Ramsay, Allan, painter, III.116 and n2, 117–18, 161n2; SJ dines with, III.161nn1,2, 188, 189; goes to Italy, IV.133 and n1; recovers mobility in Italy, IV.189, 285; death of, IV.374–75nn3,5; death ment., IV.388n1
Ranby, John, surgeon, I.23 and n7

Rann, Rev. Joseph, III.100 and n1, 161 and nn1,2, 165
Rape of the Lock (Pope), II.272n4; quoted, III.188n4
Raphael, painter, III.89n1
Rasselas (Johnson), I.178–79 and nn1,2, 5,8,9,11; ment., I.184, 185, II.12n1, III.17n4, IV.273n3; translated into Russian, II.13n7, IV.284n3; translations of, II.13 and nn5–7; Italian translation ment., II.118, III.378n5; copy sent to Pembroke College, Oxford, IV.441
Rasselas: Istoria di Rasellas Principe d'Abissinia (trans., Mei), III.378n5
Ratiken *see* Mam Ratagan
Rational Farmer, The, I.27n4
Rational Inquiry concerning Prayer (Cumming), II.140n1
Rawlinson, Richard, topographer and antiquarian, IV.79n3
Ray, Richard, wood mason, II.23 and n2
Raynes, Henry, Chancellor of the Diocese of Lichfield (1713–34), IV.104n3
reading: as antidote to mental disturbance, I.395, II.265; as prerequisite for intellectual and social life, III.288; SJ has more opportunity for, IV.130
Reading Mercury, I.170n6
reason, II.31–32; compared to fancy, II.134
Reed, Isaac, editor and literary scholar, III.319 and n3
regatta, II.236n3; England's first, II.231 and n5, 232–33, 234 and n1; as conversational topic, II.238–39
Regulating Act of 1773, IV.58nn2,5
Reid, John, sheep stealer, II.150n5
Reid, Miss, I.137
Relation of a Journey begun in 1610 (Sandys), II.269 and n1, 282
religion: and death, I.46, 301 and n2, II.313; and Richardson's *Sir Charles Grandison*, I.79 and n5; SJ differs with H. Boothby on, I.119 and n1; "Chris-

religion (*cont.*)

tianity is the highest perfection of humanity," I.269; and SJ's mother's health, I.174, 176, 177–78; advice to JB on study of theology, "it ought not to be considered a question whether you shall endevour to know the will of God," I.238; and issue of translation of the Bible into vernacular, I.269–71; "studies of the Learned are influenced by forms of Government and modes of Religion," I.309; advice to T. Barnard as he visits a part of the world "divided between bigotry and atheism," I.314 and *n*38; issue of immunities and toleration for dissenters, II.13 and *n*8, 30 and *n*3; on church now cathedral in Edinburgh, II.52 and *n*4; impressions of chapels visited in the Hebrides, II.105–6; on the Jews' annual pilgrimage to Jerusalem, II.133; on fancy and religion, II.134; and death of Harry Thrale, II.311–12 and *n*2, 313; prayer as source of tranquility, II.312; and Dr. Dodd's case, III.29, 32–33; importance of early religious education, III.211; advice to newly ordained preacher, III.311–13; SJ on S. Hardy's religious doctrines, III.315–16; and death of Henry Thrale, III.330, 332, 334, 337–38; "prayer can pass the line and the Tropics," IV.131; *see also* Johnson, Samuel—religion

Reliques of Ancient English Poetry (Percy), I.190–92 and *n*4, 194–95

Remarks on Prince Arthur (Dennis), III.225*n*3

Remarks on the Life and Writings of Dr. Jonathan Swift (Lord Orrery), I.51 and *nn*1–3, 62–63 and *n*3, v.31*n*3

Remarks on the Tragedies of the Last Age (Rymer), III.124*n*3

Remarks upon Cato (Dennis), III.225 and *n*4

Renny *see* Reynolds, Frances

Repington, Gilbert, friend of SJ: ment., I.9*n*5

— LETTER: I.7–8

Repington, John, brother of Gilbert, I.7*n*1, 8

Rerum Scoticarum Historia (Buchanan), II.126*n*4

Revenge, The (Young), III.81*n*6

Reynolds, Elizabeth *see* Johnson, Elizabeth Reynolds

Reynolds, Frances (Renny), painter, sister of Sir J. Reynolds: relations with her brother, I.173*n*21, III.151 and *n*1, v.18 and *n*2; ment., I.244, 321*n*1, 322 and *n*2, 372, 377, II.6, III.108, 198, 302, IV.33, 41; and subscription solicitation, II.201–2; pays condolence call on Hester Thrale, II.322; and O. Goldsmith epitaph, II.344 and *n*3, 345; health ment., III.102; SJ dines with, III.202–3, 209; paints portrait of SJ, III.278 and *n*1, IV.151*n*3, 188; and advance copy of *Prefaces*, III.278 and *n*2, 294; goes to Richmond, III.308; SJ to give set of *Lives of the Poets* to, III.352; failed scheme to sell paintings to Hester Thrale, III.352 and *n*2; SJ's criticism and advice on her *Enquiry Concerning the Principles of Taste*, III. 355–56 and *n*1; IV.30–31, 311, 323, 327; invited to dine with SJ, IV.231, 249–50, 258; invited to SJ's for Christmas Day, IV.261–62

— LETTERS: I.215–17, 246–47, 376–78, II.144–45, 320–21, 322–23, 343–45, 352, III.151, 177, 191–92, 194, 278–79, 352, 355–56, IV.30–31, 116, 186, 190, 212–13, 249–50, 258, 311, 323, v.17–18

Reynolds, Sir Joshua, Kt., painter: financial success of, I.173 and *n*20, 199 and *n*9, 205 and *n*5; relations with his sister Frances, I.173*n*21, III.151*n*1, IV.326, v.18 and *n*2; trip to Devon with SJ, I.206n12, 215n1, 255n2; reputation increases, I.214; ment., I.216 and n8, 376, 377, II.6, 270 and n3, 344, III.14, 67n5, 89n1, 115, 116 and n2, 132, 151n2, 161n2, 202, 244, 250, 302, 308 and n4, IV.75n1, 137, 139, 185, 186, 266, 377n2; health of, I.243–44, IV.87 and n1, 91; and Literary Club, I.251n2, 265, II.126n1; and the Hornecks, I.339n1; portraits of SJ by, I.*frontispiece*, I.372 and n2, III.127 and nn3,5,6, III.134; and O. Goldsmith's death and epitaph, II.146, 330–31 and nn2,3, 344n3, 345–46; drinks too much, II.171; and subscription solicitation, II.201–2; SJ solicits support for E. Allen, II.225, 227; and rumor concerning Harry Thrale's activities before his death, II.322–23; residences of, II.335n2; SJ dines with, II.335, III.3, 4, 198, 290; SJ asks to assist C. Paterson, II.353; SJ desires engravings after portraits by, III.192 and n2; delivers twelfth *Discourse* at Royal Academy of Arts, IV.96 and n7; and G. Crabbe, IV.116–17; SJ appeals to on behalf of M. Lowe, IV.121–22, 121n3; SJ gives R. Chambers news of, IV.126–27; J. Barry's attacks on, IV.135n8; on financial success of Royal Academy's exhibition, IV.136; portraits of the Streatham Park circle, IV.227n5; double portrait of H. Bouverie and F. A. Crewe, IV.239n9; explains *et in Arcadia ego*, IV.239n9; and Essex Head Club, IV.256–57 and n4; involved in negotiation for SJ's augmented pension, IV.342 and n3, 347; SJ gives account of his health to, IV.354; as Painter to the King, IV.375 and n5, 388 and n1, 413n3; and denial of proposed pension increase, IV.398 and nn1,2, 400, 413; on SJ in public (urban) life, IV.428 and n1

— LETTERS: I.243–44, 387, II.330–31,

345–46, 353, III.123, 329, 351, IV.87, 114–15, 116–17, 121–22, 135–36, 142, 195–96, 256–57, 329–30, 341–42, 374–75, 387–88, 407, 412–13, V.18–19

Reynolds, Mary, sister of Sir J. Reynolds *see* Palmer, Mary Reynolds

Rhetorical Grammar (Walker), IV.100n4

Rhudde, Anthony, II.179n1, 322

Rhudde, Mary Wood: and legal dispute with J. Taylor, II.179 and nn1–3, 282–83, 285–86, 296, 302–3, 328, 335, 355

Rhys, John David, grammarian, I.310n13

Riccio, David, favorite of Mary, Queen of Scots, II.52 and nn7,8

Rice, Frances (Fanny) Plumbe (Mrs. John): elopement of, II.31 and n3, 32, 33 and n3, 34n4, 36 and n6, 112 and n7, V.28n1; ment., II.234

Rice, John, II.31n3, 32, 33–34 and n3, 34n4, 36 and n6, 112 and n7; ment., II.234

Rice, Morgan, distiller, father of John, II.31n3, 32, 33–34 and nn3,4

Richard III (Shakespeare): quoted, IV.133n2

Richardson, Rev. James, III.170n3

Richardson, Martha *see* Bridgen, Martha Richardson

Richardson, Robert, Dean of Lincoln Cathedral, III.359n1

Richardson, Samuel: SJ on need of index to novels of, I.47–48, 75 and nn7,9; and C. Lennox, I.59 and n3, 60; ment., I.67n4, IV.160; death of, I.206 and n8, 215; SJ alludes to, II.328n5, III.79, 138 and n2; and H. M. Chapone, III.240 and n2

— LETTERS: I.47–48, 55–57, 69–70, 74–76, 78–80, 93, 132–33

Richardson, William, nephew of Samuel: ment., I.132 and n1

— LETTER: IV.115

Rider, Richard, Chancellor of the Diocese of Lichfield (1734–40), IV.104n3

Rider's British Merlin: quoted, III.139 and n2

Ritter, Joseph, servant of JB, II.65n16, 280 and n4, III.104 and n7

Rivarol, Antoine, author, I.321n1

Rivington, C., printer, III.174n2

Rivington, John, bookseller, I.354–55

Robert brothers, balloonists, IV.204n1

Roberts, Griffith, grammarian, I.310n13

Roberts, James, bookseller, I.33 and n6

Roberts, Judy, niece of Bennet Langton, I.163 and n7

Robertson, Margaret *see* Strahan, Margaret Robertson

Robertson, Thomas, publisher, IV.28n7

Robertson, William, historian, I.281 and n4, 289, II.52, 53n13, 128; and copyright issue, II.129n1

Robin of Doncaster *see* Byrkes, Robert

Robinson, Rev. Richard George, I.303n1

Robinson, Sir Thomas, 1st Bt., politician, I.84n6

Robson, Bateman, attorney, II.58 and n19, III.317, 339

Rochefoucauld, François de la *see* La Rochefoucauld, Duc de

Rochester, Bishop of (1713–23) *see* Atterbury, Francis

Rochester, Bishop of (1756) *see* Pearce, Zachary

Rochester, Bishop of (1774–93) *see* Thomas, John

Rochester: SJ's visit to, IV.165, 173; SJ's return from, IV.174 and n2, 178, 179; SJ on heat in, IV.180

Rockingham, 2d Marquis of (Charles Watson-Wentworth), politician, I.231n1, IV.29n4, 62n3; death of, IV.59 and n1

Roebuck, Elizabeth, friend of SJ: death of, III.48 and n3

Rogers, Rev. J. M., III.297n1, IV.288n4

Rogers, Mary Prowse (Mrs. J. M.): and E. Herne's legacy, IV.288 and n4; *see also* Prowse, Mary

– LETTER: IV.288

Rolt, Mary (Mrs. Richard), I.360

Rolt, Richard, journalist, I.360n1

Roman Catholic Relief Bill, III.268n5

Rona (Skye), II.80, 89

Roper, William, son-in-law of Sir Thomas More, I.113 and n4

Rose, Sarah *see* Burney, Sarah Rose

Rose, William, schoolmaster, IV.185 and n7

Rosmunda (Rucellai), IV.19n1

Rossdhu (Dumbarton home of Sir J. Colquhoun), II.109 and n1

Rothes, Countess of (Jane Elizabeth Leslie), wife of L. Pepys, IV.138 and n7

Rothes, Mary, Dowager Countess of (Mrs. Bennet Langton, the younger): marriage, I.351 and n2; ment., I.356, 374, 381n2, 382, 391, II.326n5, 345, III.9, 37, 67nn5,6, 71 and n7, 125, 142, 351, IV.24, 118–19, 126, 138n7, 200, 225, 313n1, 314, 350, 384, V.25; birth of first child, I.359 and n4, 387; SJ dines with, II.326 birth of Jane ment., II.350 and n7; birth of eighth child, IV.31 and n5

Rowe, Nicholas, poet and playwright: quoted, III.67n10; SJ on obscene epigram of, III.226–27 and n2; and *Lives of the Poets*, III.228, 233n5, 238, 254, 328n3

Rowley, Thomas, fabrication of T. Chatterton, II.332n9, 336n9, 339n6

Royal Academy, III.27 and n4; early exhibitions of paintings lead to formation of, I.199n8; appointment of printer to, II.225 and n2, 227; Nollekens's portrait bust of SJ intended for exhibition at, III.54n2, 108; ment. of 1778 spring exhibition, III.115 and n3; move and official opening of 1780 exhibition, III.250n14, 253; and M.

Lowe's painting, IV.121*n2*; on dinner and 1783 opening exhibition, IV.134–35 and *nn*5,6; 1783 exhibition's finances, IV.134–35 and *nn*5,6, 136 and *n*3; and SJ's godson C. Paterson, IV.142; SJ attends spring 1784 exhibition, IV.320, 321, 324, 418

Royal Library, I.303 and *n*3; advice on formation of, I.307–14

Royal Society, IV.176*n*3

Royal Suppliants, The (Delap), III.196*n*13

Rucellai, Giovanni, poet and dramatist, IV.19*n*1

Rudd, Margaret Caroline, adventuress, II.334 and *n*6, III.59

Rudd, Mary *see* Rhudde, Mary Wood

Ruddiman, Thomas, Scots classicist and antiquarian, I.58 and *n*6, 272 and *n*5, II.126*n*4

Ruffhead, Owen, miscellaneous writer, III.295 and *n*1

Rufus, William, II.48*n*10

Ruggle, George, playwright, IV.310*n*1

Rushworth, Mr., speculator, III.305

Russell, Rev. John, III.55*n*3

Ryland, Honor Hawkesworth (Mrs. John), I.128*n*4

Ryland, John, merchant: and Ivy Lane Club, I.127*n*1, IV.246, 247*n*1, 256; and Hawkesworth project, II.356 and *n*1, 359, III.16–18; SJ gives account of his health to, IV.170–71, 380, 388–89, 410, 429; oversees lettering and placement of E. Johnson's gravestone, IV.348 and *n*3, 350, 430, 435; and Essex Head Club, IV.351 and *n*4, 416 and *n*1

— LETTERS: II.355–56, 359, III.16–18, IV.170–71, 177–78, 350–51, 380–81, 388–90, 407–8, 410–11, 416–17, 429–30, 434–35

Rymer, Thomas, critic, III.124 and *n*3

S

Sackville, John Frederick *see* Dorset, 3d Duke of

Sadler, James, balloonist, IV.438*n*1

St. Albans, II.316*n*3

St. Albyn, Rev. Lancelot, IV.39–41

St. Andrews, Archbishop of *see* Beaton (Bethune), David

St. Andrews, Cathedral of, II.55 and *n*5

St. Andrews, University of, II.55 and *n*3, 56 and *n*10

St. Andrews (Fife), II.55–56; ment. of trip to, II.357

St. Asaph, Bishop of *see* Shipley, Jonathan

St. Cross (almshouse), I.255*n*3, III.36–37

St. Cuthbert, Church of (Darlington), II.49*n*17

St. Giles, Church of (Edinburgh), II.52 and *n*4

St. John, Frederick *see* Bolingbroke, 2d Viscount

St. John, Henry *see* Bolingbroke, 1st Viscount

St. John's Gate, London, I.5 and *n*2, 33*n*2, 141, 146

St. Leonard's College (St. Andrews University), II.56 and *n*11

St. Mary's Abbey (York), II.48 and *n*10

St. Mary's and St. Machar's, Cathedral of (Aberdeen), II.58 and *n*22

St. Mary's College (St. Andrews), II.56 and *n*10

St. Moluag, Chapel of (Raasay), II.89 and *n*12

St. Paul's School, St. Paul's Churchyard, IV.131 and *n*1

St. Salvator's College (St. Andrews), II.56 and *nn*10,11

Salesbury, William, lexicographer, I.310*n*13

Salisbury, Wiltshire: SJ plans to visit, IV.190, 191; Heale House described,

Salisbury, Wiltshire (*cont.*)
IV.194 and *n*3; SJ's trip from, IV.216–17

Salisbury Cathedral, IV.222

Sallust (Gaius Sallustius Crispus), historian, I.12, 221*n*6

Salter, Samuel: death ment., IV.259*n*6

Salusbury family: Hester Thrale inherits property of, II.147 and *n*4

Salusbury, Hester Maria Cotton (Mrs. John), mother of Hester Thrale: ment., I.280, 295, 327, 346, 370, 398 and *nn*1,2, 407 and *n*5, 415, II.7, V.25; death of, I.318–19 and *n*1; health and illness of, I.318–19*n*1, 362*nn*2,3, 366, 416*n*4; home robbed, I.343*n*8, 346, 347–48; health ment., I.364, 373, 378, 399, 402, 403 and *n*4, 404, 408, 409, 410, 412; illness of, II.17–18, 17 and *n*2, 18 and *n*1, 19, 28, 31, 35, 37 and *n*1, 38*n*2; impending death of, II.20–21; health improves, II.22, 23, 24; death of ment., II.37*n*1, 147*n*5; epitaph for, II.215 and *n*1, 220, 221, 223, 229 and *nn*9,10
— LETTER: I.280

Salusbury, John, father of Hester Thrale, I.280*n*1, II.112*n*13, 335*n*4; and inheritance controversy, IV.88 and *n*2

Salusbury, Lady (Sarah Burroughs), wife of Sir Thomas, I.401*n*3; dispute with Hester Thrale over inheritance, IV.88*n*1, 95 and *n*1; Hester Thrale's financial settlement with, IV.318*n*8

Salusbury, Sir Thomas, Kt., uncle of Hester Thrale, I.400–401*nn*1,3, 406; controversy over estate, II.112–13 and *nn*13,15, 114, 117 and *n*1

Samalan, island (Mull), II.106 and *n*21

Sandiland, island (Mull) *see* Samalan

Sandwich, 4th Earl of (John Montagu), II.155

Sandyland, island (Mull) *see* Samalan

Sandys, 2d Baron (Edwin Sandys), II.118*n*8

Sandys, George, colonist and poet, II.269*n*1

Sannaland, island (Mull) *see* Samalan

Sappho, III.8*n*4

Sarpi, Paolo, historian, I.13*n*3, 19–20 and *n*8

Sarum Missal, I.396*n*8

Sastres, Francesco: SJ forgets appointment with, IV.3 and *n*1, 32; ment., IV.99, 158*n*4; SJ to invite to meet C. Lewis, IV.307; ment. of lexicographic project of, IV.378 and *n*3, 390, 406, 425–26
— LETTERS: IV.32, 378–79, 390–91, 406, 425–26, 432–33, 439

Satires (Juvenal): quoted, IV.355 and *n*1, 401*n*1

Saul, Edward, author, IV.218 and *n*3

Savage, Richard, poet, dramatist, I.32–33 and *nn*1–6

Savile, Sir George, 8th Bt.: and Gordon Riots, III.267*n*1, 268 and *n*5

Sayer, Robert, print and map dealer, II.343 and *n*3

Scaliger, Joseph (1540–1609), classical scholar, IV.391 and *n*7

Scarsdale, 1st Baron (Nathaniel Curzon), II.243–44 and *n*1, III.70*n*4

Schoeffer, Peter, printer, I.310*nn*10,11, 313*n*29

scholarship *see* literature and literary scholarship

Scholemaster, The (Ascham), II.48*n*15

science: experiments using sun's rays, IV.161–62 and *n*5

Scotland, I.362–63*n*1, 389*n*7; propagation of Christian knowledge in, I.269–71 and *n*2; Langton's visit to, I.381 and *n*2; masquerades in, II.8 and *nn*3,4; plaids in, II.59; SJ on deforestation in, II.63*n*2, III.41 and *n*11; food in, II.95–96; houses in, II.97; King says not to go there anymore, II.174;

SJ speaks well of "every thing Scotch, but Scotch oat-cakes and Scotch prejudices," II.214; W. Seward visits, III.31 and n2; SJ on introduction of money into the Highlands, III.40 and n8; SJ on JB's feudalism project, III.200; and corrupt electoral system, IV.263 and n5; politics in, IV.291n2; see also Hebridean tour

Scots: on new King's relationship with English and Scots, I.198–99; SJ jokes about, II.330 and n4, 332; Scots angry at SJ's Journey, II.174 and n2; ment. of their writing English well (with specific reference to H. Blair), III.19

Scots "dialect," III.11

Scott, Anna Maria Bagnall (Mrs. William), IV.126n18

Scott, John, poet: death of, IV.404 and n1
— LETTERS: II.142–43

Scott, Mary Anne, daughter of William, IV.126n18

Scott, Susanna Thrale (Mrs. Thomas), IV.89n3

Scott, Thomas, M.P., brother-in-law of Henry Thrale, IV.89 and n3

Scott, William, classicist and jurist: ment., II.41n5, 268 and n1, III.254 and n9, 266, 268; SJ inquires about employment for a young man, IV.117–18; SJ gives R. Chambers news of, IV.126 and n18; SJ gives account of his health to, IV.417–18
— LETTERS: IV.117–18, 417–18

Scrase, Charles, solicitor, I.381 and n5, III.140–41, 195–96 and n11, 206 and n6, 217, 339 and n3; and Hester Thrale's Welsh property, II.240 and n10, 241n5; and brewery finances, II.245 and n10, 257; ment., II.327 and n4, III.188, 219, 274, 285, 294; makes loans to Thrales, III.67n9, 134n9, 241 and n6; health of, III.94–95 and n6, 219, 281 and n3; and Henry Thrale's

will, III.201 and n1, 339, 341; SJ on mind of, III.211

Scripture-Account of the Nature and Ends of the Holy Eucharist (Hardy), III.315nn1–6

Scripture Theory of Earth, The (Worthington), II.175n2

Scudéry, Georges de, poet, I.95n7

sculpture, I.311 and n18

Seasons, The (Thomson), I.150nn3,4

Secker, Thomas, D.D. Archbishop of Canterbury: and Edward Lye, I.231n4, 250

Sedgwick, Henry, childhood friend of SJ, II.297 and n6

Select Collection of Poems (Nichols), III.278n1

self-government, I.200; see also government

Selwyn, Charles, banker, IV.228 and n9

Seneca, philosopher, III.175n3, 354n1

Sententia Minuciorum, II.192, 199–200 and n1

Serious Call to a Devout and Holy Life (Law), I.72 and n7

servants, IV.73

Settle, Elkanah, poet, III.120–21nn1,3,5

Seven Years War, I.139n7

Seward, Anna ("Swan of Lichfield"), poet, I.301 and n5, 317, III.366–67, 370n3; ment., II.234; success of Louisa, IV.412 and n3

Seward, Elizabeth Hunter (Mrs. Thomas), I.301 and n5

Seward, Rev. Thomas, I.28 and n4, 301 and n5, 380, II.333

Seward, William, F.R.S., F.S.A., II.148n8, III.14n4, 31 and nn1,2, 35–36, 68 and n6, 168, 229 and n7; ment., III.310, IV.426; visits SJ before going abroad, IV.147; becomes Hester Thrale's confidant, IV.241 and n5; health ment., IV.412

Shaftesbury, 3d Earl of (Anthony Ashley Cooper), I.24n1

Shakespeare, William, i.135, 256n3, 335; quoted, i.368 and n2, 380 and n4, 381 and n3, iii.77nn5,9, 78n3, 92n7, 125n3, 140 and n10, 212n9, 308n2, 368n3, iv.46n2, 205n6; Jennens's edition of, ii.25 and n7; and *Lives of the Poets*, iii.237n10; for references to works of *see* title of individual work

Shakespeare (Johnson), i.158, 159–60 and nn1–3,6, 255–56, 335n1; SJ's *Proposals for Printing, by Subscription, the Dramatick Works of William Shakespeare*, i.135 and nn13, 140–41, 142, 146–47, 159–60 and n6, ii.201–2 and n2; and E. Hector, i.142, 146–47; terms of contract regarding free sets for SJ, i.153 and n2; ment., i.155, 164; publication date changes, i.158, 159 and n2; appendix, i.162–63 and n1; and T. Percy, i.232 and n8; published, i.246 and n1; and D. Garrick, i.247–48 and nn1,2, 251, 252; and G. Steevens, i.254 and n3, 335 and n3, 354; and J. Tonson, i.254–55; and J. Warton's subscription, i.255; and C. Burney, i.256n3; SJ's protest against discounted sets, i.258 and nn1–3; letters in newspapers on, i.265 and n8; and R. Farmer, i.335n1, 355 and n3; and Johnson-Steevens edition, i.341 and n2, 350–51 and nn2–4; revision ment., i.351 and n1, 356 and n1; and J. Rivington, i.354–55 and n1; SJ requests "sheets" of edition, v.5 and n1

Shakespear Illustrated (Lennox), i.46n1, 56n3, 63n5, 71

Sharpe, F. W., father of Mary, iv.31n6

Sharpe, Mary, friend of E. Carter: marriage of, iv.31n6

Sharp, John, Archdeacon of Northumberland, iii.38n1

Sharp, Samuel, surgeon, i.193 and n6

Sharp, W. (possibly William Sharp, surgeon), iii.38

Shaw, Mr., apothecary or physician: ment., ii.332, iii.300

Shaw, Rev. William, Gaelic scholar, iii.12 and nn3,5, 102, 321n2, 322

Shebbeare, John, surgeon and political writer, v.27 and n2

Sheffield, 1st Baron (John Baker-Holroyd) (later Earl of Sheffield), iv.33n3

Sheffield, Baroness (Abigail Way Baker-Holroyd), iv.33 and n3; ment., iv.36

Sheffield, John, poet: and *Lives of the Poets*, iii.233n5, 254

Shelburne, Dowager Countess of (Mary Fitzmaurice), iii.147 and n4

Shelburne, 2d Earl of, 1st Marquis of Lansdowne (William Petty Fitzmaurice), iv.29n4, 59n1, 62–63, 68n2, 74

Sheldon, John, anatomist, surgeon, and balloonist: and Royal Academy, iv.136n2; ballooning activities, iv.279 n2, 415n1

Shelley, Elizabeth, Lady (wife of Sir John), iii.80n22

Shelley, Henry, husband of Hester Thrale's cousin, iii.80n23

Shelley, Sir John, 5th Bt., iii.80 and nn22,23, 133 and n2, 306 and n8, 308

Shelton, Staffordshire: and Fenton, iii.247n1

Shenstone, William, poet, i.191n4, 195n3; and *Lives of the Poets*, iii.233n5

Shephard, Rev. Thomas (the elder), iv.227 and n3

Shephard, Rev. Thomas (the younger), iv.221 and n9, 227

Shepheards Oracles, The (Quarles): quoted, iii.5n4

Sherard, Bennet *see* Harborough, 3d Earl of

Sheridan, Elizabeth Ann Linley (Mrs. Richard Brinsley), singer, iv.33 and n5

Sheridan, Frances Chamberlaine (Mrs. Thomas, the younger), i.194 and n14

Sheridan, Richard Brinsley, playwright and politician, I.193*n*12; and benefit performance for T. Davies, III.110*n*2; and wife's career, IV.33*n*5

Sheridan, Thomas (the elder), schoolmaster, friend of Jonathan Swift, I.193*n*12

Sheridan, Thomas (the younger), actor and rhetorician, I.193–94 and *n*12

She Stoops to Conquer (Goldsmith), II.9 and *n*8; play rehearses and opens, II.14 and *n*10; G. Colman's concern over, II.25 and *n*5

Sheward, Mrs.: ment., IV.160, 166, 212 and *n*2

Ship Inn (Brighton), III.81*n*7

Shipley, Jonathan, D.D., Bishop of St. Asaph, II.335 and *n*3, III.258 and *n*3; ment., III.245*n*3, 250 and *n*13, IV.31 and *n*2, 96 and *n*2

Ship of Fools (Barclay), I.89–90*nn*3,4

Ship Tavern (Brighthelmston), IV.83*n*1

Shipton, John, surgeon, I.23 and *n*7

Shrewsbury (ship), I.357 and *n*2

Shute, John *see* Barrington, 1st Viscount

Siddons, Sarah Kemble (Mrs. William), actress, IV.96 and *n*5, 228 and *n*8, 232–33 and *n*7

Sidney, Sir Philip, Kt., I.348 and *n*7; quoted, III.57 and *n*2; anecdote about a painter, IV.198 and *n*2

Siècle de Louis XV (Voltaire), III.200 and *n*6

Simpson, Elizabeth Gravenor (Mrs. Joseph), V.20*n*10

Simpson, Rev. Francis, III.171*n*4

Simpson, Jane Adey (Mrs. Stephen), V.19*n*5

Simpson, Joseph, barrister, I.60–61 and *n*3, V.19–21; death ment., I.316; SJ on parental relationship of, V.19–20, 21; SJ's advice on debts, V.20

Simpson, Stephen, father of Joseph, V.19 and *n*5, 20

Sinclair, John, barrister, IV.3*n*1, 4 and *n*3

Sir Charles Grandison (Richardson) see *History of Sir Charles Grandison*

Siris (Berkeley), III.235*n*2

Sister, The (Lennox), III.201 and *n*5

"Skia" (ode, Johnson), II.102 and *n*2

Skye, Isle of, II.62 and *n*1, 69 and *n*2, 71, 77; description of, II.78–79; imprisoned on because of weather, II.86, 87; agriculture and climate of, II.97–98

Skyrmsher, Charles, probable first cousin of SJ, IV.442–43 and *n*2

Slains Castle, Aberdeenshire, II.61 and *n*9

Smalbroke, Richard, Chancellor of the diocese of Lichfield, I.233 and *n*1, II.230*n*1

Smart, Anna Maria Carnan (Mrs. Christopher), I.169–70

Smart, Christopher, poet, I.169*n*1

Smelt, Leonard, Deputy-governor to the Prince of Wales, III.250 and *n*12

Smith, Adam, political economist: ment., II.357*n*3, III.12*n*8

Smith, Edmund, poet: and *Lives of the Poets*, III.150*n*1, 152 and *nn*3,4

Smith, Sir George, 1st Bt., II.222*n*3

Smith, Rev. Haddon, becomes Reader at the Temple Church, IV.238*n*2

Smith, Henry (1724–68), cousin of Henry Thrale, II.132*n*1

Smith, Henry (?1756–89), cousin of Henry Thrale: appointed trustee of Thrale brewery, III.216*n*2; ment., III.316 and *n*1; as executor of Henry Thrale's will, III.330*n*6, 341; ment. as guardian of Thrale children, IV.337 and *n*3

Smith, J. R., engraver: engraving by ment., III.127*n*3

Smith, Jane (Mrs. Henry), II.132 and *n*1

Smith, John, Lord Chief Baron of the Exchequer in Scotland, II.52*n*3

Smith, Joseph, British consul at Venice, 1.308*n*4

Smith, Joseph, ironmonger: ment., 1.350

— LETTERS: 1.334, 353–54, 385

Smith, Lady (Catherine Vyse Smith), 11.222 and *n*3, 230, 111.166; gets new postchaise, 11.229

Smith, Mary (Mrs. Ralph), 11.132 and *n*1

Smith, Ralph, cousin of Henry Thrale, 11.132*n*1

Smith, Richard, Brigadier General, 1v.58 and *n*4

Smithson, Sir Hugh *see* Northumberland, 1st Duke of

Smollett, James, Commissary of Edinburgh, cousin of Tobias, 11.110 and *n*6, 216 and *n*8

Smollett, Jean Clerk (Mrs. James), 11.216 and *n*8

Smollett, Tobias, novelist, 1.187*n*1, 188*n*7, 11.110 and *n*6

Sneyd, John, High Sheriff of Staffordshire, 1.317*n*3

Society for Propagating Christian Knowledge in Scotland, 11.150*n*7

Society of Procurators, 1v.28*n*7

Society of Solicitors, 1v.28*n*7

Sofonisba (Trissino): quoted, 111.378 and *n*1

Solander, Daniel Charles, Swedish botanist, 1.386 and *n*4

solitude, 1.9 and *n*7, 292, 1v.247, 263; "is one of the greatest obstacles to pleasure and improvement," 1.9 and *n*7; SJ on his reclusive life, 1.42; since death of his wife SJ is "a kind of solitary wanderer in the wild of life," 1.90; "where monastic life permitted, every order finds votaries, and every monastery inhabitants," 1.200, "I cannot think it pleasant to live quite alone," 11.71; "be not solitary, be not idle," 11.118, 313, 111.201; "Here sit poor I, with nothing but my own soli-

tary individuality," 11.256; "I live in stark solitude," 111.206; "he who lives by himself has many hours of unwelcome solitude," 1v.211; feels weight of solitude very pressing, 1v.247; could bear sickness better if relieved from solitude, 1v.263; "a man unconnected is at home everywhere . . . or nowhere," v.21

Somerset, James, slave, 11.349–50 and *n*3, 349*n*4

Some Thoughts Concerning Education (Locke), 1.293*n*5

Southerne, Thomas, playwright, 11.356*n*1

South Sea Company, v.4 and *n*9

Southwark: SJ invited to, 11.22*n*2, 26*n*1; Henry Thrale's political activities in, 11.151 and *n*2, 111.254*n*4, 262, 314; Henry Thrale plans improvements at house in, 11.226 and *n*3; Thrales move to, 111.217, 218*n*8, 219; Hester Thrale campaigns in, 111.251*n*5, 258*n*6; Hester Thrale visits, 111.262*n*12; The Clink, 111.276 and *n*5

Southwell, 2d Baron (Thomas Southwell), 11.6*n*2, 1v.81*n*2; and M. Lowe, 111.114*n*1, 313

Southwell, 3d Baron and 1st Viscount (Thomas George Southwell), 111.313 and *n*1, 1v.81*n*2

Southwell, Baroness (Margaret Hamilton) (wife of 3d Baron): SJ's condolences on death of husband, 111.313–14

— LETTER: 111.313–14

Southwell, Edmond, son of 2d Baron Southwell: ment., 11.6 and *n*2

Southwell, Edward, of Wisbech Castle: tutor for, 1.198 and *n*4

Southwell family, 1v.81*n*1

Southwell, Frances ("Mrs. Southwell"), daughter of 2d Baron Southwell: ment., 11.6 and *n*2, 204 and *n*2, 111.251, 253

Southwell, Lucia (Lucy) ("Mrs. South-well"), daughter of 2d Baron South-well: ment., II.6 and *n*2, 204 and *n*2, III.251 and *n*7, 253

Spain, I.200; proposed invasion of Isle of Wight and Portsmouth, III.180–81 and *n*2, 183, 184–85, 191, 193, 197, 207

Spaulding Society, IV.84*n*2

Spence, Elizabeth Fordyce (Mrs. Joseph, M.D.), II.49–50 and *nn*21,22

Spence, Joseph, M.D., II.49*n*21

Spence, Joseph, Professor of Poetry, Oxford, II.53*n*15, III.229 and *n*7, 259 and *n*1

Spencer, Charles *see* Sunderland, 3d Earl of

Spencer, George *see* Marlborough, 4th Duke of

Spencer, George John *see* Althorp, Viscount

Spencer, Lady Georgiana *see* Devonshire, Duchess of

Spenser, Edmund, poet, I.80*n*1, 81*n*4, 88–89 and *n*8, 94

Spicer, John, student, I.8 and *n*8

Sprat, Thomas, Bishop of Rochester, I.340*n*1

Staffordshire, I.363, II.332, III.20, 24, 44, 86*nn*7,8

Staffordshire Canal, I.366–67 and *n*3

Stamford, Lincolnshire, II.47

Stamp Act, I.264 and *n*7

Stanhope, James, 1st Earl, politician, I.37 and *n*4

Stanhope, Philip *see* Chesterfield, 5th Earl of

Stanhope, Philip Dormer *see* Chesterfield, 4th Earl of

Staple Inn (Gray's Inn, London), I.184*n*1

State of the Prisons of England and Wales (Howard), IV.322 and *nn*8,9

Staunton, George Leonard, physician, I.202–3

Steele, Sir Richard, Kt., III.226 and *n*2

Steevens, George, Shakespearean editor: ment. I.254 and *n*3, 335 and *n*3, 354, 355, IV.8, 108*n*2, 168, V.27; and Jennens controversy, II.25 and *n*7; and The Club, II.126–27, 128, 129; and "Rowley" manuscript, II.332 and *n*9; to receive set of *Lives of the Poets*, III.343; ment., IV.8, 108*n*2, 168, V.27; on H. Croft's books, IV.136–37

– LETTERS: II.126–27, 129, III.10

Stephens, Rev. Robert, I.32 and *n*8

Stepney, George, poet, III.146 and *n*3

Stewart, Francis, SJ's amanuensis, I.50 and *n*2, 73*nn*1,3, III.232*n*12

Stewart, Mrs., sister of Francis Stewart, III.232 and *n*12, IV.291, 299

Steyning affair, III.316–17

Stilton, Huntingdonshire, II.47 and *n*2

Stockdale, Percival, author, II.354, III.286–87 and *nn*2–4, 291 and *n*9

– LETTER: V.21

Stockton, Mr., I.41

Stoneham, James, sailor, III.271 and *n*7

Stonehenge, IV.221–22 and *nn*11,13,14, 17

Storer, Peter, attorney, II.3*n*5

Storer, Sidney *see* Hawkins, Sidney Storer, Lady

Stormont, 7th Viscount (David Murray) (later 2d Earl Mansfield), II.271*n*6

Stourbridge Grammar School, I.3*n*2

Strahan, Andrew, son of William, IV.366 and *nn*1,2

Strahan, Rev. George, son of William: education of, I.209–10 and *nn*3,4, 217–18, 219, 220–21, 224–25, 234–35, 248; and neglect of friends, I.224; enters University College, I.244–46 and *n*1; ment., II.87; marriage, III.144 and *n*10; SJ dines with, III.158; relationship with his father, IV.68–69*nn*2–5, 79–80, 95, 105, 110–11; SJ gives account of his health to, IV.420

– LETTERS: I.217–18, 219, 220–21,

Strahan, Rev. George (*cont.*)
224–25, 234–35, 248, IV.68–69, 79–80, 105, 110–11

Strahan, Margaret, daughter of George, IV.420 and *n*1

Strahan, Margaret Penelope Elphinston (Mrs. William): ment., I.45 and *n*4, 72, 246, IV.83, 174, 371–72, 411, 420 and *n*1; illness of, III.230*n*9; at Bath, III.255; SJ's condolences on death of son, III.342–43

– LETTERS: III.342–43, IV.9–10, V.22

Strahan, Margaret Robertson (Mrs. George), III.144 and *n*10, 158, IV.420 and *n*1

Strahan, Maria Isabella, daughter of George, IV.420 and *n*1

Strahan, William, printer, M.P.: ment., I.42*n*1, 66*n*2, 132, 158, 281*n*4, II.354*n*1, III.23*n*1, 34*n*11, 202, 257, 342*n*1, IV.9, 78, 189, 317*n*7, 366 and *n*1, 395*n*1; and SJ's *Dictionary* project, I.50–51, 73 and *nn*1,4, 82*n*1; SJ on proposal for "Geographical Dictionary," I.68–69 and *n*2; acts as SJ's banker, I.82 and *n*1, 397, III.137, 325, IV.433 and *n*1, 442, 446; and *Rasselas*, I.178–79; cost of George's education, I.244–46; SJ gives opinion to on copyright issue, II.129–31; and publication of *Journey*, II.144*n*1, 155, 159; and presentation copies of *Journey*, II.155, 167, 364*n*2; SJ asks to cancel page in *Journey*, II.156–57 and *nn*2,7; asks assistance for two indigent cases, II.162–63; and Ossian controversy, II.168*n*3; and SJ's *Taxation No Tyranny*, II.184–85, 187–88; SJ wishes political evaluation from, II.250–51; and firing of J. Calder, II.293*n*1, 297; SJ offers help with Scots authors' works, II.357 and *n*3; publication of H. Blair's sermons, II.367 and *n*1; quarrel between SJ and, III.123; SJ dines with, III.187, 204; wife's illness,

III.230*n*9; and Gordon riots, III.267 and *n*3, 269, 303; granddaughter ment., III.285 and *n*10; SJ asks for political assistance on behalf of Henry Thrale, III.314; on SJ's cough, IV.46; relationship with son George, IV.68–69*nn*2–5, 79, 95, 105, 110–11 and *n*1; SJ gives account of his health to, IV.83, 87–88, 173–74, 371–72, 411, 442; resigns from Essex Head Club, IV.345 and *n*4

– LETTERS: I.50–51, 68–69, 73, 82, 178–79, 244–46, 397, II.129–31, 156–57, 161–62, 167, 184–86, 187–88, 250–51, 357, 367, III.123, 137, 314, 325, IV.83, 87–88, 95, 173–74, 371–72, 411, 442, 445–46, V.22–23

Strahan, William (the younger), printer, son of William: death of, III.342 and *n*1

Stratico, Simone, mathematician and engineer, I.207 and *n*13

Streatfeild, Anne (Mrs. Henry), III.126 and *n*2

Streatfeild, Sophia, Greek scholar, friend of Hester Thrale, III.116*n*6, 126 and *n*2, 127 and *n*4, 131, 134 and *n*7, 166

Streatham Park, I.284 and *n*3, 307*n*1, 323–24 and *n*3; ment. of "pineapple" and "strawberries and cream," in association with, I.323–24 and *n*3, 343; laboratory, I.371 and *n*1, 376; Thrales move from to economize, I.403 and *n*5; additions and improvements to, II.23 and *nn*2,3, 226 and *n*4, III.52 and *n*4, 253 and *n*1; ment., III.5, 6*n*2, 96*n*3, 177, 379, IV.38 and *n*2; lake dredged, III.52 and *n*4; "now eighth wonder of the world," III.88; SJ praises, III.166; and Gordon Riots, III.269 and *n*14; and SJ's biography of Pope, III.319 and *n*1; Hester Thrale lets, IV.91*n*7; portraits at, IV.227*n*5

Strickland, Cecilia Towneley (Mrs.

Charles), friend of Hester Thrale, II.272n5, 336–37 and n17

Strickland, Charles, II.337n17

Strictures on the Modern System of Female Education (More), III.335n1

Stuart, Col. James, son of the 3d Earl of Bute, friend of JB, III.191n11

Stuart, Rev. James, I.271 and n9

Stuart, Lady Jane *see* Macartney, Baroness

Stuart, John (1713–92) *see* Bute, 3d Earl of

Stuart, John (1744–1814) *see* Mountstuart, Viscount

success: "always produces either love or hatred," I.78

Sulpicius Severus, hagiographer, III.299 and n4

Sunderland, 3d Earl of (Charles Spencer), diplomat, statesman, and bibliophile, I.37 and n6

Suspicious Husband (Hoadley), IV.393 and n4

Sutton, Daniel, inoculator, I.282 and n4

Swan, John, M.D., III.227 and n1

"Swan of Lichfield" *see* Seward, Anna

Swift, Jonathan: ment., I.322n1, III.248n3; and J. Hawkesworth, III.17 and n3; and *Lives of the Poets*, III.233n5, 295 and n3; quoted, III.246n9, 299 and n3, IV.152n15, 336 and n2; and prophecy of Merlin, III.293 and n1

Swinburne, Henry, travel writer, III.213 and n7

Swinton, John, historian and Keeper of the Archives, Oxford, IV.445 and n1

Swynfen, Elizabeth *see* Desmoulins, Elizabeth Swynfen

Sydenham, Thomas, M.D., III.227 and n1

Sylva, or A Discourse of Forest-Trees (Evelyn), I.327 and n5

Sympson, Rev. Thomas, Priest Vicar of Lincoln Cathedral, I.264 and n3

Synod of Argyle, II.150nn7,8

T

Tacitus, Cornelius, historian, III.79n12, IV.145n3

Talbot, Catherine, author, I.67n4

Talbot, Thomas, D.D., II.210 and n16

Talisker (Skye), II.81n52, 85, 93

Talman, William, architect, I.411n3

Tamil literature, IV.127 and n24

Tasso, Torquato, poet, III.117n2

Tatler, The, IV.241 and nn2,3

Taxation No Tyranny (Johnson), II.170 and n3, 173, 174, 184–85 and nn1–3, 320n8, 325n2; changes in, II.185–86 and nn1,4; SJ wishes to present to friends at Oxford, II.187–88; to send copy to E. Hector, II.191; copy sent to J. Taylor, II.192; and Lord North, II.194n7; hostile responses appear, II.197–98 and n3; J. Wesley's use and support of, II.290 and n2

Taylor, Elizabeth *see* Galliff, Elizabeth Taylor

Taylor, Elizabeth Webb, first wife of Rev. John, I.32 and n11

Taylor, Rev. John: ment., I.8 and n5, 368, 403, III.16, 25, 45n2, 53, 55, 59n9, 67n4, 68, 74, 166, 176, 243, 264, 378, IV.152, 232 and n2, 246, 369, 371; health ment., I.77–78, 341, 342, 367, 369, 370, 373, 375, 394–95, 396; marital problems, I.225–30, 232–34, 235–37, 241–42; home and grounds of, I.347 and n3, 371; interest in animal husbandry, I.371, II.235, 244, III.59, 69, 79, 81 and n10, 83, 86, 377; post-chaise of, I.373 and n4, II.310n2, III.68, 70n4; SJ stays with, I.379, 408, 409, II.235, III.46–47, 56, 57–58, IV.340–41; and O'Toole, I.417n4; legal dispute with

Taylor, Rev. John (*cont.*)
M. Rhudde, II.179 and *nn*1,3, 282–83, 285–86, 296, 302–3, 309–10 and *n*1, 321–22 and *n*2, 324, 327–28, 334, 335, 337, 346, 354–55; and boarding of C. Carter's horse, II.236*n*4, 246; ment. concerning the harvest, II.238; hopes to see Thrales at Ashbourne again, II.239; on Henry Thrale's failure to visit, II.247, 251; SJ concerned over health of, II.285, 296, IV.74, 93, 94; SJ dines with, II.325; visits Thrale children with SJ, II.326; and JB's stay with, III.39–40, 56; improvements to house and grounds at Ashbourne, III.58–59, 79, 82*n*17; musical interests, III.59; SJ and JB use chaise of, III.68, 70*n*4; Hester Thrale on, III.79*n*21; SJ on health and diet of, III.154–55, 167, 172, 179–80, 242–43, 264–65, 296, 344–45, 370, 373, 374; SJ tries to find curate for parish of, III.170–71; and selection of new Bishop of Gloucester, III.183; bloodletting, III.242, 243, 261, IV.300, 335; lawsuit of, III.258, 261–62, 265, 296; and St. Margaret's, Westminster, III.259*n*9, 265; and deanery of Lincoln, III.359 and *n*1, 374, 377, V.24*n*1; and Collier inheritance case, IV.16*n*1, 53–54, 56–57, 60, 74, 93, 94, 101, 105–7; and silver coffeepot, IV.18 and *n*2, 60; SJ advises against an uneasy mind, IV.66–67, 335; SJ informs of his testicular sarcocele, IV.201; SJ recommends milk, IV.247, 253, 254, 269; ment. of return to London of, IV.381; SJ gives account of his health to, IV.426; charge of neglecting health angers SJ, IV.427; SJ recommends temperance, IV.427*n*2
– LETTERS: I.4, 28–32, 61–62, 103–4, 139–40, 147–49, 225–30, 232–34, 235–37, 241–42, 248–49, 253–54, 330, 391–92, 394–97, 397–98, 399,

II.10–11, 22, 39–40, 44–45, 122, 135, 151–52, 162–64, 167–68, 179–80, 191–92, 197–99, 214–15, 276–77, 282–83, 285–86, 296–97, 302–3, 309–10, 316–17, 321–22, 324, 346–47, 354–55, III.20–21, 24–25, 154–55, 163–64, 179–80, 182–83, 192–93, 220–21, 242–43, 264–65, 344–45, 359–60, IV.16, 18, 53–54, 59–60, 61–63, 64–65, 66–68, 74–75, 75–77, 93–94, 101–2, 105–7, 108–9, 148–49, 179, 193, 201, 209, 225–26, 237, 243–44, 247–48, 253–54, 260, 269–70, 276–77, 300–301, 312, 333, 334–36, 340–41, 421, 426–27, V.23–24

Taylor, John, Birmingham merchant, I.260 and *n*3, 416*n*2

Taylor, Mary Tuckfield (Mrs. John), second wife of Rev. John, I.61 and *n*4; marital estrangement and legal battle, I.226–30 and *n*1, 232–34, 235–37, 242 and *n*1

Telemachus, a Mask (Graham), II.214 and *n*8, III.9

Temora. An Ancient Epic Poem (Macpherson), II.168*n*1, 170*n*2

Temple, Henry *see* Palmerston, 2d Viscount

Temple, Sir William, 1st Bt., statesman and author, II.295 and *n*5, III.218–19 and *n*14, IV.360 and *n*3; on Ireland, I.151 and *n*5

Temple, William Johnson, friend of JB, IV.70 and *n*3

Tencin, Madame de, author, I.136*n*2

Terence (Publius Terentius Afer), I.12; quoted, III.4*n*1, 206*n*4, IV.372*n*4

Tertre, F.-J.Duport du, Jesuit author, I.150 and *n*2

Tetty *see* Johnson, Elizabeth Jervis Porter

Théâtre des États du Duc de Savoie, I.312 and *n*25

Theobald, Lewis, Shakespearean editor, I.357*n*4, III.166*n*4

Theocritus, I.12

"Thief and the Cordelier" (Prior), III.195 and n7

Thirlby, Rev. Styan, IV.84n8

Thomas à Becket, II.57n12

Thomas, John, Bishop of Rochester, Dean of Westminster, IV.269 and n4, 270 and n6

Thomas, R., bookseller, III.188–89 and n5, 195

Thomas, Rev. Dr., schoolmaster, II.36 and n6

Thomason, George, collector, I.308n4

Thompson, John, cooper: and R. Levet's death, IV.10n1, 11nn4–6

Thomson, James, poet, I.150 and nn3,4; and Lives of the Poets, III.20 and n10, 227, V.32n4; quoted, III.240n3

Thomson, Mrs. Robert Thomson, sister of J. Thomson, III.20n10

Thornhill Mansion, Bromley, Kent, I.130n8

Thorpe Constantine, Staffordshire, IV.185nn5,6

Thoughts on the Coronation (Gwynn), I.201n1, III.45n2

Thoughts on the Late Transactions Respecting the Falkland's Islands (Johnson), I.351n1, 381 and n1, II.155n2, 325n2

Thrale, Anna Maria, daughter of Henry and Hester, III.20n8; birth and death of, I.297n2, 302–3 and nn3,5; ment., II.146 and n10

Thrale, Cecilia Margaretta, daughter of Henry and Hester, III.20n8, 88 and n6, 134n11; birth of, II.340 and n2, III.7 and n3, 162 and n2; health ment., IV.120n2, 134; and J. Cator, IV.163 and n4, 275; effect of mother's marriage on, IV.339n1

Thrale, Frances Anna, daughter of Henry and Hester: birth of, II.151 and n3, 204 and n2; ment., II.221, 235, 252 and n6, III.20n8; health of, II.246 and n5

Thrale, Henrietta Sophia (Harriet), daughter of Henry and Hester, III.134n11; birth of, III.80n1, 162 and n2; on absent friends, III.375 and n5, 378; illness of ment., IV.119 and n1, 120 and n1; death of, IV.134 and n1

Thrale, Henry: introduction to SJ, I.249n1; political career and parliamentary campaigns; I.250n3, 293n2, 296, 297–98, III.244 and n1, 251n2, 254 and n4, 262, 280–81; ment., I.289, 324, 325, 332n1, 334, 346, 371n1, 375, 376, 415, II.6n4, 7, 58, 356, III.5n2, 31n2, 42, 46n6, 52, 54, 58, 62n3, 75n9, 81–82 and n14, 82, 87n1, 88, 91, 93, 95n9, 119, 139, 156, 188, 209n3, 273n8, 276, 281, 285, 372n7, V.25; SJ requests help in securing discharge of T. Coxeter, I.357; and W. H. Lyttelton, I.369n3; and SJ's chemistry experiments, I.371n1; financial problems, I.398n3, 399–400, 407 and n4, III.67n9, 241 and n6; threatened suit against, II.17 and nn1,5, 20; dispute concerning brewery, II.22 and n3; and improvements at Streatham Park and other expansion plans, II.23 and nn2,3, 226 and n4, 249, 259, III.52n4, 67n9, 75–76 and n10, 82; and quack chemists, II.31 and n2, 37; and Plumbe-Rice affair, II.31n3, 33 and n3, 34n4; and his brewery restes, II.36 and n11, III.336, 339–40; SJ wishes his company on Hebridean trip, II.94–95; SJ requests he send money to R. Levet or A. Williams, II.108; to visit J. Scott's garden and grotto, II.142–43; to visit Wales, II.147 and n4, 149n3; political opposition to, II.151 and n2, 154; SJ asks to make H. Heely the "Keeper of the Tap," II.165; entertains constituents, II.165 and n3; SJ requests character reference for C. Carter, II.182–83; and J. Crutchley, II.184n3; improve-

Thrale, Henry (*cont.*)

ments at Southwark, II.226 and *n*3, 229; fails to visit SJ and J. Taylor when in Derby, II.251, 253; trip to France, II.271 and *n*1; visits E. Hector, II.275*n*2; meets L. Porter, II.276*n*3; planned but canceled trip to Italy, II.299 and *n*22, 321, 322; grief of over Harry's death, II.317, 321, 322; after his son's death visits SJ, II.317*n*3; SJ encourages F. Reynolds to pay condolence visit to, II.321; false report of death of, III.15 and *nn*1,2, 16 and *n*2, 19 and *n*1; SJ's letter of "pure congratulation," III.16; and brewery management and finances, III.52–53 and *n*5, 67 and *n*8, 69, 91, 216 and *n*2, 217; visited Lichfield, III.55*n*1; presents *Thraliana*, III.61*n*5; SJ borrows money from, III.71, 72–73, 75; goes to Brighton, III.182*n*7; will being drawn up, III.201 and *nn*1,2; election results, III.254 and *n*4, 314 and *n*1, 318; death and funeral of, III.329 and *n*2, 343*n*1, 344 and *n*1; SJ on death of, III.330 and *n*2, 331, 332, 334, 335, 337, 349, IV.23; and SJ's coal, IV.36; SJ on attention given to him by, IV.125; SJ writes epitaph for, IV.125 and *n*9; Sophia's illness compared to that of, IV.250 and *n*2; SJ gets books for, V.26
– HEALTH OF: suffers from depression, III.126*n*1, 128, 133, 139–40 and *n*1, 141, 143; suffers stroke, III.168 and *n*1, 169, 171–73; SJ's congratulations on recovery from stroke, III.173–75, 264; "keep mind quiet," III.175; activity and exercise recommended, III.175, 195, 206, 209, 218, 305; stroke ment., III.175–76, 179, 182, 183, 184 and *n*2, 190; recovery and improvement of, III.179, 205, 219, 220, 231–32, 233, 239, 265–66, 288, 302; and bloodletting, III.185, 187, 242, 304–5; ment., III.192–93, 206,

257, 296, 299 and *n*1, 309; suffers 2d stroke, III.221 and *n*6; diet, III.229 and *n*6, 239*n*9, 241, 246, 248, 266, 283–84, 288, 294; T. Lawrence and SJ discuss, III.235, 301*n*1; abstinence suggested, III.248, 263–64; SJ's medical advice to, III.304–7; apoplexy ment., III.326–27; SJ warned against "full meals," IV.427 and *n*1
– LETTERS: I.324–25, 357, 378–79, II.99–100, 102–3, 108, 165, 182–83, 338–40, III.16, 45, 173–75, 263–64

Thrale, Henry Salusbury (Harry) (the younger), son of Henry and Hester: birth of, I.280*n*2; ment., I.343 and *n*5, 346, 365, 373, 375, 378, II.217, 221, 229, 240, III.20*n*8; education of, II.24 and *n*1; and his mother's Welsh estate, II.113 and *n*15, 240*n*10, 248; SJ on love for, II.119; owes SJ a penny, II.215 and *n*6; SJ on health of, II.245–46; death of, II.299*n*3, 311–12 and *n*1, 313, 323 and *n*2, III.162 and *n*2, 299*n*2; Conte Manucci and death of, II.325*n*3

Thrale, Hester Lynch (Mrs. Henry): pregnancies, I.250*n*2, 280 and *n*2, 364–65, 368, II.102 and *n*7, 151*n*3, 340 and *nn*1,2, 341*n*2, 341–42 and *nn*2,3, 365; and SJ-Chambers collaboration on Vinerian lectures, I.276*n*1; SJ's concern over health of, I.280, II.213, III.188, 362 and *n*5; IV.26–27, 241 and *n*5, 255, 321–22; and political campaigns of Henry Thrale, I.293, 294–96, 298, III.244, 250–51 and *nn*2,5, 252–54, 256, 258*n*6, 262; and Ladies' Charity School, I.330*n*1; ment., I.382, 388, II.100, III.3*n*5, 15*n*2, 16, 22*n*1, 31*n*2, 42, 45, 58, 99, 109, 157, 288, 328, 352, 360*n*1; and J. Beattie, I.383*n*2; and Plumbe-Rice affair, II.31–34, 36; and SJ and Mrs. Salusbury's death, II.38–39*nn*2,6; and her Welsh estate, II.58 and *nn*18,19, 147 and *n*4, 240 and *n*10, 241*n*5, 248; SJ wishes her company on Hebridean trip, II.94–95; loses uncle's estate, II.117–18; to visit J. Scott's garden and grotto, II.142–43; SJ on birth of son, II.146 and *n*10; fall from horse, II.151 and *n*3, 154; receives advance copy of *Journey*, II.159 and *n*3; assists Carter family, II.162 and *n*2, 162 and *nn*3,4, 195 and *n*2; on W. W. Pepys, II.175*n*5; and Oxford riding school scheme, II.182–83, 187, 188–89, 193, 195, 209, 211, 215, 216, 218, 219, 223, 246, 293, 308–9; given JB's Hebridean journal to read, II.206 and *n*13, 209 and *n*5; attends regatta, II.231–32, 234 and *n*1; anxiety over her children's health, II.245–46, 248, 264–65 and *n*6; and Ralph's death, II.251; and husband's health, II.266, III.187, 188, 195, 198, 205, 206, 209, 211, 218, 229, 235, 301*n*1, 304–7; trip to France, II.271*n*1; visits E. Hector, II.275*n*2; meets L. Porter, II.276*n*3; and Harry's death, II.311–12, 313–15, 316, 319, 321, 322; and Hawkesworth play, II.356; Baretti quarrels with and leaves, II.365–66 and *n*15; death of children ment., III.20 and *n*8; wishes to meet Duke and Duchess of Devonshire, III.24, 25–26; visited Lichfield, III.55*n*1; ancestral home, III.66*n*4; SJ joins at Brighton and returns with to Streatham, III.96*n*3; eye injury, III.102; and Nollekens's bust of SJ, III.108; and husband's stroke, III.167–69, 171–73, 175–76, 184–85; miscarriage, III.182 and *n*4, 183; and Gordon Riots, III.267–69, 270–77; and SJ's biography of Pope, III.319*n*1; reaction to husband's death, III.329–33, 329*n*1, 333–34, 336; and Henry Thrale's will, III.339, 340–41, 340 and *n*5, 345–46; brewery sale, III.348 and

*n*1, 349, 351, 352–53; financial concerns, III.363 and *n*1; and Povoleri verses, IV.19 and *n*1; on R. Chambers, IV.62–63 and *n*8; on health of J. Perkins, IV.63*n*1; dispute with Lady Salusbury over inheritance, IV.88*n*1, 95–96, 98; resides in London, IV.91 and *n*7; and Harriet's death, IV.134 and *n*1; and ballooning, IV.203–4, 235, 272–73; SJ advocates baths for her health, IV.255; suffers nervous breakdown, IV.255 and *n*1; and Piozzi affair, IV.322*n*7; secret marriage plans of, IV.328*n*1; impending marriage alienates daughters, IV.337 and *n*2; marriage to G. M. Piozzi, IV.338 and *n*1, 351 and *n*1; SJ urges to live in England rather than Italy, IV.343 and *n*3; *see also* Piozzi, H. L.

– LETTERS: I.249–50, 281–82, 284–85, 286–87, 289, 293, 294–96, 297–98, 299–300, 302–3, 304–5, 307, 316–17, 318–20, 322, 323–24, 325–27, 333, 336–37, 342–49, 361–62, 364–71, 372–76, 379–81, 398, 399–404, 405–12, 413–14, 415, II.5, 6–7, 16–21, 22–27, 28–29, 30–39, 46–51, 69–84, 87–98, 100–102, 103–8, 109–19, 132, 159, 165–66, 173, 174–75, 186–87, 188–90, 193–95, 204–8, 208–12, 215–18, 219–25, 225–27, 228–50, 251–62, 263–65, 268, 293, 308–9, 310–15, 317–19, 325–29, 331–37, 340–43, III.3–5, 25–27, 45–47, 48–54, 55–56, 60–63, 65–74, 115–16, 126–28, 129–31, 133–34, 138–41, 143–44, 155–56, 157–58, 165–70, 171–73, 175–77, 184–89, 194–96, 198–99, 201–3, 204–6, 208–12, 216–20, 228–30, 235–41, 243–46, 248–55, 257–59, 261–63, 265–77, 279–82, 283–86, 289–91, 294–95, 296–97, 299–300, 301, 304–8, 316–17, 329–33, 333–34, 336–38, 338–41,

Thrale, Hester Lynch (*cont.*)

345–46, 346–47, 361–68, 370–75, 377–79, IV.5–6, 7–8, 12–13, 19, 20, 31–32, 33–34, 34–35, 37–39, 41–42, 42–43, 46–48, 49–50, 51–52, 54–56, 86, 88–89, 95–99, 100–101, 107, 118–20, 134–35, 136–37, 145–48, 150–53, 154–58, 159–64, 165–66, 168–69, 171–72, 174–75, 184–86, 187–88, 191–92, 203–5, 207, 216–17, 219–22, 228–30, 232–33, 234–35, 238–40, 245–46, 248–49, 250, 254–55, 258–59, 264–67, 272–73, 275–76, 283–84, 292–93, 294–95, 297–98, 315–20, 321–22, 325–26, 328–29, 334, 336–37, 338, 343–44, V.25–31

Thrale, Hester Maria (Queeney; also "Miss"), daughter of Henry and Hester: ment., I.209$n1$, 295, 320, 343, 346, 362$n4$, 370, 373, 375, 376, 408, 409, 411, II.24, 166 and $n2$, 180, 217, 226, 229, 275$n2$, 328, III.14 and $n4$, 20$n8$, 26 and $n3$, 27 and $n8$, 45, 49, 50, 55, 62, 82, 94, 134$n11$, 141, 143, 205, 229, 238, 244, 254, 257, 262, 270, 273, 276, 281, 285, 306, 328, 329$n1$, 332, 337, 364, 371, 375, IV.35, 38, 41, 55, 163, 185; smallpox inoculation, I.282 and $nn3,4$; cabinet of, I.403 and $n1$, 409–10, 412, 415, II.112, 118, 218; birthday ment., II.75 and $n24$; letters from and lack of letters from ment., II.112, 252, 254, 333 and $n2$, 336, III.51, 53, 143, 167, 202, 205 and $n1$, 219, 236, 297, 299, 364–65 and $n2$, 365, 367, IV.169, 298, 316–17, 318 and $n7$, 325; studies Italian with G. Baretti, II.118 and $n5$, 151, 218 and $n6$; health of, II.189 and $n7$, 245–46, 313 and $n1$, 314–15, 317 and $n1$, IV.52; and guinea hen, II.228 and $n2$, 241; trip to France, II.271$n1$; attracts attention of French royalty, II.272 and $n2$, 275; meets L. Porter,

II.276$n3$; leaves for Bath after Harry's death, II.314$n1$, 316; growth of, III.65; 13th birthday, III.68 and $n1$, 98 and $n5$; dancing and dancing lessons ment., III.82, 84 and $n3$, 209, 218; Latin lessons, III.173 and $n6$, 195, 294; ment. as "youngling," III.188 and $n3$, 199, 202; and estate of Crowmarsh, III.201$n2$; SJ requests his watch be sent by, III.222; SJ gives advice on life, III.234–35, 288–89; sore eyes, III.248 and $n2$; music lessons, III.248 and $n3$; SJ on her father's death, III.342; SJ on captiousness of, III.369–70; and J. Crutchley, III.372 and $n7$; moves to London, IV.91 and $n7$; SJ urges study of arithmetic, IV.133, 138, 142–43; SJ's warning against idleness, IV.180–81; anecdote of, IV.194 and $n2$; opposition and reaction to mother's marriage, IV.331$n2$, 337 and $n2$, 339–40 and $n1$; and "speaking figure," IV.331 and $n3$; SJ on her mother's marriage, IV.339; to live with J. Cator, IV.339$n1$; SJ's two maxims for, IV.367

– LETTERS: I.378, 404, 412, III.58–60, 128–29, 212–14, 222, 234–35, 256, 287–89, 309–10, 341–42, 369–70, 376–77, IV.99, 114, 133, 138–39, 142–43, 180–81, 189, 194–95, 211–12, 227–28, 260–61, 278–80, 330–31, 337–38, 339–40, 367, 391–92, V.24–25

Thrale, Lucy Elizabeth, daughter of Henry and Hester: ment. as SJ's godchild, I.302$n4$, 324–25, 326, 327, 349; birth of, I.324 and $n4$; ment., I.343, 346, 362$n4$, 365, 376, 404, 412, II.98, 146 and $n10$; illness and death of, II.114 and $n21$, 119, 147$n5$, III.20$n8$

Thrale, Penelope, daughter of Henry and Hester, II.146 and $n10$, III.20$n8$

Thrale, Ralph, son of Henry and Hester: godfathers of, I.369$n3$, II.118$n8$;

birth of, II.102n7, 119, 146 and n10; sent to Brighton because of ill health, II.207 and n5, 241n4; health of, II.217, 221, 228, 233, 237, 239 and nn4,5, 241, 245, 248; death of, II.239n5, 248n4, 251, III.20n8; godmother of, v.31n2

Thrale, Sophia (Sophy), daughter of Henry and Hester: birth of, I.365 and n5, 367, 368, 369–70; ment., II.146 and n10, 229, III.20n8, 134n11, 244–45 and n2, IV.175; health of, II.246 and n5, 264 and n6; SJ visits, II.326 and n1; and Brighton, III.165 and n4, 281n1; writes verses, III.295 and n8; living in London, IV.91 and n7; ment. of letters to and from, IV.169, 174, 233, 235, 259, 318, 325; SJ on mathemathical and scientific proficiency of, IV.175–76, 254–55; story of ment., IV.185, 189; illness of, IV.245–46 and n1, 249 and n2, 250, 254; health ment., IV.293, 295, 298, 302; opposed to mother's marriage, IV.331n2, 337 and n2; effect of mother's marriage on, IV.339n1
– LETTER: IV.175–76

Thrale, Susanna Arabella (Susy), daughter of Henry and Hester: birth of, I.343 and n6, III.119; ment., I.346, 349, 370, II.146 and n10, 229, III.20n8, 134n11, 143; SJ on health of, II.246; SJ's "little girl," II.252; SJ visits, II.326 and n1; godfather of, III.53n8; SJ defender of, III.80 and n3, 141, 366–67; and Brighton, III.165 and n4, 281n1; with SJ at C. Burney's home, III.244–45 and n2; writes verses, III.295 and n8; living in London, IV.91 and n7; ment. of letters to and from, IV.139, 146, 153, 169, 174, 233 and n11, 235, 259, 293, 295, 325; SJ on gluttony, IV.181–82; opposition and reaction to mother's marriage, IV.331n2, 337 and n2, 339n1

– LETTERS: IV.169–70, 181–82, 197–98, 240–42, 301–2

Thrale brewery, II.20n2, 23 and n5, 115, 242n4, 245n10, 333–34; and restes, II.36 and n11, 257, 336, 339–40, 440; need for male heirs, II.365

Thrale family: F. Reynolds inquires after health of, II.344n1, 345

Thraliana, III.61 and n5; ment., III.66

Three Crowns Inn, Lichfield, I.222–23 and n6

"Three Warnings, The" (poem, Thrale), III.240 and n1

Thuanus, Jacques-Auguste see De Thou, Jacques-Auguste

Thurloe, John, secretary of Oliver Cromwell, I.30 and n21

Thurlow, Edward Thurlow, Lord, 1st Baron, Lord Chancellor: and J. Taylor's lawsuit, II.321–22 and n3, 324 and n4, 346 and n5, 354 and n2; ment., III.333n1; involved in request for increase in SJ's pension, IV.342 and n3, 398 and nn1,2, 413; SJ on denial of pension increase but on personal gratitude to, IV.399–400
– LETTER: IV.399–400

Tibullus, Albius: quoted, II.194n14, IV.353n10

Tighe, Edward, Irish lawyer, II.175 and n6

time: on tomorrow, I.110; importance of trifles in whiling away, I.199; "Time cannot be always defeated, but let us not yield till we are conquered," II.301; and quarter-days, III.95n12; SJ on, IV.147; "the opiate of musing idleness," IV.180–81; on futurity, IV.294–95

Tiridates II, Arsacid prince, I.54 and n12

"To Fortune" (Thomson), III.240n3

Tolcher, Henry, alderman of Portsmouth, I.215–16 and n3

Toleration Act of (1778), III.267n1

"To Miss Aurelia C — R: on her Weeping at her Sister's Wedding" (Collins), III.227nn1,2

Tomkison, Mr., IV.213

"To Mr. Cyriack Skinner Upon his Blindness" (Milton): quoted, III.368n2

Tom Thumb the Great (Fielding), I.380n3

"To my Honour'd Kinsman, John Driden of Chesterton" (Dryden): quoted, III.205n6

To the Honor of the Noble Captaine O'Toole (Taylor), I.417n4

Tonson, Jacob, the younger, publisher: ment., I.129n4, 153n2, 260, 274 and n1; and SJ's finances, I.274 and n1

– LETTERS: I.158, 254–55, 257–58

Tonson, Richard, publisher, I.129n4

Tooke, William, historian, IV.284 and n2

Topsell, Edward, author, I.22 and n3

Torrington, Devonshire, I.215–16nn1, 4

Tour in Scotland and Voyage to the Hebrides (Pennant), II.93n36, III.41n13, 113n1

Tour of Ireland, A (Twiss), II.205n4, 334

Tour Through Some of the Northern Parts of Europe (Wraxall), II.209–10 and n12

Towers, Joseph, miscellaneous writer, III.76n11

Townley, Charles, engraver, III.192n3

Trapaud, Alexander, Governor of Fort Augustus, II.66 and n23, III.142n6

travel, II.50 and n28, 94–95; "the use of travelling is to regulate imagination by reality," II.78; advice for long journey, IV.63–64

Traveller, The (Goldsmith), III.230n1; quoted, II.229n8

Travels in Asia Minor (Chandler), II.209 and n9

Travels through Portugal and Spain (Twiss), II.204 and n3, 209

Travels through Spain (Swinburne), III.213n7

Treatise of English Particles (Walker), I.221 and n5

Treatise on a Consumption of the Lungs . . . and of the Structure and Use of the Lungs (Barry), IV.266n6

Treatise on Asthma (Floyer), IV.303n6

Treatise on Opium (Young), I.72 and n5

Trinity College, Oxford, I.11n1; SJ presents Baskerville's *Virgil* to, I.105n6, 323 and n5; Kettell Hall, I.108n5

Trissino, Giangiorgio, playwright, III.378n1

Tristia (Ovid), IV.402n3; quoted, IV.400n1

Tuam, Archbishop of *see* Bourke, Joseph Dean

Tuckfield, John, M.P., I.227, 229 and n5, 242n1

Tully *see* Cicero, Marcus Tullius

Tunbridge Wells, III.126n1

Turner, Charles, M.P., III.267n1

Turner, William, Master of Stamford Grammar School, I.217 and n4

Turnor, Diana *see* Langton, Diana Turnor

Turton, Catherine, of Lichfield, II.228, III.51

Turton, John, M.D., III.296–97 and n9, 300

Tutbury, Staffordshire, I.229 and n7

Twelfth Night (Shakespeare): quoted, III.308n2

Twiss, Richard, travel writer, II.204–5 and nn3,4, 209, 334

Tychonis Brahei . . . vita (Gassendi), II.337 and n3

Tyrwhitt, Thomas, Chaucerian scholar: and "Rowley" manuscripts, II.332 and n9, 339

Tyson, Mr., Master of Ceremonies, Bath, III.269–70 and n16

U

Ullinish (Skye), II.81*n*52; cave at ment., II.107 and *n*24

Ulva, Isle of (Mull), II.104 and *n*7

Universal History, I.93 and *n*1

University College, Oxford, I.244–46 and *nn*3–5,7, 297 and *n*4

"Urban, Mr.," I.32–33

V

Vaillant, Paul, bookseller, I.140 and *n*1

Vanity of Human Wishes (Johnson), I.28*n*6

Vansittart, Robert, D.C.L., Fellow of All Souls College, Oxford, I.186 and *n*4, II.113 and *n*18

Vass, Lauchlan, II.65 and *n*17

Veigel, Eva Maria *see* Garrick, Eva Maria Veigel

Velleius Paterculus, Gaius, Roman historian, I.12 and *n*7

Vergilius, Polydorus, historian, I.155*n*4

Verney, Ralph Verney, 2d Earl, I.218*n*1, IV.126*n*16

Vernon, George Venables, M.P., I.4 and *n*4

Verrine Orations (Cicero), II.335*n*7

Versailles, II.272 and *n*1

Verses on Inchkenneth see Insula Sancti Kennethi

Verses on the Death of Dr. Swift (Swift): quoted, III.246*n*9, 299 and *n*3, IV.152*n*15, 336*n*2

Vesey, Agmondesham, Accountant-General of Ireland, III.27*n*5, 209, 213; elected to The Club, II.26 and *n*3

Vesey, Elizabeth (Mrs. Agmondesham), Bluestocking, III.27 and *n*5, 187, 209, 266; ment., III.157, 229, 235, 251*n*8, 276

Victor Amadeus II, King of Sicily and Sardinia, I.312 and *n*24

Village, The (Crabbe), IV.116–17 and *nn*1–4

Villette, Rev. John, Ordinary of Newgate, III.34 and *n*9, 35*n*12

Vincent, Sir Francis, 7th Bt., II.227*n*8

Viner, Charles, jurist, I.161*n*2

Vinerian lectures, I.276 and *n*1, 282*n*1, 293*n*1, 320 and *n*2, 322*n*3, 333*n*1, 413*n*1; preparation of statutes for, I.161*n*2

Virgil, I.51–55, 105*n*6, III.124*n*2, IV.390–91 and *nn*6,7; SJ's response to Lord Orrery's conjecture concerning, I.51–55; quoted, I.96 and *n*20, 286*n*2, 327*n*3, 376*n*2, II.35*n*4, 37*n*12, 125*n*3, 228*n*5, 230*n*16, 309*n*8, III.15*n*2, 19*n*3, 61*n*7, 77*nn*6,10, 301*n*2, IV.130*n*5, 139*n*11, 232 and *n*3; Baskerville edition of, I.105*n*6, 323 and *n*5

Viry (Viri), François Marie Joseph Viry, Comte de, Sardinian envoy, III.91

Vision of Theodore (Johnson): ment., I.11*n*3, IV.281*n*4

Vitellius, Aulus, Roman emperor, II.259*n*8

Vocabolario degli Accademici della Crusca, IV.426 and *n*2

Voltaire (François Marie Arouet), I.28*n*6, III.200 and *n*6

Vossius, Isaac, scholar, III.61*n*6

Voyage to Abyssinia, A (trans., Johnson), I.25*n*3, 143*n*8

Voyage to the Pacific Ocean (Cook), IV.332–33 and *n*2

Voyage towards the South Pole (Cook), III.50*nn*5,6

Vyse, Catherine Smalbroke (Mrs. William), II.230 and *n*1

Vyse, Mary, daughter of Rev. William, I.317 and *n*5; and SJ's visits to Lichfield, II.228, 230, III.166

Vyse, Rev. William (the elder), Treasurer of Lichfield Cathedral, I.317*n*5,

Vyse, Rev. William (*cont.*)
II.230*n*1; ment., III.38*n*1, 321 and *n*4,
IV.442 and *n*1
Vyse, William (the younger), Rector of
Lambeth, son of Rev. William: SJ so-
licits help on behalf of I. De Groot,
III.38–39, 44; ment., III.124*n*4, 166,
IV.320; SJ solicits help on behalf of E.
Desmoulins, III.321; SJ solicits help
on behalf of A. Macbean, III.333; and
J. Compton's conversion, IV.77–78
and *n*1; SJ suggests J. Compton's
book be dedicated to, IV.82
— LETTERS: III.38–39, 44, 321, 333,
IV.442–43

W

Wade, Mr.: ment., III.218
Wakefield, William, II.48*n*11
Wales: SJ and Thrales visit, II.147 and
*n*4, 148–49*n*1, 149, 151; has nothing
that can excite or gratify curiosity,
II.151, III.66 and *n*4; SJ returns from,
II.151 and *n*1; no community of
knowledge in, IV.211–12; *see also*
Welsh language
Walker, John, lexicographer and elocu-
tion specialist, IV.100 and *n*4
Walker, William, grammarian, I.221
and *n*5
Wall, John, M.D., I.361*n*1, 362*n*2, 366*n*5,
370
Waller, Edmund, poet: and *Lives of the
Poets*, III.109–10*nn*1–4, 116–17 and
*n*2, 122 and *n*2
Wallis, Capt. Samuel, I.386*n*3
Walloons, The (Cumberland), IV.33*n*4
Walmsley, Gilbert, Registrar of the
Ecclesiastical Court, Lichfield,
I.224*n*5, 292*n*1, III.86*n*4, 240,
IV.185*n*6

Walmsley, Magdalen Aston (Mrs. Gilbert), III.86 and *n*4, 91, 240
Walpole, Horace, I.282*n*4, 356*n*5,
392*n*3; on capture of Havana,
I.211*n*2; on Lord Lyttelton's death,
II.112*n*10; E. Tighe and, II.175*n*6; on
American political situation, II.186*n*3;
on Duchess of Kingston's bigamy
trial, II.321*n*3; on dismissal of Prince
of Wales's preceptors, II.347*n*10; on
health of T. Beauclerk, III.9*n*6; on
gout, III.193*n*5; on political situation
in 1779, III.197*n*4; on American War
debt, III.207*n*4; on H. Swinburne's
Travels, III.213*n*7; and *Mysterious
Mother*, III.225–26 and *nn*1,2; and
Gordon Riots, III.269*n*12, 272*n*2; on
severe weather, IV.36*n*1; on R. Cam-
bridge, IV.100*n*5; on heat of summer,
IV.175*n*5; on J. Opie, IV.193*n*1; on bal-
loons, IV.204*n*1
Walpole, Sir Robert, I.28*n*5, 37*n*6,
II.353 and *n*3
Walsh, William, poet, III.276 and *n*4
Walton, Brian, Biblical scholar,
IV.395*n*2
Walton, Izaak, IV.308; and Lord Hailes,
II.139 and *n*3, 145–46, 150
war, I.213
Warburton, William, Bishop of
Gloucester, I.92 and *n*1; replaced as
Bishop of Gloucester, III.183 and *n*2;
and SJ's biography of Pope, III.259*n*1,
295*n*2
Ward, William, Birmingham mercer,
I.40 and *n*3
Wardlaw, Henry, Bishop, II.55*n*3
Warley Camp, Essex, III.124*n*1, 125*n*2,
131–32 and *n*2, 142; George III visits,
III.132*n*6
Warren, servant, I.343 and *n*8
Warren, Thomas, Birmingham printer
and bookseller, I.24*n*1, 25 and *n*3, 26–
27 and *n*4, 104, 105, 125–26*n*6;
ment., I.260

Warter, Rev. Thomas, I.218*n*2

Warton, Joseph, poet and critic: ment., I.80*n*1, 89, 90, 91, 97,101, 109, 186*n*4, III.3, 37, V.34; and SJ's *Shakespeare*, I.162 and *n*1, 350–51

– LETTERS: I.67–68, 77–78, 90–91, 133–34, 255–56, 350–51, III.259–60, V.33

Warton, Mary Daman (Mrs. Joseph), I.255 and *n*1

Warton, Thomas, poet and literary historian: ment., I.86, 87, 106*n*9, 133, 155–56 and *n*1, 186*n*4, 209, III.135; and Baskerville's *Virgil*, I.323*n*5; and SJ's *Shakespeare*, I.341; commitment to reviving "antiquated literature," II.139; SJ mistakenly opens JB's letter to, III.255 and *n*3

– LETTERS: I.80–82, 87–90, 91–92, 94, 97–98, 99–101, 108–10, 112–13, 155, 162–64, 323, 341, III.255, V.33, 34

Watson, Robert, Professor of Logic, St. Andrews, II.55 and *n*4, 357 and *n*2, III.8, 165 and *n*3

Watson-Wentworth, Charles *see* Rockingham, 2d Marquis of

Watt, James, engineer, II.310*n*3

Watts, Isaac, poet, III.38 and *nn*2–4, 367 and *n*6, V.32

Way, Abigail *see* Sheffield, Lady

Way, Benjamin, M.P., III.3*n*2

Way, Elizabeth Anne Cooke (Mrs. Benjamin): ment., III.3 and *n*2, IV.33*n*3, 217; SJ thanks for pocket book, IV.132

– LETTERS: IV.35–36, 53, 132, 439, V.34

Way of the World (Congreve), III.110*n*2

Way to Keep Him (Murphy): Harry Thrale attends performance of, II.323 and *n*2

Webster, Rev. Alexander, II.120 and *n*6, 123, 124, 127 and *n*1, 128

Wedderburn, Alexander, lawyer and politician, I.207–8*n*3; and J.Taylor's lawsuit, II.324 and *n*5, 327, 346 and *n*2, 354 and *n*3; on *Evelina*, III.130

and *n*5; and Gordon riots, III.269*n*13

Welch, Anne (Nancy), daughter of S. Welch, II.328–29 and *n*9, III.106–8 and *n*2, IV.160 and *n*6; ment., III.54 and *n*3

Welch, Mary, II.366*n*1, 367 and *n*3; *see also* Nollekens, Mary Welch

Welch, Saunders, J.P.: ment., II.328–29 and *n*9, 366*n*1, 367 and *n*3, III.54 and *n*3, IV.160 and *n*6

– LETTER: III.106–8

Welsh language, I.152 and *n*6, III.136; *see also* Wales

Wesley, Rev. Charles (the elder), evangelist brother of John: ment., III.95*n*8

Wesley, Charles (the younger), harpsichordist, son of Charles, the elder, III.59 and *n*3, 95

– LETTER: V.34–35

Wesley, Rev. John, evangelist, I.295*n*1; ment., I.295*n*1, II.164, V.35; visits W. Dodd, III.34*nn*8,11; SJ introduces JB to, III.162

– LETTERS: II.290, III.162

Wesley, Mr., of Southwark, I.295–96, 295 and *n*1

Wesley, Samuel, harpsichordist, son of Charles, the elder, III.59 and *n*3, 95

Wesley, Sarah, daughter of Charles, the elder: ment., III.95 and *n*8, V.35

– LETTER: IV.233–34

Wesley, Sarah, sister of Charles, the younger, V.35

Wesley, Sarah Gwynne (Mrs. Charles, the elder), V.35 and *n*2

West, Gilbert, poet: and *Lives of the Poets*, III.233*n*5, 292–93 and *n*5

Westcote, 1st Baron (William Henry Lyttelton), M.P.: godfather to R. Thrale, I.369*n*3, II.118*n*8; ment., I.369 and *nn*5,6, III.50; and SJ's "Life" of his brother G. Lyttelton, III.291–93, 294

– LETTERS: III.291–93

Westminster School, Dean's Yard, London, I.10 and $n15$

Weston, Rev. Phipps, I.303–4, 305–6

Wetherell, Nathan, D.D., Master of University College, Dean of Hereford: ment., I.245$nn3$,4, III.46, 282 and $n7$; and Oxford riding school, II.183$n2$, 188, 189, 194, 215, 233, 246, 300 and $n4$, 303–4, 308; wishes to visit Thrale brewery, II.194, 195; and SJ's honorary D.C.L., II.197$n2$; SJ informs of bookselling practices, II.304–8; SJ to dine with, IV.52, 54

− LETTERS: II.304–8, III.170–71

Weymouth, IV.172

Wheeler, Benjamin, D.D., Regius Professor of Divinity: and inscription on "Genoa stone," II.192, 199–200; duties as clergyman, III.312; SJ to dine with, IV.55; death of ment., IV.187, 214, 305, 329

− LETTERS: II.192, 199–200, III.136–37

Whitbread, Samuel, brewer, III.53$n7$; SJ dines with, IV.138 and $n8$

Whitby, John, son of Thomas, I.11$n16$, 37$n1$

Whitby, Thomas, Staffordshire landowner, I.11 and $n16$, II.157$n4$

White, Mrs., SJ's housekeeper, IV.433

White, William, first Bishop of Pennsylvania, II.12–14

Whitehead, Paul, poet, I.15$n6$

Whitehead, William, poet, I.285$n3$

White Horse Inn, Edinburgh, II.51 and $n1$

Whiting, Ann, relative of SJ, IV.440$n3$

Whiting, Sarah, relative of SJ, IV.440$n3$

Whittell, Thomas, clerk, III.120$n4$

Whole Duty of Man (Allestree), III.158 and $n2$, 159

Wicher's Almshouses *see* George Wichers' Almshouses

wigs and hair, III.95–96

Wilcocks, Johnny, actor, II.339 and $n3$

Wilkes, John, politician: ment., I.187$n1$, 188 and $n7$, 333$n2$; political supporters oppose Henry Thrale's reelection, II.151 and $n2$; SJ dines with, II.330$n4$, 331 and $n3$, 332; and chamberlainship election, II.347 and $nn8$,9; and Gordon Riots, III.270–71 and $n4$, 272 and $n1$, 273

− LETTER: IV.139

Wilkes (Wilks), Father Joseph, Benedictine monk, II.272$n5$, 336–37, 338 and $n1$, 343, III.75

Wilkes, Mary, daughter of John, IV.139 and $nn2$,3

Wilkins, John, D.D., Warden of Wadham College, Bishop of Chester, IV.176 and $nn3$,4; flying chariot scheme, IV.273$n3$

Willcox, Johnny *see* Wilcocks, Johnny

"William and Margaret" (Mallet), IV.188$n8$

William I, King of England, II.49$n18$

William the Lion (of Scotland), II.57$n12$

Williams, Anna, poet, I.44$n5$, 78–80 and $nn1$,2,9, 216, III.9 and $n12$; failing eyesight of, I.44 and $n5$, 124; ment., I.87, 138, 205, 211, 214, 217, 221, 231, 251, 253, 334$n1$, 352, 354, 360, 375, 388, II.6, 27, 28, 119, 142$n1$, 181, 186, 273, 324, 326, 358, 359, III.6, 131, 189, 202, 204, 295, IV.82, 85, 173, V.25; SJ's plans for benefit for, I.124 and $n3$, 126, 127–28, 129, 320–21 and $n4$; and Sir J. Philipps, I.160–61$n1$, 195; residences, I.173 and $n19$, 252$n1$; and *Miscellanies in Prose and Verse*, I.185–86 and $n3$, 279 and $n5$; and Ladies' Charity School, I.330$n1$, 331; SJ asks R. Chambers and Henry Thrale to call on and lend money to, II.99, 100, 108; corresponds with Sir A. Gordon, II.120 and $n3$; and T. Cumming, II.141; and petition for charity for blind, II.152–53 and $n1$; health ment., II.194, 206, 246, 283, 360–61, 365, III.41–42, 58, 60,

68, 78, 95, 99, 102, 119, 189, 203, 296–97, 300, IV.9 and $n2$, 15, 23, 126, 130–31, 160, 167–68; and F. Chambers's letter, II.245, 252; Hester Thrale visits, II.259; death of, III.36$n20$, IV.187 and $n1$, 198, 214; relationship with R. Levet and E. Desmoulins, III.127, 134, 139, 140, 191, 209, IV.137 and $n8$, 139 and $n9$; at Kingston, III.288; and Gordon Riots, III.288$n2$, 290, 303; last illness of, IV.186, 187, 189, 191, 192; effect of her death on SJ, IV.195 and $n1$, 199, 202, 203, 204–5, 212, 213, 219 and $n5$, 225, 230, 236, 265, 312, 389, 404; and E. Montagu, IV.203, 217

Williams, John, sailor, III.271 and $n7$

Williams, Zachariah, inventor, father of Anna, I.44$n5$

Willison, John, author, II.150$n7$

Will of King Henry VII (Astle), III.354$n1$

Wills, Rev. John, Rector of Tydd St. Mary, V.24 and $n2$

Wilson, Thomas (1663–1755) (the elder), D.D., Bishop of Sodor and Man, IV.103 and $n1$

Wilson, Rev. Thomas (*c.* 1704–84), D.D., Prebend of Westminster Abbey, I.103 and $n1$, III.258, 259$n9$, 265; death ment., IV.326

Wilson, Rev. Thomas (1747–1813) (the younger), schoolmaster: and *Archaeological Dictionary*, III.357–58 and $nn1,5$; SJ on dedication of book by, IV.102–3

– LETTERS: IV.102–3

Wilson v. Smith and Armour, II.9 and $n9$

Wilton, Frances *see* Chambers, Frances Wilton

Wilton, Joseph, II.127$n2$, 215$n1$, 220

Winchester: SJ visits, I.255 and $n2$, III.260 and $n2$

Windham, William, M.P., scholar and mathematician: and Essex Head Club, IV.140$n1$, 257$n2$; visits SJ in Ashbourne, IV.386 and $n2$, 387, 408

– LETTERS: IV.140, 375–76, 413–14, 439

Wingate, Edmund, mathematician, IV.138 and $n5$

Wise, Rev. Francis, Radclivian Librarian, I.88 and $n2$, 89, 94, 97, 108, 109, 112, 113, 114, 155, 165

Wishart, George, tutor of John Knox, II.56$n9$

Witlings, The (Burney), III.188$n3$, 196$n12$

Woffington, Margaret, actress, III.22$n1$

women, I.214; SJ on power of, I.228; and inheritance rights, II.288–89, 291; and gluttony, IV.181

Wonderful Curiosities, Rarities, and Wonders in England, Scotland, and Ireland (Burton), IV.267 and $n3$

Wood, Alexander, surgeon, III.103 and $nn2,3$

Wood, Anthony, antiquarian, I.115 and $n2$, 133$n2$, IV.79 and $n3$

Wood, Mary (Mrs. Ralph) *see* Rhudde, Mary Wood

Wood, Ralph, nephew of John Taylor, II.179$n1$, 283, 355, III.164; ment., II.335$n6$

Woodcock, Mr., solicitor, I.228 and $n1$, 229, 232–33

Woodward, Francis, M.D., II.332 and $n4$, 336, III.236, 238, IV.249 and $n2$, 250

Word to the Wise, A (Kelly): SJ's prologue for benefit performance of, III.27 and $nn6,7$; SJ's prologue ment., III.49

workhouses, III.51 and $n7$

Works of George, Lord Lyttelton (ed. Ayscough), III.292 and $n4$

Works of the English Poets, with Prefaces, Biographical and Critical (Johnson) *see Lives of the Poets*

World, The: and *Dictionary* notices, I.95 and $n5$

World Displayed; or, a Curious Collection of Voyages and Travels, I.187$n3$

Worthington, William, D.D., Prebendary of York, II.175 and nn2,3; death of, III.131

Wraxall, Nathaniel William, 1st Bt., memoir writer, II.209–10 and n12; and J. Macpherson, II.168n2; ment., III.235

Wray, Sir Cecil, Bt., IV.306n4

Wright, Mr., printer, I.246n10

Wright, Rev. Thomas, curate, III.170n3

Wrottesley, Sir John, 4th Bt., IV.185 and n5

Wyndham, Sir Charles see Egremont, 2d Earl of

Wynn, Sir Watkin Williams, 4th Bt., I.296 and n2

X

Xenophon, I.12, II.361 and n5, III.136 and n5, IV.304n2, 345, V.3 and n1

Y

Yalden, Thomas, poet: ment., V.32n4

York, II.47–48 and nn7,9

York, Archbishop of see Drummond, Robert Hay

York, Edward Augustus, Duke of: and S. Foote, II.366n19

Yorke, James, Bishop of Gloucester, III.183n2

Yorktown, Battle of, IV.65n5

Young, Edward, poet: quoted, I.364n4, III.81n6; and Lives of the Poets, III.233n5, 295, 296, 322nn1,2,4,5

Young, Frederick, son of Edward, III.322 and n2

Young, George, medical writer, I.72 and n5

Young, John, classicist, IV.168–69 and n3

"Young Coll" see Maclean, Donald

youth, III.234–35; "every new action or practice is a kind of experiment," I.142; confidence of at 21 years, I.171; immaturity of juvenile years, I.198; "too rigorous in our expectations," I.225; "the transition from the protection of others to our own conduct is a very awful point of human existence," II.199; and learning, II.263–64

Z

Zaphira (Palmer), II.172n1

Zobeide (Cradock), IV.107n1

Zodiac signs: ment., III.277 and n10; the Virgin, III.294

Zon, Giovanni Francesco, Venetian resident, I.85 and n1, 87